From the Margins of Hindu Marriage

From the Margins of Hindu Marriage

Essays on Gender, Religion, and Culture

EDITED BY
Lindsey Harlan
Paul B. Courtright

New York Oxford
Oxford University Press
1995

Oxford University Press

Oxford New York
Athens Auckland Bangkok Bombay
Calcutta Cape Town Dar es Salaam Delhi
Florence Hong Kong Istanbul Karachi
Kuala Lumpur Madras Madrid Melbourne
Mexico City Nairobi Paris Singapore
Taipei Tokyo Toronto

and associated companies in
Berlin Ibadan

Published by Oxford University Press, Inc.,
198 Madison Avenue, New York, New York 10016-4314

Library of Congress Cataloging-in-Publication Data
From the margins of Hindu marriage :
essays on gender, religion, and culture /
edited by Lindsey Harlan and Paul B. Courtright.
p. cm. Includes bibliographical references and index.
ISBN 0-19-508117-X (cl).—ISBN 0-19-508118-8 (pbk.)
1. Marriage—India. 2. Hinduism—India.
I. Harlan, Lindsey. II. Courtright, Paul B.
HQ670.M35 1994 306.81'0954—dc20 93-51040

2 4 6 8 9 7 5 3

Printed in the United States of America
on acid-free paper

For Robert, Devon, Kirin,
and Peggy

Acknowledgments

We would like to thank each of our contributors, especially for their patience as this volume took shape. Julia Leslie deserves our special thanks. It was at the Conference on Women in South Asia she organized at Oxford University that the idea to create such a volume was born during a teatime conversation. We are grateful to Jack Hawley for practical advice on the nitty-gritty aspects of editing. We thank Cynthia A. Read and Peter Ohlin at Oxford University Press for their characteristic editorial skill and good humor. For their kindness and generosity we thank Yves Vequad, Mary Lanius, Catherine Weinberger-Thomas, David White, Eric Adler, Joseph Elder, Ray Owens, and Cynthia Atherton.

New London, Conn. L.H.
Atlanta, Ga. P.B.C.
February 1994

Contents

Contributors

PAUL B. COURTRIGHT, professor of religion and chair of the department at Emory University, is the author of *Gaṇeśá: Lord of Obstacles, Lord of Beginnings* (Oxford, 1985) and *The Goddess and the Dreadful Practice* (Oxford, forthcoming). His work has focused on Hindu mythologies and ritual practices in the context of social and cultural life. Currently he is researching the relationship between scholarship and ideology in nineteenth-century colonial India.

WENDY DONIGER (formerly Wendy Doniger O'Flaherty), Mircea Eliade Professor of the History of Religions at the University of Chicago, has published numerous works on mythology and religion in India and elsewhere. Her publications include: *Hindu Myths: A Sourcebook, Translated from the Sanskrit* (Penguin, 1975); *Women, Androgynes, and Other Mythical Beasts* (Chicago, 1980); *The Rig Veda: An Anthology of 108 Hymns Translated from the Sanskrit* (Penguin, 1981); *Dreams, Illusion, and Other Realities* (Chicago, 1984); *Tales of Sex and Violence: Folklore, Sacrifice, and Danger in the Jaiminiya Brahmana* (Chicago, 1985); *Other Peoples' Myths: The Cave of Echoes* (Macmillan, 1988); *The Laws of Manu*, with Brian K. Smith (Penguin, 1991); and *Mythologies*, the English-language edition of Yves Bonnefoy's 1,300-page *Dictionnaire des mythologies* (Chicago, 1991). Among her works-in-progress are: *The Mythology of Horses in India; The Bed Trick: An Encyclopedia of Sexual Masquerades;* and a novel tentatively titled *Horses for Lovers, Dogs for Husbands.*

ANN GRODZINS GOLD, assistant professor of religion at Syracuse University, has published extensively on popular Hinduism and oral traditions in Rajasthan. Her works include: *Fruitful Journeys: The Ways of Rajasthani Pilgrims* (California, 1988); *A Carnival of Parting: The Tales of King Gopi Chand and King Bharthari as Sung and Told by Madhu Natisar Nath* (California, 1992); and (with Gloria Goodwin Raheja), *Listen to the Heron's Words: Reimagining Gender and Kinship in North India* (California, 1994). Gold's current research is on cultural constructions of the environment.

MARY E. HANCOCK has been appointed assistant professor of anthropology at the University of California, Santa Barbara, and is currently a National Endowment for the Humanities Fellow at the School of American Research in Santa Fe, New Mexico. Prior to that she was a Mellon Foundation Postdoctoral Fellow in the Social Sciences and associate member of the Department of Anthropology and the Committee on South Asian Studies at the University of Chicago. She is currently revising her doctoral dissertation for publication.

LINDSEY HARLAN, associate professor of religious studies at Connecticut College, is the author of *Religion and Rajput Women: The Ethic of Protection in Contemporary Narratives* (California, 1992), and is currently writing a book on hero veneration. Her interests include women's ritual and narratives, social change, and heroic tradition, especially in Rajasthan and its environs.

RALPH W. NICHOLAS, William Rainey Harper Professor of Anthropology at the University of Chicago, carried out field research in West Bengal and Bangladesh beginning in 1960 and continuing until 1981, when he became dean of social sciences at the University of Chicago. He is the author (with Ronald Inden) of *Kinship in Bengali Culture* (Chicago, 1977). He has worked in the areas of village politics and kinship. Most recently he has studied Hindu rites and the interaction of Hinduism and Islam in rural Bengali society.

GLORIA GOODWIN RAHEJA, associate professor of anthropology and chair of the department at the University of Minnesota, is the author of *The Poison in the Gift: Ritual, Prestation, and the Dominant Caste in a North Indian Village* (Chicago, 1988), and coauthor (with Ann Grodzins Gold) of *Listen to the Heron's Words: Reimagining Gender and Kinship in North India* (California, 1994).

SUSAN S. WADLEY, professor of anthropology at Syracuse University, has written extensively on women, ritual, and social change in north India. She is the author of *Struggling with Destiny in Karimpur, 1925–1984* (California, 1994) and *Shakti: Power in the Conceptual Structure of Karimpur Religion* (Chicago, 1975), and has edited several volumes—on women in India, oral epics, and religion and the media. In addition, she has written numerous articles on women, oral traditions, and social change in north India. Her work has focused primarily on one community in northern India, although more recent research has focused on a regional epic tradition called Dhola.

Guide to Pronunciation

Words from various Indian languages and dialects are transliterated according to accepted conventions. Although most transliteration is consistent throughout, the editors have allowed for variations in some cases to reflect differences in regional dialects and languages (hence *pūjā* in Hindi and *pūja* in Tamil) and to accommodate contributors' preferences (such as the partially Anglicized transliteration of *jungli rani* in the essays by Gold and Harlan). Geographical names appear without diacritical marks, as they would in signs. Names of deities and of characters in literature and folklore appear with diacritical marks, as do the names of famous historical personages. Names of contemporary individuals appear without diacritics, as would the names of published authors in bibliographies. Words commonly found in English dictionaries appear without diacritical marks. Foreign words that recur in the essays are given brief definitions in the Glossary.

From the Margins of Hindu Marriage

1

Introduction: On Hindu Marriage and Its Margins

LINDSEY HARLAN AND PAUL B. COURTRIGHT

This book explores some of the fundamental presuppositions about and experiences of marriage in South Asian culture. It traces a variety of conceptual and imaginative boundaries delineating the institution of marriage and reveals crucial notions about marriage that are best or sometimes only revealed at its margins, at those thresholds of entry, exit, renunciation, and violation in which marriage is undertaken, severed, resisted, or idealized. Our purpose is to discover how marriage actually works as a social and imaginative reality by considering the various experiences and perceptions of those who have crossed or transgressed its borders.

Implicit in this pursuit is a recognition of the multiple conceptions of marriage by people at various stages of their lives and situated in differing circumstances. The institution looks quite different to those who have experienced it at varying times and at different points along its periphery. If marriage is viewed as a circle comprising these points, then the experiences of people participating in or reflecting on the institution constitute something like a rather intricate spirograph tracing in which their collective experiences and perceptions confirm the existence of the circular perimeter, whereas their individual experiences and perceptions intersect within the perimeter in a number of ways.

Many studies of Hindu marriage predominantly focus on prescriptive literatures, especially the Sanskrit moral–legal texts (*dharmaśāstra*s), which interpret marriage as a set of normative rules and attitudes to be pursued in order to achieve merit and engender social harmony.[1] Other studies approach the subject more quantitatively by surveying attitudes or practices among various communities.[2] The essays in this volume draw upon these interpretive traditions but take the analysis of marriage in a different direction. Rather than explore presentations of marriage as an ideal or normative human transaction and relationship—a view from the center, as it were—these essays look at marriage from the margins, from places where the idealized constructions reveal their flaws and vulnerabilities as well as their enduring capacities. The main vehicles for access to these neglected areas of marriage are stories, songs, and narrated explanations of life experiences in which these marginalities are revealed. Many of these narratives are quite old and have been adapted to the circumstances of contemporary life. Others have only now made the transition from oral tradition to printed text.

The statuses of women located at different points along the margins of marriage have widely divergent social valuations. Some are generally considered normative, such as the daughter who becomes a wife. Others are usually viewed critically, such as the wife who becomes a widow. Still others are generally thought to be both admirable and potentially threatening, such as a wife who becomes a *bhakta* or celibate. And then there are those women—such as the wife who becomes a *satī*, a practice now largely consigned to history but still influencing contemporary understandings of and attitudes toward marriage—who receive radically divergent evaluations, depending on the religious, social, political, and cultural commitments of those doing the evaluating. In short, whereas work on marriage has often concentrated on the normative state—marriage leading to death before that of a husband—and then contrasted this with other states, our approach is to concentrate on variously valued statuses outside marriage and on alternations between married and nonmarried states.

While the essays in this volume do not exhaust the possibilities for interpreting Hindu marriage from its marginal perspectives, they do provide examples of reflexive approaches that enlarge our understanding of the multilayered, multidimensional nature of this most enduring and complex human institution in the context of Hindu culture.[3] Our purpose is not to draw a detailed map of marital experience but to sketch some of the perspectives from which it may be viewed. This volume consists of reflections on various discourses within Hindu culture, including patriarchal or dominant discourses on women and marriage as well as various challenges to and subversions of these discourses.

In soliciting contributions along these lines, we pursued two additional aims. First, we wanted to make this an interdisciplinary volume combining insights from anthropology, Indology, folklore, and the history of religions. Second, we attempted to include among our ideal readers those with interests in gender studies or cross-cultural studies on marriage and those who themselves may have encountered the marginalities of marriage in their own lives. For those less familiar with Hinduism and its traditions and interpretations of marriage, we present the following overview.

Hindu Marriage and the Social and Religious Construction of the Person

Anthropological research on kinship and caste in India has contributed much to our understanding of the infrastructure of rules and attitudes that have shaped the understanding and negotiation of marriage. More textually oriented Indological scholarship has investigated the classical texts, the *dharmaśāstra*s, on moral and legal discourse in which marriage is understood and prescribed. Marital ideologies, practices, and beliefs are complex and vary considerably from region to region in India and among various Indian communities or castes. Nevertheless, some general principles seem to be recognizable through most of Hindu culture.

Contemporary understandings of Hindu society have been profoundly shaped by the work of the French anthropologist Louis Dumont. Dumont argues that whereas Western society tends to be individualistic in outlook, Indian society tends to be holistic: it understands the cosmos as a whole, of which society is a constituent part. As society plays its role within the natural order of the universe, so people play roles within society, but these people are not individuals with strictly discrete identities. Rather, they are interdependent parts of society, parts organized in terms of hierarchically ranked castes with relationships that are roughly equivalent among caste members.[4]

Ranking, according to Dumont, is based on the fundamental opposition between the pure and the impure. Thus the Brahman, the ritually purest of all persons, stands at the head of the cosmosocial body, and the naturally impure *Śūdra,* or servant, stands at the feet, with the other caste groups falling in between. The marriage arrangement becomes the primary context for sorting out where a particular family, lineage, and kin group ranks in relation to others. Through marriage a family's status may be maintained, strengthened, or weakened. Because a marriage affects the status of the entire family and its lineage, it is deemed too important a decision to leave to the persons actually getting married. Rather, the decision rests with the heads of extended family units. Consequently, arranged marriages are the norm; marriages undertaken by the marrying parties themselves, so-called love marriages, are considered deviant, even dangerous.

An important part of the traditional understanding of marriage is the notion that social status and human capacities are embedded in the very bodily substances themselves, especially blood. Within the institution of marriage, descent is patrilineal: blood is inherited in the male line through the intermediary of women. The purity of caste is to be found in blood, which is conceived not just as a substance but as the basis of personal and family character. It can be rendered more or less pure according to the actions and circumstances of those possessing it.[5] Blood defilement or pollution results from contacts with less pure persons and substances, which taint or dilute character.

Intercaste marriages or affairs produce relatively impure issue. According to a widely shared Hindu understanding of physiognomy, blood condenses to form semen in men and sexual fluid in women. Conception occurs when the male and female "bloods" merge during sexual relations. A child inherits whatever purity is contained in parental blood.[6] Line-preserving liaisons occur between persons from the same caste group (*jāti*). For this reason it is expected that men who marry only one woman, as the Hindu Marriage Act of 1954 requires, will marry within their own caste.[7] A liaison between a higher-caste man and a lower-caste woman is considered *anuloma*, or with the grain. It results in offspring who, though possessing less purity and status than the father, are ascribed membership in some caste community and accorded a certain degree of legitimacy within society.[8] Such an arrangement preserves the hierarchical and partriarchal structure of society. In contrast, a liaison between a higher-castle woman and a lower-caste man is considered *pratiloma*, or against the grain. Such an arrangement violates the structure of society and results in offspring who are typically ascribed very low status or regarded as outcasts. These notions make it clear that the purity of women is especially crucial to the maintenance of the position of the family within the social hierarchy.

Purity is determined not only by the circumstances of one's birth but also by the actions one performs during one's life. Actions appropriate to caste and subcaste maintain and fortify the blood purity of the individual and so also of descendants. In contrast, actions that are inappropriate defile the integrity of the line. Because responsibility for maintaining the blood purity of the husband's line falls heavily upon the wife who marries in from another family and line, there is special concern that her actions be consistent with the rules and expectations of her conjugal kin. A woman is expected to preserve her chastity and to perform rituals that will maintain household purity and promote the well-being of her husband and his household.

Purity, however, is not the only interpretive axis for understanding Indian culture; it is joined and challenged by auspiciousness (*maṅgala* in Sanskrit), which derives in part from the actions of women as they perform their roles as wives, mothers, and protectors. Frédérique Marglin's influential book on the *devadāsīs*, or temple dancers, of the sacred city of Puri shows that the principle of auspiciousness is as essential as the notion of purity for understanding the dynamics of social organization.[9] Previous discussions of purity tended to assign a positive value to pure acts and substances, and a negative one to acts and substances causing pollution. This discourse obscured recognition of the fact that both sexual intercourse and birth are positively valued but highly polluting activities. The temple dancers whom Marglin studied performed daily rituals for God but were regarded as impure because of their various sexual liaisons with male temple servants and with the king. Yet these same women were considered auspicious because they were married not to mortals but to God. Hence, they could never become widows; they were "daily wedded" by their liaisons with God and his human representatives. The dancers' rituals pleased the God Jagannath, who was responsible for the good fortunes of the area, particularly fertility of the land, animals, and people. Like Jagannath, the king, who was considered the walking incarnation of Jagannath, was held responsible for fertility of the fields. His authority and legitimacy were tied to his power to bring about good fortune.

In *The Poison in the Gift,* Gloria Raheja explains the notion of auspiciousness not just as a quality that inheres in a person or thing but as one that can be transferred through ritual exchange. The auspiciousness of women is not something that wives simply have and widows lack; it is something that women can receive, carry, and pass on. In the wedding ceremony itself, the episode of *kanyā dān*, or "gift of a virgin," requires that the father give away the bride to the husband and his family. Though considered the very embodiment of auspiciousness, the bride transfers a measure of inauspiciousness from her natal family to the conjugal family. The wedding conjoins two things, like an eclipse. This inauspiciousness must be passed on by the groom's family through the offering of gifts, or *dān,* to Brahmans and wedding attendants from lower castes. The gifts serve both to contain the inauspiciousness of the marital exchange and to compensate the recipient for taking on the dangers contained therein. By looking at the moment of marriage, the moment at which the margin between virginal and married life is ritually marked, Raheja shows how families transfer auspiciousness through *kanyā dān* but, in a parallel way, how dominant castes maintain their good fortune by distributing gifts.

In arranging marriages families give weight to the status of prospective partners, but they also try to find their children partners with comparable or greater economic resources. Personal rapport, which is of primary importance in Western marriages, is often consigned to last place in their list of priorities and is generally determined as much by astrological reckoning as by assessments of personality and personal appearance. In the selection of a marriage partner, the welfare of the kinship line and its maintenance through mixture of pure blood take precedence. Grooms and brides—especially brides—are admonished to constrain their own desire to conform to family expectations and needs.

As is apparent from the concerns attending the selection of marriage partners, individual identity is heavily contextualized by the ideal of family solidarity and lineage preservation. Hence, in the Hindu household, after marriage, persons tend to address and to refer to each other not by proper names but by kinship designations. This is true of relations by blood (father, mother, daughter, son, etc.) and by marriage (husband, wife, mother-in-law, etc.). Thus, throughout India, kinship has an elaborate and specific terminology. For example, in Hindi a wife's elder brother-in-law is her *jet* and her younger brother-in-law her *devar,* while a mother's brother is a *māmā* and a father's brother a *kākā.* Specific terms like these subsume individual personality under designations of familial roles, responsibilities, and privileges. Ritual observances—for example, the custom of *ghūṅghaṭ,* which requires women to veil their faces in front of senior, especially male, affines—reinforce the more formal arrangement within the relatively intimate familial environment.

When a bride marries into her husband's family, she enters into this complex web of human relationships. While she is expected to obey and please her husband, she is also expected to serve the interests of his family as a whole. She has to walk a delicate and at times perilous path between her husband and the other members of his family, especially the other significant women, his mother and sisters. Her conjugal family may seek to limit and structure her time with her husband to keep her from earning his loyalty and affection at the expense of his devotion to his family. A wife is supposed to integrate the family as she preserves its line. She must serve her function as *pativratā* (literally, she who takes a vow [*vrat*] of devotion to her husband [*pati*]), by respectfully fulfilling obligations to all senior family members, including senior women, and by directing and caring for junior family members. To understand more fully the way in which she is understood to perform the functions incumbent upon her as a wife, it is necessary to look closely at the fundamental propositions about female character and duty that have been discussed in some of the scholarship on Hindu women.

The Nature of Hindu Women

One useful avenue for understanding the cultural representations of women and Hindu marriage is to look at portrayals of the female in the mythic traditions. Although Hindu goddess do not necessarily serve as paradigms for social values, they do demonstrate certain suppositions about female behaviors, powers, desires, and character. As Wendy Doniger has shown, the mythic, especially the Puranic, traditions have much to reveal about constructions of not only metaphysical but also social realities and norms in Indian culture.[10]

Students encountering the study of India for the first time often ask why, if goddesses are so revered, women are so oppressed? Their question assumes that women are powerless pawns in a male game, or that the power women do wield within the domestic and religious spheres in society is not worthwhile, or at least is not as important as the power wielded by men in the public world. While many people in India agree that the power women wield is insufficient and so are fighting for greater social and political equality, most do not see women as utterly powerless. Social convention, patrilineal inheritance, and patrilocal residence impose many limitations on women, but women do have certain powers that are not obvious to outsiders or valued by all insiders. These powers are made visible in mythology and folklore, where female figures, women and goddesses, exercise considerable power. The veneration of goddesses, as virgins, mothers, and warriors, and its attendant valuation of the female suggests certain important assumptions about the character and abilities of women in society.[11]

While Hindu goddesses have many names and forms, they are often thought of as ultimately identifiable with a unified female deity, often referred to simply as Devi, "the Goddess." Although the Goddess, who is frequently addressed as Mātā, or "Mother," is understood as a single power and presence, she has no single form that captures or conveys the depth and complexity of her character. In fact, she has some characteristics that are logically opposed. These tend to be identified with two different types of personae and iconographies: one fierce, the other docile. The fierce form is often represented as dark or malevolent, whereas the docile form is represented as light or benevolent. There are, however, problems with each of these oppositions, as we shall see.

The dark form is most clearly illustrated by the goddess Kālī, or the "Dark One," who is depicted with pointed, shriveled breasts, a sharp tongue dripping with the blood of demons, a garland of skulls, and a wild tangle of locks. The light form is illustrated by Gaurī, the "Golden One," who is also Pārvatī, "Daughter of the Himalaya," depicted with fulsome breasts, a gentle smile, lovely jewelry, and properly braided or chignoned hair. The complexions and iconographies of these goddesses, however, become mixed in other goddesses. For example, there is Durgā, a warrior goddess who, like Kālī, slays demons but is often described or depicted as having a radiant complexion, a gentle expression, and copious breasts. Moreover, even the personalities represented in the forms of Kālī and Gaurī are fluid and transmutable. This fluidity is instantiated by the famous myth in which Śiva teases his wife Kālī about her dark complexion. In India, dark complexions are generally considered less desirable than light ones, and marriage negotiations often take into account the fairness of the bride. So, embarrassed, Kālī goes to a "cosmic beauty parlor"[12] and returns with radiant golden skin, which is suitable to the wife of the great Lord Śiva.

While these representations of Kālī and Gaurī set out contrasting modes of the feminine, their volatility and fluidity point to the mixture of these modes in actual women. The goddesses' opposing iconographies represent disjunctive dimensions in the depiction of women, who, though ideally docile, can be angry, fierce, and destructive. Psychoanalytic perspectives locate this ambivalence about the powers of the goddess as part of a complex cultural processing of the infant's experience of the mother as the omnipotent and alternatively giving and withholding figure.[13] Traditional legal texts and popular belief affirm that the woman who feels mistreated is understood to have the capacity to curse, and so harm or destroy, those who have wronged her.

It is worthwhile noting that in myth and society female rage and destructive capacity are often thought more devastating and ruinous than male rage. Thus in Hindu mythology, when the gods are in danger of losing their heaven to their enemies, the demons, they produce from their combined wrath a goddess who is capable of destroying the demons that so overwhelm them. This goddess Durgā produces from her own wrath Kālī, the dark warrior who finishes what Durgā started. Kālī destroys the forces of anarchy with her power, her *śakti*.

Sometimes Kālī's rage is so violent as to deprive her of discrimination. Destroying the demons, Kālī loses control and becomes frenzied; she is calmed only when she sees Śiva, her husband. When Kālī is uncontrolled, her power is unchanneled and indiscriminate; but within the constraints of her marriage to Śiva, her power is directed toward the establishment of order and well-being. She is responsible not only for defeating the forces of disorder but for promoting creativity and fertility.

This notion of controlled *śakti* as promoting social order finds expression in the widely shared understanding that women should never be independent. Women should not be left to their own devices but should be supervised and protected by men. The main concern behind this notion is not that women will go about indiscriminately killing and maiming like the frenzied Kālī but that they might succumb to sexual temptation, which will destroy their purity and the purity of their lineage. The connection between female freedom and sexual license is made in mythology: the goddess fighting various demons is often portrayed in a kind of sexual combat. Fighting the demon Mahiṣa, the goddess is also engaged in battle flirtations, as only an unsupervised woman could.

Women in society must be protected from such temptations by social strictures; they cannot roam as the Goddess does, or society will disintegrate. For society to prosper, women's power must be channeled toward procreation and the protection of the family. Representations of control and privation are found throughout the world in which women operate. Symbols of binding and confinement show up in many female customs and manners. A proper wife wears a chignon or a braid; loose hair implies a lack of sexual restraint.[14] She also wears jewelry that symbolizes her married status, including bangles, whether of gold, silver, glass, iron, or ivory, which she must relinquish at the moment she becomes a widow.[15] Often her jewelry includes some type of precious-metal ankle bracelets; metal or cotton necklaces on which are strung embossed representations of deities are common as well. In western India, for example, many Rajput women wear both images of their husbands' lineage goddess and the sneeze goddess (Chiṅk Mātā) to keep her from causing sneezes, which would be inauspicious at important ritual moments.[16] In various places nose rings and forehead ornaments that are tied back into chignoned hair also symbolize a woman's attachment to a husband and his family. Finally, there is the sari, which is wrapped around the body to conceal carefully the contours of the woman's sexual characteristics.

Along with wearing these various items and styles associated with control, women are expected to show dependence and deference through their observance of a number of conventions. Many women observe *ghūṅghaṭ*, or veiling of the face, in front of male in-laws, particularly if the in-laws are senior to their husbands. In some households women do not address seniors unless spoken to, and then respond only in hushed voices, which further reduces the possibility of easy verbal intercourse. An even more dramatic example of restriction is found in the convention of *pardā*, practiced in many communities. *Pardā*, which literally means "curtain," refers to the seclusion of women within the household. *Pardā* keeps women from being seen by men who are not members of the household. With *pardā* the world of women literally becomes the world of the household. This practice has been pervasive among groups of high-caste women; low-caste women have often been too poor to be able to afford the luxury of doing only women's work in the household.

Many of these representations of controlled sexuality also connote auspiciousness and the fertility that it encompasses. Thus the jewelry represents control in marriage but also good fortune, of which children are the primary expression. The wedding sari is red, which is the color of auspiciousness and is often linked to menstrual blood and the blood of childbirth in various ritual and mythic contexts.[17] The bride so adorned is often compared to the Goddess, who when united with her husband is the source of worldly fertility and prosperity. The same notions of auspiciousness are attached to the vermilion that married women wear in their hair parts or the *bindi*s, or dots, they wear on their foreheads.

The confinement of women to a female sphere with its various symbolisms of binding, then, is generally seen as controlling and channeling power toward approved ends. The stricture of *pardā*, however, actually relegates to women a number of decision-making processes. Within the household, women have control over certain types of activities, chiefly domestic ones. The mother-in-law often makes major decisions about the distribution of goods within the family and coordinates the various work details performed by daughters and daughters-in-law.

Aside from these areas of authority, *pardā* also gives to women a measure of freedom from the constant surveillance by men. Although many women find *pardā* frustrating and speak wistfully of their natal villages where as daughters they could walk about unveiled, many also say that *pardā* allows them to speak and act more freely than would otherwise be possible given the other conventions of deference that women must obey. In *pardā* they feel they can be relatively relaxed and can have the space to complain about and be critical of men and their rules.[18]

The idea of the women's sphere as a place where some dissension is inevitable is widespread in India. In most households where space is limited, there is at least some tension among wives who have married into their households from different families with different customs.

These features of women's spheres of life find expression in women's songs. Many songs give voice to resentment about treatment of wives and express women's threats to leave the household and take their husbands with them if their treatment does not improve. These songs often speak of the power of wives and the influence of their sexuality on men. Indeed, they often ridicule men, whom they portray as sexually dependent and even childlike. Some of the songs are taunting or even abusive, particularly those that accompany marriage. Festive songs often proclaim women's power to make men respect their wishes and celebrate women's sexuality and fertility.

Women's power is also understood as encompassing the ability to preserve the lives of husbands. A wife is charged with the immense responsibility for protecting her husband's longevity. To this end a woman performs various rituals to ensure her husband's long life. For example, women keep *vrat*s, or vows, to various deities in order to enlist divine aid in protecting their husbands.[19] These vows, which typically involve fasting, are accompanied by stories that illustrate the power of the *vrat* when properly executed or that celebrate the devotion of legendary *pativratā*s, such as the famous Sāvitrī, whose devotion brought her husband back to life. A model *pativratā*, Sāvitrī is considered the perfect embodiment of wifely auspiciousness. Sāvitrī has the capacity to protect and to withdraw protection. Similarly, women have the power to protect; by implication, their withdrawal of protection can result in destruction or harm to others.

These ideas about the control of women and women's power are also shaped by the *dharmaśāstras*, classical legal texts in which we see a normative and idealized pattern of the life cycle. According to the *dharmaśāstras* Hindu males should pass through four distinct stages, or *aśramas*. As youths they should study and serve their teachers, as young men they should marry and support the family and community, in middle age they should retire from active worldly life and engage in study and spiritual practices, and in old age they should renounce the world and become holy men. Many men understand renunciation as a higher calling, especially for those who have repaid their debts to their ancestors by fathering sons to perpetuate the lineage.[20] Although few men actually pattern their lives after this ideal structure, the norm of renunciation sometimes causes or exacerbates ambivalence about marriage as a lifelong commitment. Nevertheless, most couples remain together in the household until one or the other spouse dies. The classical tradition formulates two basic roles for women: daughter and wife. In contrast to male lives, in which the norms pertinent to the four stages of life are honored more often in principle than in practice, women's lives and their two stages actually approximate the cultural ideals set forth in the literature.

According to various texts composed by Brahmans for high-caste audiences, and contemporary norms, particularly those of high-caste people, it is auspicious for the wife to die first. A woman should be married: a widow is not married, or rather, not married any longer. Outliving a husband reflects badly on the wife because it means that she has failed to protect and nurture him. She is to some extent responsible for his death, if not from injuring or neglecting him in this life, then from the ripening of the negative consequences of actions she committed in a previous one. Because of this, the widow is expected to live out her years doing penance, which though socially sanctioned is usually self-imposed. She should lead a simple life, a life without the luxuries of jewelry, fine clothes, and rich, spicy food. Rather, she should devote herself to religion and to serving the household in whatever ways she can. Furthermore, she should avoid wedding celebrations and various other auspicious occasions, lest her presence bring bad luck. For the same reason, she should not remarry. On the whole, widow remarriage is practiced only by low-caste and tribal people, those who have been least influenced by the Sanskritic tradition and who can least afford to support widows.

By contrast, men are allowed, and even encouraged, to remarry, particularly if they have not yet contributed sons to their lineage. Thus, even though ideally marriage is only one of four stages for men, in fact it is the most important stage, for without their marriage the line disintegrates. After they have produced sons, however, the men are theoretically free to leave the household to seek liberation. Whereas for women, ideally and practically, the end of life is marriage, for men ideally the end of life is renunciation of marriage. Hence, we have seen that though very few actually do renounce marriage, many speak wistfully of the superiority of renunciation, which, they say, they might perform were they not so weak-spirited or so essential to their family's economic survival.

Much of the scholarship on Hindu tradition has focused on conceptions of liberation and the renunciatory and contemplative lifestyle that is conducive to liberation. This fascination with soteriology, as T. N. Madan has pointed out in his book *Non-Renunciation*, has tended to contribute to an understanding of the domestic life that men share with women as a lesser mode of existence and as one relatively uninteresting. Madan's work has contributed to efforts to demystify and de-exocitize India by exploring the householder tradition, which values karmic rewards instead of condemning them as bonding those who pursue them to the karmic chain of reincarnation (*saṃsāra*).

Recent scholarly focus on the domestic sphere has also benefited from a burgeoning scholarship on women. This research has tried to correct Western views that see women as powerless in a patriarchal culture. These views are themselves grounded in the pervasive Western image of India as backward and inferior to Western culture, an image that has its roots in the colonial era. There has been great fascination with the notion of *śakti*, or female power, at both the divine and the social level.[21] Yet this fascination has been tempered with concern that portraying Indian women as empowered and trying to rebuke or bracket "colonialist" perspectives may run the risk of remystifying women who are, in many ways, disadvantaged by the devaluation of their gender. Some of the most interesting scholarship that tries to address this dilemma examines women's life histories and folk narratives to detect patterns of resistance to gender and class dominance.[22]

Much contemporary writing on Indian society, especially that of the subaltern school of social historians and feminist interpretations of colonial and postcolonial representations of women in India, takes seriously the issue of who is representing whom, and why.[23] Patterns of thought that pervaded the colonial relationship continue to haunt Western writers, and thus many Indian writers are understandably sensitive to having their culture written about. Doing our best to avoid reifying and exoticizing marriage, in this volume we try not to look at marriage as some sort of cultural monolith possessing an essential character but to show that there are myriad perspectives that can be brought to bear on just what marriage is or is not. We see the experience of marriage as manifold and often discontinuous. Reflecting on the shifting peripheries of marriage, we focus attention on the diversity and ambiguity that inheres in our subject.

The Essays

The essay by Gloria Goodwin Raheja explores the dynamics between ritual traditions and local practices of marriage in rural north India. Some of these traditions stress the separation of a woman from her natal kin at the moment of marriage yet at the same time define her presence in her husband's home as a potential threat to the unity and solidarity of her new conjugal family. These traditions often disadvantage women because, as Raheja points out, women may come to feel they have no one to call "one's own" if they are experiencing difficulties with their husbands or their husbands' kin. The essay explores genres of women's songs that comment critically on the social structures and practices within which rural women live.

Mary Hancock's contribution shows how possession and renunciation shape the religious devotion (*bhakti*) of eminent Brahman women devotees of goddesses in Madras and demonstrates that devotion both affirms and tests marriage. *Bhakti* allows these women to redefine their roles within their families, to assert their authority to make decisions for the household, and to reconceive the domestic space to allow public access.

Susan Wadley's examination of widowhood contains a comparison of the experiences of high- and low-caste widows and a discussion of how the differing expectations of women in these positions inform their understanding of marriage. Wadley also shows that a woman's attachment to her blood relatives, which she is expected to renounce in marriage, carries on into widowhood and that even a woman whose husband is alive may be symbolically widowed by the death of a brother.

Ann Grodzin Gold's essay describes the continuity of identity that women maintain despite their movement between statuses. Drawing from a folk narrative that displays a woman's unflagging *bhakti* in the face of familial objections, Gold shows how women may respond critically, with discontent and disapproval, to the experience of being perceived as split between identities as members of natal families and members of conjugal families. Instead, women see themselves as whole persons who have complex and subtle reflections on female powers and virtues.

Ralph Nicholas's essay discusses the ways in which notions of divorce reflect and shape the dominant cultural constructions of marriage as portrayed in Bengali texts and examines the effectiveness of the wedding ritual in achieving the transformation of persons.

Wendy Doniger's essay turns to ancient legal and mythological texts to explore the discourse regarding adultery and *niyoga,* the practice of giving a widow to the deceased's brother so that she may conceive a child belonging to her conjugal lineage. Her analysis uncovers Indian culture's deep and pervading ambivalence about sexuality at the margins of marriage.

Paul Courtright's essay takes up the image of the *satī,* a woman immolated on the pyre of her deceased husband. By exploring conflicting interpretations of the powers and responsibilities of women in marriage, he identifies a paradox inherent in the sacrificial dimension of *satī* immolation. His essay then turns to what appears to be a recent adaptation of *satī* ideology to traditional forms of feminine sainthood as a consequence of the abolition of *satī* immolation, and explores some surprising ways in which tradition and modernity interact.

Lindsey Harlan's essay focuses on Mīrā Bāī, a medieval Kṛṣṇa devotee, who draws family condemnation. She explores contemporary constructions of Mīrā's story by Rajput women and suggests that the ambivalence women feel about Mīrā's unorthodox behavior may be due in part to the many ways in which Mīrā is positioned at the margins of marriage. Mīrā is a daughter, a wife, a widow, a *bhakta,* an adulteress, a dancer, an ascetic, and, in some sense, a *satī.* Her transgressions of marital convention both defy and delineate Hindu marriage.

NOTES

1. An excellent example of this approach is Raj Bali Pandey's *Hindu Saṃskāras* (Delhi: Motilal Banarsidass, 1976).

2. An example is the ethnographic analysis of local marriage practices found in Lina Fruzzetti, *The Gift of a Virgin: Women, Marriage, and Ritual in a Bengali Society* (New Brunswick, N.J.: Rutgers University Press, 1982).

3. Other marginalities of marriage that might be considered would include female ascetics and *devadāsīs*, or temple dancers. Excellent work on asceticism has been done by Lynn Teskey Denton ("Varieties of Female Asceticism," in *Roles and Rituals for Women,* ed., Julia Leslie, [London: Pinter Press, 1991], pp. 211–32) and Lawrence A. Babb (*Redemptive Encounters: Three Modern Styles in the Hindu Tradition* [Berkeley: University of California Press, 1987]); on *devadāsīs* regarding asceticism; see Frédérique A. Marglin, *Wives of the God-King: The Rituals of the Devadasis* of Puri. (Delhi: Oxford University Press, 1985), and Amrit Srinivasan, "Reform and Revival: The Devadasi and Her Dance" *Economic and Political Weekly,* 20, no. 44 (1985), 1869–76.

4. Dumont's analysis is presented most fully in *Homo Hierarchicus: The Caste System and Its Implications* (Chicago: University of Chicago Press, 1970).

5. The transmutability of code and substance is discussed in McKim Marriott and Ronald Inden, "Towards an Ethnosociology of North Indian Caste

Systems,'' in *The New Wind: Changing Identities in South Asia,* ed., Kenneth David, (The Hague: Mouton, 1977), pp. 227–38.

6. See Akos Östör, Lina Fruzzetti, and Steve Barnett, eds., *Concepts of Person: Kinship, Caste and Marriage in India* (Cambridge, Mass.: Harvard University Press, 1982), pp. 27–28; Nur Yalman ''On the Purity of Women in the Castes of Ceylon and Malabar,'' *Journal of the Royal Anthropological Institute* 93 (1963): 40; and Wendy Doniger O'Flaherty, *Women, Androgynes and Other Mythical Beasts* (Chicago: University of Chicago Press, 1980), pp. 17–64. A contrasting view is presented in Marglin, *Wives of the God-King,* pp. 58–64.

7. Before this act was passed or in situations where it is not enforced, men are expected to marry in caste at least for their first marriage and then may choose to marry women from castes ranked beneath their own.

8. For further discussion of these notions, see Stanley Tambiah, ''From *Varna* to Caste Through Mixed Unions,'' in *The Character of Kinship,* ed. Jack Goody (Cambridge, Mass.: Harvard University Press, 1982), pp. 191–229.

9. Marglin, *Wives of the God-King.*

10. See, for example, her book *The Origins of Evil in Hindu Mythology* (Berkeley: University of California Press, 1976), pp. 1–13.

11. This is one reason for the proliferation of articles and books treating goddesses. Recent examples include Eveline Meyer, *Aṅkāḷaparmēcuvari: A Goddess of Tamilnadu, Her Myths and Cult* (Stuttgart: Steiner Verlag, 1986); Giles Tarabout, *Sacrifier et donner à voir en pays Malabar: Les Fêtes de temple au Karala (Inde du Sud)* (Paris: Ecole Française d'Extrême-Orient, 1986); William Sax, *Mountain Goddess: Gender and Politics in a Himalayan Pilgrimage* (New York: Oxford University Press, 1991); Kathleen Erndl, *Victory to the Mother: The Hindu Goddess of Northwest India in Myth, Ritual, and Symbol* (New York: Oxford University Press, 1993); David Kinsley, *Hindu Goddesses: Visions of the Divine Feminine in the Hindu Religious Tradition* (Berkeley: University of California Press, 1986); and Lynn Bennett, *Dangerous Wives and Sacred Sisters: Social and Symbolic Roles of High-Caste Women in Nepal* (New York: Columbia University Press, 1983).

12. This is Wendy Doniger O'Flaherty's phrase; see *Women, Androgynes, and Other Mythical Beasts,* p. 93.

13. This interpretation has been developed by Sudhir Kakar in *The Inner World: A Psycho-analytic Study of Childhood and Society in India* (Delhi: Oxford University Press, 1978); and most recently by Stanley Kurtz in *All Mothers Are One: Hindu India and the Cultural Reshaping of Psychoanalysis* (New York: Columbia University Press, 1992).

14. For elaborations on the symbolism of hair, see Gananath Obeyesekere, *Medusa's Hair: An Essay on Personal Symbols and Religious Experience* (Chicago: University of Chicago Press, 1981); and Alf Hiltebeitel, ''Draupadī's Hair,'' *Puruṣārtha* 5 (1981): 179–214.

15. A widow is expected to be chaste and to be supervised by the male head of the household, even if he is her son. A widow who does not remain defined by devotion to her deceased husband is viewed as potentially loose and a threat to the integrity of the family. It is therefore not surprising that words for widow and prostitute are the same in many Indian languages.

16. For a discussion of similar practices in south India, see Holly Baker Reynolds, ''The Auspicious Married Woman,'' in *The Powers of Tamil Women,*

South Asia Series no 6, ed., Susan S. Wadley, (Syracuse, N.Y.: Maxwell School of Citizenship and Public Affairs, 1982), pp. 35–60.

17. See especially Bennett, *Dangerous Wives and Sacred Sisters*, pp. 224–29, 240–43.

18. For a general introduction to the strictures and freedoms of *pardā*, see Hanna Papanek, "Purdah: Separate Worlds and Symbolic Shelter," in *Separate Worlds: Studies in Purdah in South Asia*, ed. Hanna Papanek and Gail Minnault, (Delhi: Chanakya Publications, 1982), pp. 3–53. For comparative perspectives on *pardā*, see Lila Abu-Lughod, *Veiled Sentiments: Honor and Poetry in Bedouin Society* (Berkeley: University of California Press, 1986); and Patricia Jeffery, *Frogs in a Well: Indian Women in Purdah* (London: Zed Press, 1979).

19. For background on *vrats*, see Susan S. Wadley, *Shakti: Power in the Conceptual Structure of Karimpur Religion* (Chicago: University of Chicago, Dept. of Anthropology, 1975), pp. 35ff.; Reynolds, "The Auspicious Married Woman," pp. 50–60; Lindsey Harlan, *Religion and Rajput Women: The Ethic of Protection in Contemporary Narratives* (Berkeley: University of California Press, 1992), 57–60, Bennett, *Dangerous Wives and Sacred Sisters*, pp. 215ff.; and Mary McGee, "Feasting and Fasting: The Vrata Tradition and Its Significance for Hindu Women," Ph.D. diss., Harvard University, 1987.

20. Morris Carstairs, *The Twice-Born: A Study of High-Caste Hindus* (Bloomington: University of Indiana Press, 1967), pp. 96–97.

21. See Wadley, *Shakti.*

22. See especially Gloria Goodwin Raheja and Ann Grodzins Gold, *Listen to the Heron's Words: Reimagining Gender and Kinship in North India* (Berkeley: University of California Press, 1993).

23. For illuminating overviews of these perspectives, see Ranajit Guha and Gayatri Chakravorty Spivak, eds., *Selected Subaltern Studies* (New York: Oxford University Press, 1988); Kumkum Sangari and Sudesh Vaid, eds., *Recasting Women: Essays in Indian Colonial History* (New Brunswick, N.J.: Rutgers University Press, 1990); T. Niranjana, P. Sudhir, and Vivek Dhareshwar, eds., *Interrogating Modernity: Culture and Colonialism in India* (Calcutta: Seagull Books, 1993); Gyan Prakash and Doug Haynes, *Contesting Power: Resistance and Everyday Social Relations in South Asia* (Berkeley: University of California Press, 1992); and Ashis Nandy, *The Intimate Enemy: Loss and Recovery of Self Under Colonialism* (Delhi: Oxford University Press, 1983).

2

"Crying When She's Born, and Crying When She Goes Away": Marriage and the Idiom of the Gift in Pahansu Song Performance

GLORIA GOODWIN RAHEJA

Authoritative South Asian textual traditions, composed or performed by males, have many things to say about the transformation women undergo as they are married, as their identity as daughter and sister is eclipsed by their identity as wife and daughter-in-law, and as they move from *pīhar* to *sasurāl,* from natal home to conjugal place. These textual discourses, and a good deal of everyday talk as well, tend to stress ideas concerning the ideal wife's assimilation into her husband's kin group and the attenuation of her ties to her own natal kin following her marriage so that the authority of her husband's kin is not undermined by her reliance on her brothers. In such texts it is assumed that the virtuous wife, the *pativratā,* will show deference to her husband's senior kin and honor her husband, while restraining her own desires for intimacy and rapport with him so as not to undermine the unity and solidarity of his family and kin group. These are very powerful and persuasive ideologies in South Asia, and they place women in disadvantaged situations in which they are distanced from their natal kin yet viewed as potentially threatening to their husbands' kin; it is seen as dangerous for a woman to be close to her brothers, and dangerous for her to draw near to her husband.

Despite the authority of these normative characterizations, women articulate critical responses to them in songs they sing at births, weddings, and festival occasions; in doing so, they set forth alternative perspectives on the transformation from daughter and sister to wife. This essay focuses on women's interrogations of male-authored discourses about marriage and female identity, voiced in ritual songs about gift giving. The idiom of the gift seems a particularly apt language for such critiques, since the marriage ritual itself is understood as a gift (*kanyā dān*, or "the gift of a virgin") and since kinship relations themselves are often spoken of in terms of the gifts deemed essential to them.[1] Thus, women's critical commentaries on gift-giving relationships strike at the very heart of patrilineal kinship in north India and its pronouncements on marriage and female identity.

Women's sung commentaries on the dual positioning of women after marriage, and the contradictory expectations engendered by this positioning, are cast largely in terms of a discourse about the gifts given in dowry and the gifts a woman expects to receive thereafter from her natal kin, the gifts a woman is expected to give to her husband's sister, and the gifts a woman may wish to receive from her husband. Women's songs from Pahansu[2] do not speak with a single voice of the contradictions and ambiguities involved in the giving and receiving of gifts; rather, divergent perspectives are given voice in songs that speak from the position of sister and songs that speak from the position of wife.

Money, Power, Sex, and Love: What Are Women Talking About When They Talk About Gifts?

Some gifts a woman receives from her natal kin have critical economic significance in her married life. Jacobson has traced the economic importance for women in central India of the jewelry gifted to them, showing that women have the most control over and the most undisputed rights to jewelry given them by their natal kin,[3] and Vatuk and Vatuk have documented, for rural Uttar Pradesh, the significance for women's lives and women's solidarity of an informal system of private savings, a system in which gifts of cash and jewelry to daughters and sisters are often enormously consequential.[4] And women can sometimes expect to be humiliated, ill treated, and even, in urban India, burned alive if the dowry expectations of the husband's family are not met.[5] Certainly, then, when women speak of the cloth, cash, and jewelry they expect to receive from their natal kin, their economic well-being is very much on their minds. But is this all that women speak of when they speak of gifts, or does their talk of *bhāt* and *neg* and *dahej* and *milāī* and all the other specifically named prestations that are regularly given and received in north India signify something more about female perspectives on marriage, kinship, and gender?

Answering this question is not easy because embedded within it are critical and complex issues of voice, subjectivity, agency, and positionality. Related to these are issues of the representation of South Asian women in scholarly literature.[6] How, for example, has gift giving, and dowry in particular, been understood in anthropological writing on north Indian society, and how have women's presences and women's perspectives been represented in this writing? Broadly speaking, there have been two general approaches to the explication of gift giving in north Indian kinship. Dumont and Vatuk were both concerned with understanding the nature of affinity in north India, the relationships between groups of kinsmen as givers of brides and receivers of brides. They were particularly struck by the fact that these affinal relationships, like consanguineal relationships in many Western societies, persist from one generation to the next. Dumont argued, for example, that a person's mother's brother is in many ways regarded as an affine; his relationship to his sister's son is partly a function of the affinal relationship he has with his sister's husband, particularly insofar as gift-giving obligations are concerned.[7] Both Dumont and Vatuk suggested that the primary focus of gifts given to married daughters and sisters and to their husbands' kin lay in the enduring relationships of groups of men linked by marriage, but Vatuk also recognized that the continuing relationship of a married woman to her natal kin was equally at stake in these gift transactions, an observation that I will be elaborating upon in this essay.

Dumont's work on marriage alliance in north and south India set the terms, then, for the first approach to the interpretation of marriage gifts, which focuses on alliances between groups of male kinsmen. This represents an extremely important set of insights into kinship in India, but it is problematic if women are viewed primarily as objects of exchange, and if their perspectives on these transactions and their active role in marriage negotiations are not attended to.

Several of Dumont's remarks in "Hierarchy and Marriage Alliance in South Indian Kinship" ground the second general set of interpretations of dowry as well. Dumont wrote that in patrilineal societies in which significant prestations accompany the bride, property is transmitted from one generation to the next under two forms: that of inheritance from father to son, and that of gifts from father-in-law to son-in-law. For Dumont this "double transmission of property" underlined the distinction between kinship and alliance, though he in no way suggested that gift-giving obligations could be understood only or primarily in relation to property rights; he stressed, rather, the ritual and social meanings of these obligations.

For Tambiah, however, such a "transmission of property," but to daughters rather than sons-in-law, was seen as constitutive of north Indian social practices connected with dowry. Though he argues that dowry expresses a status relation between wife givers and wife receivers,[8] he sees this as meshing with a more fundamental notion of "female property rights."[9] Dowry represents, for Tambiah as for Goody,[10] a "pre-mortem inheritance" to which a daughter is entitled, bestowed upon her at the time she is married, as a "share" of the estate that will be inherited primarily by her brothers. Tambiah is unequivocal on this point:

> Dowry is property given to the daughter to take with her into her marriage. Technically it is her property and in her control though the husband usually has rights of management. A husband cannot transfer the dowry to his sister, partly because he requires his wife's consent, but more importantly because it is against the spirit of the dowry institution, which is that dowry given a wife and in her legal possession should form part of the conjugal estate, to be enjoyed by the husband and wife and to be transmitted to their children.[11]

Tambiah also argues that a woman's husband and his kin acquire no "jural" interest in this property, and that the woman's daughters are expected to inherit after her death. This transmission of property through the female line is held to be the "core" meaning of dowry in north India. In a discussion of Dumont's view concerning inhe: 'tance and affinal prestations, Tambiah observes rightly that Dumont interprets property transmission through gifts as arising from a much more fundamental creation of alliances between givers and receivers of brides. Tambiah rejects this interpretation and argues instead that the double transmission of property is the prior and more basic fact.

Much of Tambiah's argument is, as he readily admits, constructed on the basis of "traditional Indian legal concepts" abstracted from the classical Sanskrit legal and moral treatises called the *dharmaśāstras*. Though he alludes to the facts that the British colonial regime undertook the recovery and translation of these works in order to administer what they imagined to be Hindu law to the Hindus, and that considerable "modification" of customary practice resulted from this textualization, he argues nonetheless that "traditional custom" concerning dowry continues to prevail in the villages, and that practices connected with marriage prestations can be interpreted directly in terms laid down in the texts.[12] This ahistorical reading of the place of textual traditions in contemporary social life is problematic, given recent studies of nineteenth-century colonial attempts to actively construct a unitary Hindu "law" concerning marriage and inheritance; textual traditions were often invoked in order to homogenize and rigidify fluid and variable local customs.[13] But even in terms of the ethnography available in 1973,

Tambiah's assertion that dowry represents the transmission of female property rights is difficult to accept.

Tambiah's 1973 essay relies rather heavily, for the north Indian portion of his exposition, on a statement made by T. N. Madan concerning a woman's "jural rights" to the *strīdhan* (female wealth) given to her in dowry.[14] A careful reading of Madan's text, however, belies Tambiah's understanding of the ethnography. Madan does indeed refer to the notion that "jurally speaking" *strīdhan* is a woman's exclusive property, but it is clear from his footnotes here that he is speaking of rights specified in the Sanskritic textual tradition. Kashmiri Pandit customary practice seems to be quite different. Madan makes it absolutely clear that female family members, whether daughters/sisters or spouses, have no rights of ownership or disposal of property; he says that daughters and sisters have "rights" to periodically visit and receive gifts from their natal kin. They receive *strīdhan* at their marriage, and despite the legal tenets concerning her exclusive rights to that property, "in practice her parents-in-law show immense interest in her *strīdhan,* and may take away the best of her personal possessions to give to their own daughters. The domestic utensils and other household effects which she brings with her are, in any case, put into household use and treated as joint property."[15] Tambiah quotes this last passage from Madan's ethnography in a footnote, but he adds that this sort of appropriation of the dowry "is certainly not customary or publicly condoned."[16] Tambiah similarly disregards as "not customary" other practices he finds to be contradictory to textual formulations. He acknowledges that there are "deviations" whereby portions of a daughter-in-law's dowry may be given on by the husband's parents at the marriage of their own daughter, but he asserts, without citing any ethnographic evidence, that this is considered "somewhat contemptible."[17]

In a recent reformulation, Tambiah has considered later ethnographic evidence that indicates quite unambiguously that his notion that dowry represents the transmission of "female wealth" is grossly inaccurate.[18] Here he discusses the ethnography of Vatuk, Parry, van der Veen, and Hershman, all of which indicates that much of the dowry is specifically intended for particular recipients among the husband's kinsmen and kinswomen.[19] He draws, then, what he sees as an essential contrast between the dowry goods that are kept in a woman's locked trunk and those that become the property of members of the groom's joint family. He states:

> Recent ethnography has clearly established that typically the *dahej* can be divided into three portions—one part, not insubstantial, that the bride may keep as her personal property, the second part, the most substantial, being controlled by the groom's joint family (especially his parents) and susceptible to use as "circulating goods" in the marriage of its daughters, and the

> third part meant as gifts to the women of the groom's joint family and his married sisters and father's sisters.[20]

But, in the final analysis, Tambiah does not see this evidence as seriously undermining his original formulation.

> The domestic-cycle dynamics of the Indian joint family revolve around the process of partition by which at a certain point—usually with the death of the parents, sometimes earlier or later—the joint family disaggregates into nuclear families of married brothers. In this sense it is correct to say that in due course joint-family assets—whatever remains after dowrying the "daughters of the house"—break up into the conjugal funds of the married brothers. Thus, after all, when due notice is taken of the joint family as a corporate group potentially destined to partition into its conjugal pairs and conjugal funds, the essential theses of *Bridewealth and Dowry* remain unshaken. These theses are that in propertied India there is usually a diverging devolution or double transmission of property to and through males and females and that this transmission emphasizes vertical bonds between parents and children at the cost of lateral lineage bonds.[21]

Thus, in "revisiting" the question of dowry and marriage prestations in South Asia, Tambiah once again imprisons the issue in a discourse of "property," "assets," "inheritance," and purely economic valuations. Despite growing evidence to the contrary, he assumes that resources within the joint family ultimately will be equitably redistributed among men and women.

The tin trunk figures prominently in Tambiah's analysis as a supposed repository of female wealth over time. Yet in Pahansu, as elsewhere in north India, the chief function of this trunk is to store the cloth that a woman receives from her natal kin throughout her marriage, cloth that is almost always "given onward" to her husband's sisters, her daughters, and others to whom she has gift-giving obligations. Even a particular item of jewelry she receives at her marriage may be demanded by her husband's sister, as a *neg* prestation at the birth of her children.[22] And the portion of the dowry that is given directly to the husband and his kin may be long dispersed—either in gifts at the weddings of female members of the household or in ordinary expenditures—by the time the joint family is partitioned.

Jack Goody has more recently expanded upon such arguments that interpret dowry in terms of a diverging devolution of property to the daughter analogous to a son's inheritance of land and other wealth. He argues that the dowry should be viewed in terms of a daughter's property rights because "the gift of dowry is made to her, to the conjugal estate and to its heirs, rather than to the groom's kin, or even to the groom."[23] In *The Oriental, the Ancient and the Primitive* he constructs a critique of anthropological analyses that stress the incorporation of a bride into her husband's family. He remarks at length on the persisting importance of the brother–sister tie in north India and speaks eloquently of the double positioning of married women and of the contradictions in kinship ideology that arise from this situation. But Goody attributes the importance of a woman's enduring ties to her brothers and other natal kin to the fact that she is supposedly entitled to property transfers at her marriage and afterward, in the form of dowry and gifts from her natal kin. Like Tambiah, he speaks of the "diverging devolution" of property in north India, to sons via inhertance and to daughters via dowry.

Goody dramatically overstates the degree to which dowry gifts are given to the daughter, rather than to her husband and his kin. Moreover, as he quite justifiably critiques the anthropological stress on the idea of a wife's incorporation into the kin group of her husband, he fails to see that this ideology does in fact represent one particular indigenous perspective on kinship relations, a perspective that may often serve the interests of powerful males in the *sasurāl* while placing women in subordinate positions. And he fails to ask whether women's insistence on the importance of natal ties in north India might in effect be a strategy of resistance to the authority of those affinal men, who may not always look favorably upon the maintenance of a woman's close relationships to brothers and other natal kin, precisely because such ties may be used to challenge their own authority over the wife.[24] In thus ignoring the positionality of the men and women who speak of dowry and kinship ties in rural India, Goody's analysis obscures the issues of women's subjectivity and women's agency, and the issue of women's particular placement in these gendered power relations.

In a somewhat critical reply to Tambiah's 1989 attempt to recuperate his earlier interpretation, van der Veen expresses a basic agreement with Tambiah concerning dowry as representing a "diverging devolution" of property.[25] He suggests that Sharma's ethnography from Panjab and Himachal Pradesh, in northwest India, indicates that women are aware of their "rights" to a share of the property of their natal kin. Sharma writes that "a woman will talk about 'my land' or 'our land' referring to the land held in the name of her father or by her husband's father. Women do not speak as though they felt excluded from ownership."[26]

This is a crucial moment. For the first time we hear a woman's voice. She utters the words "our land" with respect to the fields of her father and brothers. Such words are presumably subsumed by Tambiah and Goody as well in a discourse only about property, assets, ownership, and "rights."[27]

In Pahansu I frequently heard married women use the words "our village" and "our land" in connection with their *pīhar*, their natal home. Moreover, I often heard women speak of their expectations that natal kin would give generously to them. But, as Madan made clear long ago, and as more recent ethnography reiterates, much of the dowry in fact goes directly to the husband and his kin, and much goes indirectly, when the bride herself takes on obligations to give cloth, jewelry, and other items that came from her natal home onward to her husband's married sisters.[28] Some of the jewelry, cash, and cloth a woman receives from her natal kin does in fact benefit her economically: she has some control over a relatively small portion of the dowry, and she may use it in many ways for her own benefit and that of her children. But the bulk of these gifts are given directly to or are controlled by her husband, her mother-in-law, and her husband's senior male kin. Furthermore, they are more likely to be put into circu-lation at the marriages of her husband's sisters or to be otherwise expended, than to be held as "assets" awaiting a division into a conjugal fund.

Why, then, do women speak so provocatively and profoundly of their ties to their natal place and to their kinsmen there? As I try to explicate women's words as they sing of gifts and of natal kin, I shall suggest that as women talk of *bhāt* and *dahej, milāī* and *neg,* and of "our land," we hear not so much a discourse on economy as a poetic discourse on power and the possibility of women's resistance to patrilineal authority and patrilineal pronouncements on female identities. Women sometimes die in urban India because the economic value of their dowries does not meet the expectations of their husbands' families, and many more women in town and village alike are made to feel insecure and unwanted in such circumstances; to speak, then, of dowry as a form of "inheritance" for women skirts these overwhelmingly important issues of power and authority. In listening to some words spoken by rural and urban women alike, we may come to see that women think not just of gaining their share of the wealth but of contesting the power relations that make them so vulnerable when they marry and go away. They speak of transforming the feelings of love, attachment, and sexuality that are defined and constrained by those relations. It is this fact of women's contestation, voiced in the idiom of the gift, that is absent in the analyses made by the alliance theorists, and by Tambiah and Goody.

Giving to "One's Own," Giving to "Another": Ambiguities at Marriage

Patterns of gift giving[29] are deeply implicated in female identity and in the relative valuation of sons and daughters from the very beginning of a woman's life. After the birth of a son, for six nights women gather in the mother's courtyard to sing *byāī gīt,* songs celebrating the auspicious birth of a son and the happiness of the new mother. When a daughter is born, there is no singing and no celebration. Learning of the birth of a girl, women who come to visit the new mother express their sympathy by saying that "it's a matter of fate," or they resign themselves to the fortune that has been meted out by saying simply, "Whatever God has given has been given."

There are many reasons why sons are desired in north India, reasons connected with land inheritance, the security of parents in later life, and the necessary performance of death rituals. Despite recently enacted legislation concerning daughters' rights in the parental estate, only sons inherit land in rural north India and only sons may perform the final rites at a parent's death. Since a daughter moves away to her husband's house, sons are desired so that mothers and fathers will not be alone as they advance in age. But the chief reason, according to Pahansu women, that the birth of a daughter brings sorrow, and the reason that songs are not sung at her birth, is the anticipation that "it will be necessary to give much in dowry." Such apprehension is voiced in a number of Hindi proverbs. When, for example, a family is worrying about the financial burden of providing an adequate dowry, a neighbor or kinsman may comment: "Without a daughter, without a daughter's husband, one enjoys what one earns" (*dhī na dhiyānā āp hī kamānā āp hī khānā*). The very giving away of a daughter to her husband's family means, in many north Indian communities, that a hierarchical relationship will be established between kinsmen, such that the family of the bride assumes an inferior status. A *banī kā gīt* (song of the young bride) sung in Pahansu in 1988 tells of the connection between a girl's birth, the sorrow of her natal kin, and their "defeat" at the time of her marriage.

Banī kā gīt

In a corner of the Color Palace, a little girl was born.[30]
When the little girl was born, her grandfather was woebegone.
[Girl speaking, just after her marriage:][31]
Grandfather, why are you the loser, and why is my grandfather-in-law the winner?[32]
[Grandfather speaking]
Dear girl, because of you I've lost, but because of my grandson I've won.
In a corner of the Color Palace, a little girl was born.

In the stanzas that follow the young bride questions her father's elder brother, her father's younger brother, her mother's brother, and her own father in the same way.

Rajavati, a wife in the house in which I lived, sat with me as I translated this song, and she remarked that the "girl's people" (*laṛkīvāle*) are considered to be "little" (*choṭā*) and the "boy's people" (*laṛkevāle*) are considered to be "big" (*baṛā*), and that is why the latter enjoy such advantages as being privileged to sit at the head of a cot when they meet, while the bride's people must sit at the foot.[33] That, she said, is why the grandfather is woebegone at the birth of a daughter, and why he "wins" at the birth of a son.[34]

Despite these disadvantages, *kanyā dān,* the unreciprocated giving away of a daughter along with substantial amounts of jewelry, cloth, brass cooking vessels, cash, and, most recently, TVS, "sofa sets," and motorcycles, has such significant ritual and social consequences that many people say it is important that each married couple have at least one daughter to be given in marriage.[35] There is a Hindi proverb, heard mostly among women, that gives voice to this perspective: "For those who have no daughter, the threshold becomes like a daughter" (*jiske dhī nahīṅ uskī dehalī dhī*). In other words, if one cannot give meritorious gifts to a daughter, one is bereft and can give to beggars at the threshold. And though there may be little joy at the birth of a daughter, there is also a recognition of the irony that though a daughter's birth may bring sorrow, her departure from her parent's home when she marries is equally sorrowful for her natal kin. This double-edged grief and its ironies are expressed in another Hindi proverb: "One has to somehow endure a daughter's birth; there's crying when she's born and crying when she goes away" (*beṭī kā dhan nibhānā hai āte bhī rulāye jāte bhī rulāye*). Other proverbs speak of the enormity and the emotionally wrenching aspects of the *kanyā dān,* the giving away of one's own beloved daughter: "If one has given a daughter, what has one kept back?" (*jisne beṭī dī usne kyā rakhā*).

The songs that women sing at births, marriages, and calendrical festivals consistently focus on their experiences of these seemingly contradictory perspectives on marriage prestations and the giving away of a daughter, and their experience of the shifting emotional valences of ties with daughters and sisters to whom gifts must be given. Because married women assume the gift-giving obligations of their husbands, and because they almost always arrange for the gift giving to their husbands' sisters, they focus also on women's experiences as givers, as well as recipients, of such gifts. I shall suggest that women's understandings and valuations of marriage are multiple and shifting, and that their polyphonic discourse on relations to natal kin and conjugal kin are voiced largely in talk about giving and receiving, from their double positioning as both wives and sisters. Women who appear in the songs as wives construe these gifts in one way, and women who appear in the songs as sisters construe them in another.

Throughout north India, the marriage ritual is frequently spoken of as *kanyā dān,* the unreciprocated giving away of a daughter along with lavish gifts for herself, for her husband, and for his kin. She is given away in the course of a complex set of ritual actions that are in part designed to effect her transformation from "one's own" (*apnī*) to her natal kin to "other" (*dūsrī*) and "alien" (*parāyī*) to them. The woman is often said to undergo a transformation at the wedding, in which she becomes the "half body" of her husband, of one substance with him. His kinsmen become her own kinsmen, and her ties with her own natal kin are transformed as well; people in Pahansu say that unmarried girls share a "bodily connection" (*śarīr kā sambandh*) with their natal kin, but that after marriage there is only a "relationship" (*riśtā*).

This ideology of the separation of the bride from her natal kin also plays an important role in some of the ritual meanings of marriage and the gift in north India. The term *dān* is used to refer to prestations given to many kinds of recipients and in many different ritual contexts. But all *dān*, Pahansu people say, is given "to move away inauspiciousness" (*nāśubh haṭāne ke lie*) from the donor and transfer it to the recipient, who is thought of as a "receptacle" (*pātra*) for the inauspiciousness contained within the gift. *Dān* is never given within one's own family, because if it were given to those who are "one's own," the inauspiciousness would stay and not be moved away. *Dān* is always given, then, to those who are "other" (*dūsrā/dūsrī*) or "alien" (*parāyā/parāyī*) to the donor, so that the inauspiciousness will "go to another house."

The giving of *kanyā dān*, then, like the giving of other *dān*, removes "evil" (*pāp*) and "danger" (*saṅkaṭ*) from the family of the donor.[36] The greatest danger comes, villagers say, if a daughter remains in her father's house after she has begun to menstruate. She must be given in *dān* because to allow her to remain in her natal home would generate inauspiciousness and misfortune. Inauspiciousness is transferred to the groom and his family through their acceptance of the *kanyā dān* and the many prestations that follow. This idea appears to have a very long history in Indic texts. In a hymn from the *Rg Veda* describing the marriage of Sūrya, the daughter of the sun, and Soma (verses of which are used in marriage rituals even today), there is a similar inauspiciousness attached to the blood of defloration. The marriage gown on which the stain of blood appears causes the bride's own family to prosper, but her husband's family is "bound in the bonds," and her husband himself may become "ugly and sinisterly pale" if he comes into contact with it. "It [the blood] burns, it bites, it has claws, as dangerous as poison is to eat." Some of the inauspiciousness involved in the acceptance of the *kanyā dān* is, in Pahansu, passed on to the groom's family Brahman priest, and this is the case in the Vedic hymn as well: "Throw away the gown, and distribute wealth to the priests. It becomes a magic spirit walking on feet, and like the wife it draws near the husband. . . . Only the priest who knows the Sūrya hymn is able to receive the marriage gown."[37]

Though a bride is also viewed as an auspicious bringer of fortune to her husband's family, this notion that the acceptance of a bride involves the acceptance of danger as well is unambiguously articulated in the Sanskrit verses that are recited at every wedding ritual, and much of the ritual is, in Pahansu, structured around this central concern. The first ritual act in the long sequence of marriage rites, for example, is the *sagāī*, the betrothal ceremony at which a "letter" (*ciṭṭhī*) formally opening the sequence of *dān* prestations and formally announcing the astrologically auspicious date for the *kanyā dān* is given by the bride's family to the groom. This *ciṭṭhī* embodies both the auspicious and life-affirming aspects of the marriage gifts as well as the inauspiciousness that is transferred to the groom. The letter, which has been prepared by the Brahman priest who serves the bride's family, and which may be opened only by the groom's priest, is daubed with auspicious turmeric and rice, and it is marked with other auspicious signs. But it also contains one and one-quarter rupees, a ritually significant sum that is often utilized in transferrals of inauspiciousness. Before the groom may safely accept this initial gift, he must be seated just outside his house upon a ritual design called *ṭakkarpūrat* (protection from harm) that absorbs some of the inauspiciousness and transfers it onward to the family Barber, who accepts the flour from which the design was made as *dān*. The Barber also receives coins that are circled over the groom's head by the men of his family, and these coins too remove some of the harmful qualities that accompany the *ciṭṭhī*. But still the letter may not be opened. The Barber's wife, meanwhile, has drawn another *ṭakkarpūrat* design in the courtyard of the groom's house. Carrying the letter in the end of his shawl, the groom stands over this design while the women of his house and his neighborhood circle dishes of grain over his head. This grain, along with the flour from this second *ṭakkarpūrat*, is then given to the Barber's wife as *dān*, again for the protection of the groom. It is only after these two sets of protective actions have been performed that the letter may be opened. The one and one-quarter rupees are taken out of the letter and kept in the groom's house. Because of the inauspiciousness that it contains, it may not be spent or otherwise used by the family. It is kept in a large clay pot for four or five years, after which it is usually given in the *ciṭṭhī* of a sister of the groom, or, if it is a silver rupee, it may be melted down and fashioned into an ornament to be given in *dān* at the time of her wedding. Inauspiciousness is thus dislodged from the house in which the silver had been kept and "given onward" (*āge denā*) to the people who in turn receive a bride.

This theme of the dangers inherent in the acceptance of *dān* from the bride's family recurs throughout the course of the many rituals connected with marriage and a woman's first years in her conjugal home. The most important rite in this protracted series of performances and giftings is the *pherā* (the circling of the fire) by the bride and groom that definitively transfers the bride from natal to conjugal kin. The *pherā* takes place in the courtyard of the bride's house. The priests of the bride's family and of the groom's, men from both sides, and the groom himself are seated around the place where the sacrificial fire will be lit. After some preliminary worship of the deities established at the site, and the ceremonial welcome of the groom by the bride's father, *dān* is offered to the groom: a small sum of money that in fact signifies all of the gifts that will later be bestowed upon him is given as *gau dān* (the gift of a cow). Immediately upon receiving this gift from the bride's father, the groom gives a portion of this money onward as *dān* to his own Brahman *purohit.* The Sanskrit verse spoken by the groom at this time indicates that this *dān* is given to the priest "to remove the faults caused by the acceptance of a cow" (*gau pratigraha doṣa nivāraṇārtham*). The sacrificial fire is then lit, and the bride's mother's brother leads the bride herself, very heavily veiled, into the courtyard and seats her at the side of the groom. The bride's father or the oldest man of her family recites the Sanskrit "resolution" (*saṅkalp*) for the giving of *kanyā dān.* In this resolution the groom is addressed as *śarmanne var* (protecting groom) because of his role as recipient of *dān* from the bride's family. The groom pronounces that the gift has been received, and he says to the bride's father, in Hindi, "may auspiciousness be yours" (*tumhārā kalyāṅ ho*), thus indicating that the giving of *kanyā dān* assures the well-being of the donor. Immediately following his acceptance of the *kanyā dān,* the groom himself makes a resolution for the giving of a *gau dān* to his Brahman *purohit.* This resolution pronounces that this *dān* is given "to remove the faults caused by the acceptance of a wife" (*bhāryā pratigraha doṣa nivāraṇārtham*). A sum of money is given as *dān* to the priest, and he is said to be one who "protects" the groom from some of the dangers involved, just as the priest in the Ṛg Vedic hymn receives the bloodstained bridal gown in order to protect the husband from its evil.

The *pherā* rite not only confers this *dān* upon the groom, it also transforms the bride's relationship with her natal kin. Before she is gifted away, she is "one's own" (*apnī*) to her natal kin, and she is said to have a "bodily connection" (*śarīr kā sambandh*) with them; but afterward people say that this is no longer the case. Just after the groom accepts the *kanyā dān,* the bride's mother's brother provides a piece of white cloth called a *kaṇjol,* measuring one and one-quarter *gaj.* The end of the bride's shawl is tied to the clothes of the groom with this cloth, and small stalks of grass, a few grains of rice, and a coin are tied in the knot of the *kaṇjol.* This cloth remains tied to the bride's clothing for several days. It may not be kept in the house after that, because of the inauspiciousness it contains; it is given to the *purohit* of the groom's family, in order to transfer the danger to him. The Sanskrit verses recited by the bride's family priest as the *kaṇjol* is tied affirms that this action is done "to protect the two masters" (i.e., the bride and the groom) from any inauspiciousness that would affect their future offspring, wealth, or longevity, inauspiciousness that is generated because of the joining together of the bride and the groom. The tying of the *kaṇjol* both unites them and contains the negative qualities thereby set loose. After this tying together of the bride and the groom, and the circling of the sacrificial fire that follows, the bride is no longer "one's own" to her natal kin. She is now said to be "alien" (*parāyī*) to them and "of another house" (*begānī ghar kī*), and though she will always have a "relationship" (*riśtā*), she no longer shares a "bodily connection" with them.

Because she thus becomes in some respects "alien" to her natal kin, the bride is now deemed to be an appropriate recipient herself of *dān* prestations from them, for only one who "goes away to another house" can take away the inauspiciousness conveyed in the gift. She will return frequently to her *pīhar*, her natal village, throughout the course of her life, and on many of these occasions she will be the "appropriate recipient" (*pātra*) of prestations that ensure the well-being and auspiciousness of her brothers and their children. People say that it is her "obligation" to accept these gifts when sons are born to her brother, when his sons marry, and at certain times in her own life when inauspiciousness may afflict her brother (such as the death of her husband, or when the first tooth of one of her own children appears in the upper rather than the lower jaw), and at a number of calendrical rituals observed by married women for the protection of their brothers.[38] The most common Hindi word for "dowry," *dahej*, is used in speaking not only of the gifts given at marriage but of these later *dān* prestations as well.

These are some of the meanings of *dān* as they appear in the marriage ritual itself. This set of meanings enters explicitly into actors' intentionality as gifts are given to married daughters and sisters and their husbands. When people in Pahansu are asked why they give *dān*, they inevitably reply that it is given "for one's own well-being achieved through gift giving" (*apne khair-khairāt ke māro*) or "to move away inauspiciousness" (*nāśubh haṭāne ke lie*). In this regard, people often pointed out to me that it is the "right" of the donor to give such gifts, and the "obligation" of the recipient to accept, and they frequently commented on the aptness of the proverb "Daughter, daughter's husband, and daughter's son, these three are not one's own" (*dhī jamāī bhānjā ye tīnoṅ nahīṅ apnā*) in such considerations. Only those who are not considered as "one's own" are appropriate recipients of *dān*.

This particular set of cultural propositions about marriage and the dissimilation of the married woman from her natal kin has played a critical role in anthropological understandings of kinship and social life in South Asia. Inden and Nicholas, for example, write that the bodily transformation of the Bengali wife is such that the people with whom her husband has a "shared body" relationship (*jñāti*) become her *jñāti*, and the people with whom her husband has a relationship defined by the gifting appropriate to relatives through marriage (his *kuṭumba* relatives) become her *kuṭumba* relatives. This includes her own natal family; after her marriage she is said to have only a "residual *jñāti*" or a *kuṭumba* relationship with them,[39] just as in Pahansu a woman's natal kin may say that they have only a *riśtā* connection with a married daughter or sister.[40]

The arguments of Inden and Nicholas are grounded largely in textual analyses, yet ideas about the alienation of the bride from her natal kin are not confined to Sanskrit texts or esoteric ritual. In their study based on fieldwork in rural Bijnor district in Uttar Pradesh, Jeffery, Jeffery, and Lyon stress the importance of a woman's continuing ties to natal kin in her resistance to the authority of her husband's kin, and the ways in which the ideology of a bride's necessary alienation from her brothers and parents and her incorporation into her husband's kin group may be invoked in order to limit her contacts with natal kin and to curtail such resistance. Men in Bijnor say, for example, that there will be too much "interference" if a woman visits her natal village too frequently or if marriages are arranged at too close a distance in the first place.[41] The ideology of alienation from natal kin thus moves from the realm of a purely textual discourse to the realm of power relations in the conjugal village. Similarly, in the Uttarakhand region of north India, men are apt to question the value of a woman's continuing relationship with her natal kin, because to acknowledge its importance would be to weaken their own power over their wives.[42] Thus, if women construct a critique of this discourse of alienation, they are simultaneously constructing a critical commentary on the power relations that frame their lives.

The overwhelming significance of a woman's ties to her brothers is evident in women's songs and everyday social practices. There is of course the pervasive notion that a woman undergoes a bodily transformation at marriage such that she no longer has a "bodily connection" (*śarīr kā sambandh*) with her natal kin but becomes the "half body" of her husband. Yet, in contrast to that image of alienation from her brothers, a married woman frequently bears a tattoo of her brothers' names upon her arm. Those names are thus irrevocably inscribed upon her body, though from one perspective they no longer share a "bodily connection."

The importance of ties to brothers is also evident in the blessing recited by senior women of the conjugal village when junior daughters-in-law of the village perform the deferential act of massaging the senior women's legs. The senior women murmur *sāī jīte raho bhāī jīte raho beṭā de bhagvān* ("May your husband live long, may your brother live long, and may god give you a son"). The importance of all three of these relationships—with the husband, with the brother, with the son—are thus voiced in that blessing.

Women are generally inconsolable upon the death of a brother. I have observed a few instances in which women took off all emblems of their marital auspiciousness—their glass bangles, toe rings, and so forth—in token of their extreme sorrow (*sok*). The removal of these emblems and embodiments of *suhāg* (good fortune) is prescribed only upon the death of a husband. When these women "take off good fortune" upon the death of a brother, they perhaps are indicating in a subtly ironic and indeed subversive fashion that they consider the tie with the brother as important as that with the husband. It is particularly significant, in relation to the argument I pose in the present essay, that sorrow at the death of a brother is here semiotically conjoined with sorrow at the death of a husband. Though the relationship with the brother is defined, in terms of the overt structure of north Indian kinship and its dominant discourse, as dramatically different from and less enduring than the relationship with the husband's kin, in their actions these women comment on and interrogate the dominant discourse that represents them as "other" to their natal kin.

The link between gift giving and the emotional attachment of brothers and sisters is less overtly evident in *dān* prestations than in gifts of another sort that explicitly foregound not the "otherness" of married daughters and sisters but their enduring ties with their natal kin. Apart from the ritually significant *dān*, daughters also have the "right" (*hak*), throughout their lives, to expect numerous other prestations whenever they visit their natal village or whenever a brother or other man from their natal village visits their conjugal village. It is often in terms of the quantity and quality of these latter gifts in particular that daughters and sisters gauge the degree of love, affection, and "unity" (*mel*) with which they are regarded by their natal kin.[43] One such prestation is *milāī*. Translated literally, this term means "meeting," "joining," or "mixing," and *milāī* is given, people say, "to increase mixture" (*mel baṛhāne ke lie*) between brothers and sisters. The most common situation in which *milāī* is given is when a brother visits the conjugal village of one of his "sisters" (his own sister, a woman of his own clan, or a woman from his own village). He is then expected to visit her home and give her a small gift, usually one or two rupees. Sisters, however distantly they may in fact be related, complain bitterly if a brother fails to pay such a visit and thus fails to exhibit in her conjugal village the degree to which he holds his sister in regard. When he does give *milāī*, the sister and her in-laws alike carefully consider every possible degree of intimacy and affection expressed in the act of gift giving. Did the brother give the *milāī* and then leave hastily, or did he drink a cup of tea and talk with his sister? Did he stay for a meal in his sister's house? Did he make the appropriate inquiries about her welfare and that of her children? If he had other affairs to attend to in the village, did he visit her first and stay longest in her courtyard, or did his actions imply that those other affairs took precedence over his feelings for his sister? Thus, while a brother might be in compliance with the "rule" that *milāī* should be given to one's sister, it is altogether possible that the style in which it is given might partly subvert, in the eyes of his sister, the emotional meaning of the gift. In any event, the sister does not experience the event simply as the fulfillment of a cultural expectation that the brother is obliged to give *milāī*. She experiences it largely in terms of the strategies and improvisations that contextualize the act and reveal the intentionality and the feelings of the donor, her brother.[44]

Another prestation, usually called *vādā*, that evokes a similar set of considerations is that given to a woman by her mother and her brothers whenever she returns to her conjugal home after visiting her natal village. When *dān* is given, there is often a fixed number of sets of cloth, or a fixed quantity of grain, or a certain number of brass vessels that should be given. In the case of these *vādā* prestations, however, while there are certain factors that should be taken into account (for example, how long the woman has stayed in her natal village and how long it has been since her previous visit), there are no ritually specified quantities that must be given. Thus it is all the more likely that women will interpret the amounts that are given in terms of the closeness of their tie with their natal kin. For married daughters and sisters, the primary significance of *milāī* and *vādā* prestations is that they bring to the fore their continuing identity as "one's own" to their brothers. In contexts in which *dān* is given, women are described as "other" (*dūsrī*) and "alien" (*parāyī*) to their natal kin, and they are referred to as *dhiyānī*, a word that has the referential meaning of "married daughter" or "married sister," and the pragmatic effect of creating distance and otherness, because it is used only in contexts in which the giving of *dān* to those who are "alien" is at issue. But in contexts in which *milāī* and *vādā* are given, the term *dhiyānī* never occurs. The more usual terms *beṭī* (daughter), *laṛkī* (girl), and *bahan* (sister) are always used, and on these occasions married women are never described as "other" or "alien," but as "one's own" to their natal kin. This shift in perspective is evident in a proverb that women often use in conversations about *milāī* and *vādā* prestations: "Daughters and sons are one's own, but the daughter-in-law is other" (*dhī pūt to apnī bahū begānī*). The pragmatic and emotional force of this proverb contrasts with that of the proverb "Daughter, daughter's husband, and daughter's son, these three are not one's own" that is invoked in talk about the giving of *dān*. The former proverb is clearly inappropriate as a commentary on aspects of relationships involved in the giving of *dān* and its ritual efficacy, since in that context the married daughter, the *dhiyānī*, is explicitly conceived of as alien and other. Despite the contradictory meanings of these proverbs, both are used in Pahansu to comment on women's relationships to natal kin and conjugal kin; it is the contextuality and pragmatic force of the proverbs that are thus at issue.

Crucial as this distinction between the two kinds of prestations (*dān* on the one hand and *milāī* and *vādā* on the other) may be in north Indian social life, there is nonetheless a sense in which the contrast is blurred in everyday experience. Though the ritual meanings of the *dān* that brothers give to their sisters foreground the "otherness" of the sister and her "obligation" to accept the gift to ensure her brother's auspiciousness and well-being, the degree of attachment and regard that a brother feels for his sister is often gauged by the quantity and quality of the gifts that he gives in *dān,* as well as those he gives in *milāī* and *vādā*. Thus, all gift giving takes on affective significance for sisters, and moves them to consider over and over again the depth of a brother's attachment.

Married women in Pahansu often commented to me that, for women, relationships "from the direction of the natal village" (*pīhar kī taraf se*), "from where one's birth took place" (*jahāṅ apnā paidā huā*) are the "closest" (*zyādā nazdīk*) of all relationships.[45] Thus, while there is an explicit ritual enactment of the severance of a "bodily connection" between a woman and her natal kin, and the creation of a "one's own" relationship with her husband's family, the emotional force of the idea of such a transformation may not, in all contexts, equal the force of the persisting tie to the natal kin and the expectations it generates.

An investigation of the rhetorical devices in women's expressive traditions that deliberately juxtapose and comment upon these disparate cultural propositions and discursive forms reveals the reflexivity of speakers and the manner in which they evaluate the relative salience and persuasiveness, and the relative force, of their cultural tropes. The rhetorical forms and recurrent themes of north Indian women's oral traditions consistently center on an awareness of the shifting and divergent images of women's ties to natal and conjugal kin in north Indian culture, and their differing emotional resonances. These themes may be seen as a reflexive commentary upon a number of pervasive north Indian assumptions about the appropriate valences to be placed upon a set of kinship relationships.

At the moment in the wedding ritual when a woman becomes "other" to her natal kin and "one's own" to her husband, she becomes subject to what Sudhir Kakar has called a "formidable consensus" concerning the injunctions placed upon a married woman. She is to remain obedient and deferential to her husband and his kin, and most importantly, she is to subordinate her desire for intimacy with her husband to the preexisting bonds of loyalty and affection with his natal kinsmen.[46] In this view, Kakar suggests, the wife represents a pernicious threat to the unity of the husband's family, and her intimacy with him must not be allowed to disrupt his relationship with his parents and siblings. In particular, the sexual relationship between husband and wife must not be publicly acknowledged or alluded to. In the presence of his parents and siblings, a woman veils her face before her husband and may not speak. A man may be severely criticized if he appears to give priority to his relationship with his wife rather than to his ties to his mother, sisters, or brothers.[47] Yet there is a recognition that though it must be relegated to the "back stage" of everyday life, sexuality creates a very strong bond between husband and wife.[48] This bond is subjected to restrictions not only in the public space of courtyard and lane but also in more private spaces. A mother-in-law may often be able to regulate the frequency with which a daughter-in-law may sleep with her husband, thus restricting the development of a relationship that might threaten the son's loyalty to his mother and his siblings.[49] And a husband may himself view his intimacy with his wife as a dangerous threat to his own natal kin.[50]

Sudhir Kakar has written of intimacy and desire as they are represented in many varieties of South Asian narrative traditions and in the personal narratives related by north Indian women in interviews in Delhi slums and in his clinical practice.[51] He observes that a profound yearning for a missing or culturally devalued intimacy with the husband is an overwhelming issue in contemporary north Indian fiction and in the life stories he recorded. Like the subversive Pahansu "dancing songs" I have discussed elsewhere that valorize a woman's decisive action in the face of a treacherous *sās* (husband's mother) or *nanad* (husband's sister),[52] such stories form a counternarrative to the perhaps more loudly voiced view that a woman should subordinate these desires to the value placed on preserving the unity of the husband's family of birth.

Women are thus caught in a web of contradictions and ambiguities upon their marriage. They are expected to distance themselves from their natal kin at marriage, for ritual reasons and for reasons connected with the power to be wielded over them by their husbands. Yet they are discouraged, by those same considerations of power and authority, from forging intimate bonds with their husbands. Thus they may often come to feel that they are "one's own" to no one at all. Women's ritual songs in Pahansu construct a commentary on cultural discourses concerning kinship and gender, and the contradictions and deprivations posed therein. These songs focus particularly on relationships between brother and sister on the one hand, and husband and wife on the other. In the songs I consider here, the question of the relative salience, the relative emotional force, of the two relationships is the focus of the commentary. The songs indicate that women are acutely aware of the conflicting emotional currents set into motion at the moment of marriage: a woman expects to enter into an intimate relation with her husband but may do so only if her husband is prepared to deemphasize the loyalty and affection he feels for his sister.[53] But the same woman, as sister, may bear a tattoo of her brother's name upon her body, and she will almost certainly expect that his affection and regard for her will be as enduring as the name scripted on her flesh.[54]

These ambiguities and contradictions in north Indian kinship have for long been seen as complicating the ideology of *kanyā dān* and the idea that a woman is unequivocally transferred from natal kin to conjugal kin at her marriage. Jacobson has stressed the informal but enduring ties between a woman and her natal place, and Vatuk has analyzed the importance of gifts in sustaining a woman's links to natal kin.[55] Women's own perspectives on these complexities are given voice in the songs I recorded in Pahansu, which reveal the double perspective of sisters and of wives. As women give voice to their vision of gifts and of their ties to brothers and to husbands, their words undermine the north Indian ideology of the *pativratā*, the ideal wife who moves silently and submissively from natal kin to conjugal kin and makes no claims of her own.[56]

Songs and Gifts

Songs sung when a brother comes to give the gifts called *bhāt*, at the marriage of his sister's children, contain some of the most compelling commentaries on married women's relationships with their natal kin, from a sister's point of view.[57]

Bhāt song 1

> I've put on my forehead ornaments, and I'm standing here
> behind the *pardā* wall.
> Give all the *bhāt* gifts, your sister is in want.
> Give a thousand rupees on a platter, and gold coins in a
> jug.

Other verses follow in which the sister says that she has put on other ornaments worn by a married woman.

The first words of this song highlight the speaking woman's identity as wife; she has put on the ornaments that embody her *suhāg* (marital good fortune), and she stands in the *oṭā*, an enclosure around the hearth specifically designed to conceal married women from affinal men who may enter the courtyard. Yet she speaks as a sister, imploring her brother to give generously to his sister who lives in poverty (*ṭoṭā*). An ironic awareness of the double positioning thus pervades this song; the woman speaks from the *oṭā*, but she speaks as a sister nonetheless.

A similarly compelling juxtaposition of identities is found in another *bhāt* song that I have analyzed elsewhere.[58] In that song a sister asks her brother to give generously, telling him (in an insistent refrain that is sung after every line of the song) that she is "born of the same mother" (*māṅ jāī*) as her brother. But she also says, in just one line, that she has become "other" (*parāyī*) to her natal kin. In thus juxtaposing her birth from the same mother with her otherness, the sister comments ironically on this contradiction in the ideology of kinship in north India. But in asking her brother to sell his house and fields and his own wife's jewelry in order to give the gifts, she tells him in no uncertain terms how she intends the ambiguity to be resolved. It is that birth from the same mother that echoes through the song and is seen as most enduring, despite the distance that a marriage may create.

In-laws may seek to minimize the importance of that tie, precisely because a woman's continuing reliance on her natal kin may threaten their own power over the young bride.[59] *Bhāt* songs tell of attempts made by the people of her conjugal village to rob the wife's connection to her natal place of its significance and of their attempts to convince her that she means nothing to her brother.

Bhāt song 2

[Wife speaking]
Husband-lord, bring me a *bindī*, and my brothers will bring a *ṭīkā*.[60]
[Husband speaking]
Be quiet, woman, let's just see what your brothers will bring.
They'll bring five rupees and say they've brought twenty-five.

Similar verses follow in which the wife asks her husband to give different kinds of ornaments, saying that her brothers will bring analogous ones.

Bhāt song 3

I'm waiting for you, my brother, and watching from the window.
My mother-in-law says, "Look here, your *bhāt* has not yet come."
And I say, "Mother-in-law, don't speak so harshly,
My brother's in a court case.
Today his court date's come, and his wife's given birth to a son."

Further verses follow in which other women of the *sasurāl* comment pointedly that the gifts have not yet come.

In both of these *bhāt* songs the wife is subjected to taunting by her husband and his kin. In the second song she speaks up to defend her brother and to insist that she is indeed important to him: only a court case and the birth of a son could keep him away from her. In these two songs a woman must struggle against her husband's kin to assert the importance of her natal ties. In such assertions, gifts often play an important part. North Indian women sometimes speak of taking cash or cloth secretly from the husband's home when they visit their natal kin, and then, if their brothers' *vādā* gifts are meager, they may, when they return to their *sasurāl*, pretend that the cash and cloth were given by their brothers.[61] They do this because a woman's position and influence in her *sasurāl* are in some measure dependent on her in-laws' perception of the degree to which she is held in esteem by her natal kin. If they give generously to her and treat her with respect, then her husband's kin know that they will also come to her defense if she is mistreated. In situations in which a mother-in-law or an older sister-in-law comes from a family less able to provide lavish gifts than the family of a younger bride, these older women may begin to criticize the quantity or quality of the gifts given to that bride by her brothers in order to assert their own authority within the family.[62] A bride whose family gives meager gifts is a bride disparaged in her husband's house.[63] Thus, as these *bhāt* songs speak of husbands and mothers-in-law berating a woman's brothers, they speak also to critical issues of power and control in a woman's conjugal home.

If gifts are signs of love and regard, then refusals to give are signs that one's loyalty and affection lie elsewhere. Many songs from Pahansu speak, in a celebratory mode, of a woman's refusal to give to her husband's kin. A defiance of the norms stressing wifely submission and a defiance of the idea of a woman's assimilation into her husband's kin group are both expressed in this "birth song" (*byāī gīt*) from Pahansu. The *bahū* (daughter-in-law) speaks in this song to the men of her *sasurāl*, of sweets that have come from her natal home.

Byāī gīt 1

The father-in-law, sitting in the *gher*, said this:[64]
Bahū, give me a *laḍḍū*,
A good spiced *laḍḍū*.[65]

[*Bahū* speaking]
If I break up the *laḍḍū*, my fingers will hurt.
And father-in-law, I won't give a whole one,
A good spiced *laḍḍū*.

The older brother-in-law, working the plow,
 said this:
Bahū, give me a *laḍḍū*,
A good spiced *laḍḍū*

[*Bahū* speaking]
If I break up the *laḍḍū*, my fingers will hurt.
And brother-in-law, I won't give a whole one,
A good spiced *laḍḍū*.

The younger brother-in-law feeding the cows
 said this:

Sister-in-law, give me a *laḍḍū*,
A good spiced *laḍḍū*.

[*Bahū:* speaking]
If I break up the *laḍḍū*, my fingers will hurt.
And brother-in-law, I won't give a whole one,
A good spiced *laḍḍū*.

In thus expressing her unwillingness to share the *laḍḍū*s, the wife voices her disapproval of the demands made on her by her husband's male kin. And because the sharing of food is in South Asia so much a mark of kinship solidarities and so much enjoined on the wife as she enters her husband's home,[66] she intimates, in no uncertain terms, that she values other ties above those in her *sasurāl*.

A new mother is expected to give gifts called *neg*, particularly to her husband's sister (her *nanad*) and also to his mother, in "payment" for the performance of various ritual services after a birth. (These *neg* "payments" are not *dān*, and they do not transfer inauspiciousness.) A birth song (*byāī gīt*) tells of the excuses a woman might make to avoid giving to her husband's sisters, as she speaks to the husband, her beloved (*piyā*).

Byāī gīt 2

REFRAIN
When Sethpal was born, I called my three *nanad*s, beloved.
The oldest *nanad* asked for my forehead ornament.
The middle one asked for my sandalwood necklace,
beloved.
The youngest one asked for our bicycle.
But I can't give the bicycle, beloved, there's an evil omen
on it.[67]

In this song the new mother says she can't give because *ān* has befallen the bicycle, that is, because some particular inauspicious circumstance (a death in the family, for example, that may have occurred at the time the item was acquired) is linked with the bicycle that would make it dangerous to give or receive. I asked Asikaur, the *dādī* (grandmother) of the house in which I lived, to help me understand this song. As she sat in her courtyard spinning cotton thread, she told me that the new mother in the song doesn't want to give anything at all to her husband's sisters, and so she has fabricated this story of the *ān*. "She won't give anything," Asikaur said, and she set aside her spinning long enough to mimic the abusive thumb gesture (*ṭhosā*) that the young wife might make as she refused to give the gifts.[68] Now Asikaur, like other women I knew in Pahansu, would not in fact hesitate to give these gifts, except in the face of severe economic difficulties. The wife's refusal in the song is thus, as women acknowledge, a provocative claim about their own valuation of natal ties over conjugal ties, in the language of the gift, a claim they might make in practice, even when they do in fact give the gifts to their own husbands' sisters. Thus, the songs are not in essence necessarily about actual refusals to give; they are representations of women's emotional commitments to their various kin and of the extent to which they might possibly resist the authority of their conjugal kin.

Many songs from Pahansu depict a reluctance to give *neg* to people in the *sasurāl*. Often such refusals are explicitly concerned with not letting go of things that have come from one's natal kin. Another birth song, for example, speaks of sweets that have come from the bride's natal place (*pīhar*), but here the husband is pointedly enlisted as an accomplice in a woman's assertion of the priority of her own natal ties.

Byāī gīt 3

[Wife speaking to her husband]
Sweetly spiced *laḍḍūs* have come from my natal place.
My *sās* stole one of the *laḍḍūs*.
Grab my *sās'* hand and give that *laḍḍū* back to me,
And bring me a lock from Lahore for my *sās*.
If she won't be locked up, then take a stick and beat her up.

Other verses follow in which the husband's brothers' wives and the husband's sisters take the place of the mother-in-law, the *sās*.

This song is particularly interesting because here the wife expects her husband to side with her; he is called upon to take a stand against his own mother and sister, to protect his wife's relationship with her natal kin. If he does this, he will also be asserting the primacy of the conjugal bond over his ties to his own natal kin. In another birth song, too, the husband is again portrayed as his wife's accomplice, as the new mother (*jaccā*) refuses to give gifts to his mother and his sister when they perform the ritual services of laying out the bed and washing the *jaccā*'s breasts before she feeds her child for the first time.

Byāī gīt 4

The *jaccā* has gone upstairs, how has it happened?

[*Jaccā* speaking]
My *sās* comes to arrange the bed, she'll ask for her *neg*.
When the time comes to give, I'll say my beloved has gone away.
He's gone away and taken the key, how has it happened?

My *nanad* comes to wash the breasts, she'll ask for her *neg*.
When the time comes to give, I'll say my beloved has gone away.
He's gone away and taken the key, how has it happened?

A woman stores the cloth and ornaments that the husband's sister has the right to receive as *neg* in her locked tin trunk. In this song the new mother fabricates a story that her husband has gone away with the key, and thus it is impossible for her to give. In referring to the husband as her "beloved" (*piyā*) just as his purported absence serves as a convenient excuse for her not to give to his own mother and sister, there is an intimation that perhaps, in the wife's estimation, his real loyalties lie with his wife rather than his own natal kin.

Thus, as the young wife in all of these songs asserts the closeness of her tie with her natal home, she simultaneously draws her husband away from his parents and his sisters, and into an intimate conjugal bond. This bond, too, receives an explicit validation in an idiom of the gift, in a great many women's songs.

Dancing song

[Wife speaking to husband]
Whether you go and sell my *sās*, or go and sell my *sūsar* standing there,
I won't regret it, just bring me a sari with a border.
Bring me a sari with a border, bring me a comb inlaid with mirrors.
Bring me two black tassels to twine in my long, long hair.

Other verses follow in which the wife tells her husband to sell his elder brother and his wife and his younger brother and his wife, to bring her the presents she wants.

In demanding adornments for her body purchased at the price of her husband's mother, father, and other kin, the wife is in fact making a moral claim concerning the appropriate resolution of a central contradiction in women's experiences of marriage. Expected, in the terms of the dominant male discourse, to distance herself from her natal kin upon her marriage, she arrives in her conjugal home, where she is also told not to forge a too-intimate bond with her husband, lest she disrupt the solidarity of his patriline. Here in this song, though, as in countless others, a woman's voice undermines this set of ideals and claims the right to redefine the terms of the marital relationship. In the following "bridegroom's song," the young wife sets aside the claims of patrilineal kinship, as she asks her husband for a *ṭīkā* (a forehead ornament).

Bane kā gīt

[Wife speaking to husband]
Bridegroom, *ṭīkā*s are being sold, bring me a *ṭīkā*.
Sell your grandmother and bring me a *ṭīkā*.
Sell your father's elder brother's wife and bring me a *ṭīkā*.

[Husband speaking to wife]
Will you have me sell my grandmother?
Will you have me sell my aunt?
Then who will you show the *ṭīkā* to?

[Wife speaking to husband]
It doesn't matter who I show the *ṭīkā* to.
Bridegroom, *ṭīkā*s are being sold, bring me a *ṭīkā*.

The final song from Pahansu that I wish to consider is a *sītnā* (insult song) sung by the women of a bride's natal family just as the formal wedding rite (*pherā*) is conducted by a Brahman priest and the men of the bride's family.[69] As the men perform ritual acts of deference to the groom's side, these women of the bride's side sit just a few feet away and sing *sītnā*, which insult and ridicule the groom's family. The sexual promiscuity of the groom's mother is perhaps the most common theme in these songs. Women sing, in the *sītnā* I have translated here, of a particular kind of embroidered fan that is always given in dowry in Pahansu, and in doing so they criticize the mother-in-law for another sort of stand on sexuality and intimacy.

Sītnā

[Bride speaking]
My grandfather has given the dān,
My grandmother has given an embroidered fan.

[Bride's kin speaking to the groom's mother]
Take it, you wanton woman, take it you slut, go ahead and take the fan.
But our beloved girl's bloom is fading, she's yearning for that lost fan.

In the verses that follow other kin terms are substituted for grandfather and grandmother in the first lines.

I did not record this *sītnā* at an actual wedding performance. When Bugli, an amiable, animated, and gracious Pahansu woman in her seventies, heard that I had been taping these songs, she called me to her courtyard and announced that she would sing some for me. She sang into my microphone, sitting on a cot in the company of her daughters-in-law and a few young girls from neighboring courtyards. As she began the *sītnā* she faltered a bit as she tried to recall the words and the melody of the song she wanted to sing. But when she came to the third line, she unhesitatingly spat out the words *udhaṛiyā* and *chanālaiyā*, and I was a bit surprised to hear the venomous tone in which she hurled these insults, translated here as "wanton woman" and "slut," at the mother-in-law.[70]

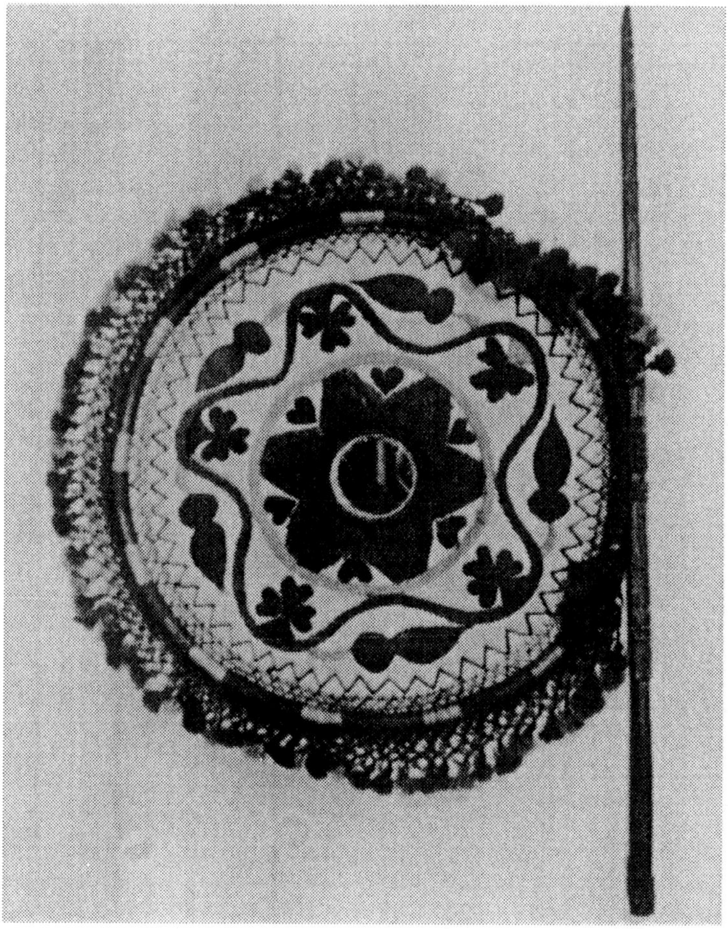

Figure 2.1 Embroidered fan (*bījnā*). From Robert F. Bussburger and Betty Dashew Robins, *The Everyday Art of India* (New York: Dover, 1968), p. 176. Reproduced by permission.

When I first heard Bugli sing this song, I was inclined to read it as a simple statement about the appropriation of "property," items given in dowry, by the groom's kin, though it was puzzling to me why so much desire was connected specifically with an embroidered fan, a relatively inexpensive item among the many things given in dowries, and an item whose use I had never actually witnessed in the village (see fig. 2.1). I remember thinking, why not complain about the likelihood that a mother-in-law might appropriate the far more valuable items—jewelry, cloth, saris, TVs, and "sofa sets"—that are given in dowries nowadays. But if we interpret this song in terms of a purely economic

Figure 2.2. Dhirju tells about the *bījnā*, in Pahansu, 1988. (Photograph by Gloria Goodwin Raheja)

logic, it will in fact be drained of all its complex significance and its implications for the politics of family life.

When I later sat in another courtyard and asked about the fan in this song, Dhirju, a middle-aged daughter of the village who had returned to Pahansu after her marriage, reminded me that such an embroidered fan (*bījnā*) is always given in the *dahej* (dowry) (see fig. 2.2). Just as

Figure 2.3 Twentieth-century Maithili painting showing Pārvatī using a *bījnā* to arouse Śiva from his ascetic withdrawal from her. From Yves Vequad, *Women Painters of Mithila* (London: Thames and Hudson, 1977), p. 56. Reproduced courtesy of Yves Véquaud.

the bride leaves her natal home at the ceremony of departure (the *bidā*), a large papier-mâché bowl filled with sweets and covered with the *bījnā* is placed in her lap by the wife of the family's Barber. This is a very auspicious act; it is important for the bride's future ability to bear children that "the lap not be empty" (*god khālī na ho jā*) as she leaves for her husband's home.

Throughout north India, embroidered fans just such as these enter into many kinds of representations not only of fertility, as in this ritual act, but more frequently and more explicitly of sexual intimacy. In paintings and women's songs from Rajasthan in the west to Orissa in the east, embroidered fans appear as emblematic of sexual union, whether it is strongly suggested as in Maithili paintings executed by women (see figs. 2.3–2.5) and in Orissan *paṭ* paintings,[71] vividly alluded to in a Rajasthani women's song translated by Ann Gold,[72] or explicitly depicted in eighteenth- and nineteenth-century erotic paintings from Rajasthan and from Kangra in the Panjab hills.[73] The iconicity of the fan itself—the fact that it is made from a carved stick or piece of bamboo and a stiffened piece of cloth on which the form of a lotus (emblematic of female genitals in many contexts) is often embroidered—is relevant here, as the bamboo and

Figure 2.4 Twentieth-century Maithili painting depicting Krishna and his lover, Rādhā. The peacock, like the *bījnā*, is a sign of sexuality. From Yves Vequad, *Women Painters of Mithilda* (London: Thames and Hudson, 1977), p. 51. Reproduced courtesy of Yves Véquaud.

the lotus come, in a Maithili women's song, to stand for the penis and the vagina that will come together in the marriage chamber. Such fans are also shown cooling the partners and dispelling the "heat" of sexual intercourse in a number of paintings.[74]

I am less interested in this overdetermined sexual imagery itself than in the way these meanings are deployed in the song from Pahansu. The appropriation of the fan by the mother-in-law signifies not just her desire to control the dowry goods but, more importantly, her attempt

Figure 2.5 Twentieth-century Maithili painting depicting the corners of the marriage chamber (*kohbar*), in which four female companions await the arrival of the groom. From Yves Vequad, *Women Painters of Mithila* (London: Thames and Hudson, 1977), p. 77. Reproduced courtesy of Yves Véquaud. Maithili song of the marriage chamber: "O wife of the bride's brother, / Paint the chamber / So that it charms the eyes, / O wife of the bride's brother, / On the walls of the chamber paint the ideal marriage / Between the bamboo and the lotuses." From W. G. Archer, *Songs for the Bride: Wedding Rites of Rural India*, ed. B. S. Miller and M. Archer (New York: Columbia University Press, 1985), p. 113. Reproduced by permission.

to regulate the creation of a dangerously intimate sexual bond between the husband and his new bride, a bond that could threaten patrilineal authority and solidarity. It is this act that provokes the abuse heaped on the mother-in-law by the bride's natal kin.

A woman's natal kin must publicly affect a total indifference to her sexuality; a woman can go about her natal village with her face uncovered precisely because her sexuality is so disconnected from all relationships there. But Veena Das has pointed out that, in private, a bride's natal kin may be intensely concerned about her sexual satisfaction and her ability to establish an intimate bond with her husband. A woman's mother or grandmother may never question her directly about these matters, but it may be appropriate for a mother to ask a new bride's brother's wife to make such inquiries, "through direct questioning and half-serious banter about the husband's virility."[75] Thus, the song's depiction of the interest of the bride's natal kin in the matter of her intimacy with her husband, couched in talk about the *bījnā*, may point to important emotional realities that are hidden by the official ideology stressing the separation of natal and conjugal spheres.

This *sītnā*, then, constructs a critique of the pervasive and often-voiced view that the ideal wife does not question a restriction of her intimacy with her husband, a restriction that might be implemented to preserve the unity of his patrilineal kin. Although, as Jeffery, Jeffery, and Lyon point out, a mother-in-law may sometimes use her position in the household to regulate the frequency of sexual intercourse between her son and his wife as she seeks to preserve the husband's loyalty to his own natal kin, women's songs consistently protest against the power relationships in the *sasurāl* that make this possible. Once again these critiques are uttered, in the *sītnā* Bugli sang, in the idiom of the gift.

The songs I have begun to explicate here are complex, and they speak of many ambiguities, contradictions, and inequities women face as they marry, move away from their natal kin, and take up their lives as wives in a patrilineal milieu. Each song, however, addresses these difficulties from the distinctive vantage point of either sister or wife. The claims made from these different positions are at odds with one another. Yet both positions subvert the idea of wife as *pativratā*, as unquestioningly submissive to the husband and his kin, and they subvert the idea that it is dangerous to patrilineal solidarities for a woman to be either too close to her brothers or too close to her husband. Songs sung from the point of view of the sister challenge the *pativratā* ideal by rejecting its requirement that women distance themselves from brothers who might side with them against their in-laws in times of crisis. Songs sung from the point of view of the wife challenge this ideal by rejecting its requirement that intimacy with the husband should be controlled so that his ties to his own patrilineal kin take first precedence, and its requirement of wifely obedience to the husband's senior kin.

As we hear these claims of rights to give and receive and claims that refusing to give might be a moral act, we may come to see that despite the economic importance of the very small portion of the dowry that a woman can in fact control, the tin trunk in which she stores her cloth, cash, and jewelry is less a place of hoarding and safeguarding a "conjugal estate" than a place from which a woman draws forth these items, to "give them onward" (*āge denā*) in varying amounts and with varying emotional dispositions. In doing so she may thus be able to subtly redraw the lines of kinship solidarities and perhaps to challenge expectations of wifely subordination.[76] Whereas women certainly welcome gifts, from brothers or from husbands, for their economic value, women sing more often, more critically, and more eloquently of the power relationships that frame each act of exchange and render married women not quite "one's own" to natal kin nor yet fully "one's own" in their conjugal place, and thus dependent on gifts to give them a measure not so much of economic security as of a position of authority and status in their *pīhar* and *sasurāl*.

That these potent challenges to patrilineal orthodoxy are more significant and more salient to the singers than simple requests for gifts as economically valuable commodities is perhaps indicated in a comparison of these Hindi songs with the following south Indian woman's song recorded in Tamil Nadu by Margaret Trawick Egnor.[77] The beginning of this beautifully translated song is very similar to the Pahansu *bhāt* song in which a woman repeats over and over again that she and her brother are "born from one mother."

I wore a silk sari,
O mother who bore me, O father, and I went to see the town where I was born.
Today the wife of my first older brother, thinking that I come for my share,
Has set a screen in my way, and has put out two pariah dogs for protection.
I didn't come for my share, mother;
I, poor sinner, came to see the town where I was born, and cry.
I wore a printed sari,
And I, younger sister, came to see the foreign land where I was born.
Today the wife of my second older brother
Has set a wall in my way and has put out two red dogs for protection.
I didn't come for riches, mother.
I, poor sinner, came to see the foreign land where I was born, and cry.

In the verses that follow the sister addresses her brothers and asks them if they have forgotten her birth.

The north Indian *bhāt* song begins with a woman's journey to her natal village, where she speaks to her brother as one who was born of the same mother. This south Indian song begins with a similar journey and similar images of a common place of birth. The north Indian song culminates in requests for costly gifts, while the Tamil singer renounces any such interests. Yet in response to a similar situation in which women, at their marriage, move away from natal kin and in which a man's interest in his sister is represented as conflicting with his interest in his wife, both songs voice a claim to love and identity, in the idiom of the gift.[78]

That Pahansu women's songs frame a shift in perspective, from that of wife to that of sister, and thereby frame a shifting set of emotional and relational valences, seems hardly surprising, in view of the particular contours of kinship in north India, and perhaps in other areas of India as well. Women are undoubtedly aware, as they sing, of the contradictory claims they make from their dual positions as sister and as wife: men are urged to hold onto the love and loyalty they feel for their sisters, yet they are also urged, in other songs sung by the same women, to give first place to their wives. From an ironic awareness of such discrepant readings, women give voice to a critique of the norms of patrilineal kinship that pronounce them "alien" to their natal kin upon their marriage and yet subordinate to and never unambiguously "one's own" to their conjugal kin. Given the emphasis on gift giving and receiving in this transactionally oriented culture, it also should not be surprising that these shifting perspectives on love and power and the ideal wife should be communicated in an idiom of rights to give and rights to receive.

NOTES

I wish to thank Lindsey Harlan, Doranne Jacobson, Patricia and Roger Jeffery, and Sylvia Vatuk for conversations and correspondence that helped me to revise an earlier draft of this essay. I also wish to thank faculty and students of the department of anthropology at the University of Minnesota, who offered gentle criticism of some of my earlier ideas, thus prompting me to rethink portions of the argument after a preliminary draft of this essay was presented at a departmental colloquium in 1990. And, as ever, most of all I thank the women of Pahansu who for fifteen years have been changing the way I see the world.

1. For important discussions of gifts and kinship relations in South Asia, see Nicholas Dirks, *The Hollow Crown: Ethnohistory of an Indian Kingdom* (Cambridge: Cambridge University Press, 1987); Louis Dumont, *A South Indian Subcaste: Social Organization and Religion of the Pramalai Kallar* (Delhi: Oxford

University Press, 1986); idem, *Affinity as a Value: Marriage Alliance in South India, with Comparative Essays on Australia* (Chicago: University of Chicago Press, 1986); Zekiye Eglar, *A Punjabi Village in Pakistan* (New York: Columbia University Press, 1960); Anthony Good, "The Actor and the Act: Categories of Prestation in South India," *Man*, n.s., 17 (1982): 23–41; Ronald Inden and Ralph Nicholas, *Kinship in Bengali Culture* (Chicago: University of Chicago Press, 1977); Gloria Goodwin Raheja, *The Poison in the Gift: Ritual, Prestation, and the Dominant Caste in a North Indian Village* (Chicago: University of Chicago Press, 1988); Sylvia J. Vatuk, "Gifts and Affines," *Contributions to Indian Sociology* 5 (1975): 155–96; and Sylvia Vatuk and Ved Prakash Vatuk, "The Social Context of Gift Exchange in North India," in *Family and Social Change in Modern India*, ed. Giri Raj Gupta (Delhi: Vikas, (1976), pp. 207–32. Vatuk's 1975 essay is a particularly significant contribution to the understanding of north Indian kinship and gift giving.

2. Pahansu, the north Indian village in which I carried out field research in 1977–79 and again in 1988, is located in Saharanpur district, in northwestern Uttar Pradesh. I also recorded women's songs in the village of Hathchoya in 1990. All songs in this essay are from Pahansu.

3. Doranne Jacobson, "Women and Jewelry in Rural India," in *Family and Social Change in Modern India*, ed. Giri Raj Gupta (Delhi: Vikas, 1976), pp. 150–52, 156–77.

4. Ved Prakash Vatuk and Sylvia Vatuk, "On a System of Private Savings Among North Indian Village Women," *Journal of Asian and African Studies* 6 (1971): 179–90. This article is also important because of the way it illustrates women's ability to turn some of the conventions of patrilineal kinship to their own advantage. Women appear not as victims but as agents in their social worlds. Vatuk and Vatuk thus counter many of the problematic assumptions made in some academic writing about South Asian women. (I thank Ingrid Pars for conversation on this point.)

5. For a range of Indian feminist perspectives on these "dowry deaths," see the numerous articles published in the journal *Manushi* on this topic in the 1980s.

6. For an extended discussion of some of these problems involved in the explication of women's words, see my introduction to Gloria Goodwin Raheja and Ann Grodzins Gold, *Listen to the Heron's Words: Reimagining Gender and Kinship in North India* (Berkeley: University of California Press, 1994).

7. Louis Dumont, "Marriage in India: The Present State of the Question. III: North India in Relation to South India," *Contributions to Indian Sociology* 9 (1966): 90–114; Sylvia J. Vatuk, "Gifts and Affines." While this persistence of an affinal relationship is particularly obvious in south India, Dumont pointed out that such a conceptualization of the mother's brother is relevant for the north as well.

8. See Raheja, *The Poison in the Gift*, pp. 118–21, for a somewhat different view of the relationship between the "hypergamous ethos" and dowry.

9. Stanley J. Tambiah, "Dowry and Bridewealth and the Property Rights of Women in South Asia," in *Bridewealth and Dowry*, by Jack Goody and Stanley J. Tambiah (Cambridge: Cambridge University Press, 1973), pp. 59–169.

10. Jack Goody, "Bridewealth and Dowry in Africa and Eurasia," in *Bride-*

wealth and Dowry, by Jack Goody and Stanley J. Tambiah (Cambridge: Cambridge University Press), pp. 1–58.

11. Tambiah, "Dowry and Bridewealth," p. 62.

12. Although I would not want to suggest that Hindu textual traditions are irrelevant for the study of contemporary social life, one must be able to discern, through careful ethnography, the points at which such texts are relevant, and one must be able to see also the extent to which these Sanskrit texts obliterate women's voices and women's perspectives on kinship and gender.

13. See Lucy Carroll, "Law, Custom and Statutory Social Reform: The Hindu Widows' Remarriage Act of 1856," in *Women in Colonial India: Essays on Survival, Work and the State*, ed. J. Krishnamurty (Delhi: Oxford University Press, 1989), pp. 1–26; and Prem Chowdry, "Customs in a Peasant Economy: Women in Colonial Haryana," in *Recasting Women: Essays in Colonial History* ed. Kumkum Sangari and Sudesh Vaid (New Delhi: Kali for Women, 1989), pp. 302–36.

14. Tambiah, "Dowry and Bridewealth," pp. 71, 161 n. 6.

15. T. N. Madan, *Family and Kinship: A Study of the Pandits of Rural Kashmir* (Bombay: Asia Publishing House, 1965).

16. Tambiah, "Dowry and Bridewealth," p. 161 n. 6.

17. Ibid., p. 62.

18. S. J. Tambiah, "*Bridewealth and Dowry* Revisited: The Position of Women in Sub-Saharan Africa and North India," *Current Anthropology* 30, no. 4 (1989): 413–35.

19. Jonathan Parry, *Caste and Kinship in Kangra* (London: Routledge and Kegan Paul, 1979); Klaas van der Veen, *I Give Thee My Daughter: A Study of Marriage and Hierarchy Among the Anavil Brahmans of South Gujarat* (Assen: Van Gorcum, 1972); Paul Hershman, *Punjabi Kinship and Marriage* (Delhi: Hindustan Publishing, 1981); Sylvia J. Vatuk, "Gifts and Affines."

20. Tambiah, "*Bridewealth and Dowry* Revisited," pp. 425–26.

21. Ibid., p. 426.

22. On the right of a husband's sister to demand such gifts, see Raheja, *The Poison in the Gift*, p. 95.

23. Jack Goody, *The Oriental, the Ancient and the Primitive* (Cambridge: Cambridge University Press, 1990), p. 227.

24. See, for example, Patricia Jeffery, Roger Jeffery, and Andrew Lyon, *Labour Pains and Labour Power: Women and Childbearing in India* (London: Zed Books, 1989), pp. 34–36.

25. Klaas van der Veen, "Reply," *Current Anthropology* 30 (1989): 431–32. Van der Veen's point that claims on one's "own" people are involved in speaking of dowry anticipates part of the argument I make in this essay.

26. Ursula Sharma, *Women, Work and Property in North-West India* (London: Tavistock, 1980), p. 53.

27. Sharma's excellent discussion in "Dowry in North India," in *Women and Property—Women as Property*, ed. Renee Hirshon (New York: St. Martin's Press, 1984), pp. 62–74, makes it very clear, however, that much of the dowry is given directly to the husband and members of his family, and that the bride has very little control over the property transferred in dowry.

28. For particular and detailed listings of dowry prestations and their recipients, see Raheja, *The Poison in the Gift*, pp. 139–43. Even many of the gifts given

by a woman's brothers at the marriage of her own daughter are specially earmarked to be "given onward" to the new bride's husband's kin, as illustrated in the *bhāt* gifts listed in *The Poison in the Gift*, p. 131.

29. To provide background on marriage and patterns of gift giving in north India, this section draws on arguments about gifts and kinship relations that I have made elsewhere, particularly in *The Poison in the Gift* and in chapter 3 of Raheja and Gold, *Listen to the Heron's Words.*

30. In *A Carnival of Parting: The Tales of King Gopi Chand and King Bharthari as Sung and Told by Madhu Natisar Nath of Ghatiyali, Rajasthan, India* (Berkeley: University of California Press, 1992), p. 315, Ann Grodzins Gold writes of some of the meanings that a "Color Palace" (*rang mahal*) may have in a Rajasthani oral epic: "As implied by its name, the Color Palace is a place of passion and strongly associated with . . . intimate relationships." In this song from Pahansu the words may conjure up the same sense of intimacy, an intimacy from which the daughter will later be sent forth. Its concrete referent here, though, is simply "inner rooms of the house."

31. Women's songs in north India frequently unfold in the form of conversations in which varying perspectives on kinship relations are voiced by as many as five or six different kinsmen. The songs are sung however by women in chorus, as a group, and the different parts are not performatively distinguished. The "speakers" are not always explicitly identified in the songs, but the women who explicated these songs for me could always say exactly who the speaker was meant to be. I have provided these identifications in brackets.

32. Though it has been pointed out that the conception of "in-law" relationships is alien to Indian kinship (Inden and Nicholas, *Kinship in Bengali Culture*), I translate the term *dādā* as "grandfather-in-law" for two reasons. First, to render it as "my husband's grandfather" would be misleading, because a young wife would not generally utter the words "my husband," lest she be thought of as lacking in modesty. More importantly, words such as *dādā* are, in these songs, pointedly juxtaposed to the terms for a woman's own natal kin, and the "in-law" suffix brings out in English this sense of difference and distance.

33. Relationships between bride's family and groom's family among the Gujars of Pahansu are far less hierarchial than in many north Indian castes, yet they do share this extremely prevalent notion of the status difference between wife givers and wife receivers. See Raheja, *The Poison in the Gift*, pp. 120–21, 263 n. 16.

34. Women's songs do not always or unequivocally contest the dominant discourse of female subordination. This is an example of a song that seems only to restate rather than resist those authoritative pronouncements about female inferiority. Yet the "beloved girl" does at least question her natal kin about why they have been "defeated" by her birth, and it is only her male kinsmen, in the song, who utter these views about their "defeat," and not the bride or her female kin.

35. See Sharma, *Women, Work and Property in North-West India*, pp. 135, 174–75 n. 1.

36. For a lengthy discussion of the nature of this inauspiciousness, and the many ritual occasions at which it is dispersed through the giving of *dān* in Pahansu, see Raheja, *The Poison in the Gift*. On this idea of the evil in the gift,

see also Jonathan Parry, "Ghosts, Greed and Sin: The Occupational Identity of the Benares Funeral Priests," *Man*, n.s., 15 (1980): 88–111; and idem, "*The Gift*, the Indian Gift and the 'Indian Gift,' " *Man*, n.s., 21 (1986): 453–73.

37. These quotations from the Ṛg Veda are from the translation by Wendy O'Flaherty, *The Rig Veda* (Harmondsworth, Eng.: Penguin, 1981).

38. For descriptions of these rituals, see Raheja, *The Poison in the Gift*, pp. 176–78; Indira Peterson, "The Tie That Binds: Brothers and Sisters in North and South India," *South Asian Social Scientist* 41 (1988): 25–52; and Holly Baker Reynolds, "Sisters Protect Brothers: Two Tamil Women's Rituals," paper presented at the conference "Women's Rites, Women's Desires," Harvard University, 1988.

39. Inden and Nicholas, *Kinship in Bengali Culture*.

40. For other discussions of this transformation women undergo as they are married, see Kathleen Gough, "Brahmin Kinship in a Tamil Village," *American Anthropologist* 58 (1956): 826–53; T. N. Madan, "Is the Brahmanic *gotra* a Grouping of Kin?" *Southwestern Journal of Anthropology* 18 (1962): 59–77; Thomas Trautmann, *Dravidian Kinship* (Cambridge: Cambridge University Press, 1981), especially p. 291.

41. Jeffery, Jeffery, and Lyon, *Labour Pains and Labour Power*, pp. 31–36.

42. William S. Sax, *Mountain Goddess: Gender and Politics in a Himalayan Village* (New York: Oxford University Press, 1991), pp. 77–78.

43. These gifts, the most important of which are *milāī*, *vādā*, and *neg*, differ from *dān* in that they are not thought to transfer inauspiciousness. For further discussion of the differences among these kinds of gifts, and their implications for kinship relations, see Raheja, *The Poison in the Gift*.

44. A sister is invariably far more interested in this display of her brother's commitment to her than in the two or five or ten rupees she receives in *milāī*.

45. See Gloria Goodwin Raheja, "Kinship, Caste, and Auspiciousness in Pahansu," Ph.D. diss., University of Chicago, 1985, pp. 395–422; and Raheja and Gold, *Listen to the Heron's Words*, for discussions of the implications of such a perspective for anthropological understandings of north Indian kinship and gender relations.

46. Sudhir Kakar, *The Inner World* (Delhi: Oxford University Press, 1978), p. 74.

47. Veena Das, "Masks and Faces: An Essay on Punjabi Kinship," *Contributions to Indian Sociology* 10 (1976): 1–30; Kakar, *The Inner World*, pp. 74–75; Alan Roland, *In Search of Self in India and Japan: Toward a Cross-Cultural Psychology* (Princeton, N.J.: Princeton University Press, 1988), p. 152.

48. Das, "Masks and Faces," p. 6.

49. Jeffery, Jeffery, and Lyon, *Labour Pains and Labour Power*, p. 29.

50. Das, "Masks and Faces," p. 13.

51. Sudhir Kakar, *Intimate Relations: Exploring Indian Sexuality* (Chicago: University of Chicago Press, 1990).

52. Raheja and Gold, *Listen to the Heron's Words*.

53. That the juxtaposition of the two relationships is viewed as problematic is perhaps indicated in the north Indian rite of *bāhar rukāī*. When a bride arrives at the threshold of her husband's house for the first time, the husband's sister ritually bars the door to her, until she is given a "payment" (*neg*) for allowing the bride to enter.

54. Jeffery, Jeffery, and Lyon have also commented on this tension between wife and husband's sister, but they attribute it almost exclusively to the wife's supposed resentment of the respite from work that the husband's sister experiences when she visits her natal home, and to the economic difficulties posed by gift-giving expectations (*Labour Pains and Labour Power*, pp. 58, 144). For a suggestion of the form in which such tensions are represented in south India, from a vantage point more like my own, see Margaret Trawick Egnor, "Internal Iconicity in Paraiyar Crying Songs," in *Another Harmony: New Essays on the Folklore of India*, ed. Stuart Blackburn and A. K. Ramanujan (Berkeley: University of California Press, 1986), pp. 294–344.

55. Doranne Jacobson, "Flexibility in North Indian Kinship and Residence," in *The New Wind: Changing Identities in South Asia*, ed. Kenneth David (The Hague: Mouton, 1977), pp. 263–83; Sylvia J. Vatuk, "Gifts and Affines." See also Leela Dube, "On the Construction of Gender: Hindu Girls in Patrilineal India," *Economic and Political Weekly*, April 30, 1988, pp. 11–19.

56. Most of the songs that I translate in this essay speak of women's relationships to their husbands in connection with relationships to mothers-in-law, sisters-in-law, and other kinsmen of the husband, and they may appear to assume the existence of joint family arrangements. My research focused on Gujars in western Uttar Pradesh, and joint families are in fact common in this landholding community. But I think these songs speak more generally of profound tensions, ambiguities, and divided loyalties in north Indian kinship that surface even in the absence of joint living arrangements.

57. *Bhāt* is a *dān* prestation that ensures the auspiciousness of the brother, but women nonetheless interpret a brother's generosity partly in terms of his regard for his sister.

58. Raheja and Gold, *Listen to the Heron's Words*.

59. Jeffery, Jeffery, and Lyon, *Labour Pains and Labour Power*, pp. 31–36.

60. In women's songs, husbands are frequently addressed as *raja* (king or lord). I have translated this as "husband-lord." One sometimes has the sense, though, that the word is used with a mocking or ironic tone. Both *bindī* and *ṭīkā* are varieties of forehead ornaments that the brothers may be expected to give in *bhāt*.

61. Vatuk and Prakash Vatuk, "On a System of Private Savings Among North Indian Village Women," pp. 185–86; Doranne Jacobson, "Women and Jewelry in Rural India," pp. 165–67, 174. I occasionally heard women allude to this practice in Pahansu.

62. I saw this happen a number of times in Pahansu. An example of such "bitter words" spoken by a mother-in-law occurs in the well-known north Indian story of "Narsi's *bhāt*," as it was told to me in 1978 by Mangal Singh, a Pahansu Gujar man. Though much of the talk in the story concerns the prestige (*izzat*) to be gained by men as they give such gifts, the plight of the daughter-in-law, as Mangal Singh narrated it, illustrates some very feminine concerns about gifts, love and power. As Mangal Singh explicated the tale of Narsi's *bhāt* to me, he pointed out that the situation in the story paralleled the relationship of mother-in-law and daughter-in-law in several families we knew in the village.

63. In this brief essay I do not have the space to discuss the horrible consequences that sometimes befall urban women when lavish and expensive dowry

gifts are not forthcoming from their natal kin. While the burning of brides for this reason, in cities throughout north India, is of course connected to "traditional" expectations about gift giving and to the position of wives in north Indian kinship, it is perhaps more directly attributable to the interpenetration of these kinship practices with an increasingly insistent consumer culture in India. I do not discuss this issue here because this paper is based on research in two villages of Uttar Pradesh, and during the time I lived in Pahansu and Hathchoya this terrifying wave of dowry-related crime against women had not reached these rural areas.

64. The *gher* is a cattle pen and men's sitting place, sometimes connected to the house but more often a separate building in the family's fields. It is very much a male space from which women are excluded unless they have specific work to do there.

65. *Laḍḍūs* are ball-shaped sweets made from chick-pea flour and sugar. They are often given along with *dahej* and *vādā* gifts in Pahansu.

66. On this point see especially Inden and Nicholas, *Kinship in Bengali Culture.*

67. The usual item given in *neg* is a piece of jewelry, and perhaps cloth and cash. I am not sure why the bicycle, an item that would never actually be given in *neg,* is said to have an evil omen on it; it may be that to say that an omen is on a woman's jewelry, the embodiments of her *suhāg* that usually figure so prominently in women's songs, would itself be inauspicious for the women who sing these songs. In "Internal Iconicity in Paraiyar Crying Songs" (pp. 331–35) Trawick Egnor mentions that in south India, upper-caste women chastized Untouchable women who sang songs in which they likened their sufferings to the trials of widowhood; to speak thus when one is not in fact a widow was viewed as an unacceptable challenge to the value of marital auspiciousness held by those landowning women. It may be that the Pahansu women who sing this song have a similar disinclination to speak of *ān* in the same breath as women's items of *suhāg,* and that may be why they sing of a bicycle instead of the expected item of adornment in this song.

68. In another *byāī gīt* from Pahansu, a woman denies her husband's sister's request for a silver bangle by actually saying, "You take this thumb, husband's sister." For the text of this song, see Gloria Goodwin Raheja, "Negotiating Kinship and Gender: Essentializing and Contextualizing Strategies in North Indian Song and Narrative Traditions." Paper presented at the conference on "Language, Gender, and the Subaltern Voice: Framing Identities in South Asia," University of Minnesota, April 1991.

69. These songs are also called *gālī* (insult). Gold explicates several Rajasthani *gālīs,* in chapter 2 of Raheja and Gold, *Listen to the Heron's Words.* For an insightful discussion of similar north Indian insult genres, see Pauline Kolenda, "Untouchable Chuhras Through Their Humor: 'Equalizing' Marital Kin Through Teasing, Pretence, and Farce," in *Divine Passions: The Social Construction of Emotion in India,* ed. Owen Lynch (Berkeley: University of California Press, 1990), pp. 116–53.

70. Rajavati told me later that women might speak these potent insult words in particularly virulent quarrels with their mothers-in-law, their husbands' brothers' wives, or their husbands' sisters.

71. See the twentieth-century *paṭ* painting of Rādhā and Kṛṣṇa in Robert F.

Bussburger and Betty Dashew Robins, *The Everyday Art of India* (New York: Dover, 1968), p. 148.

72. Gold indicates that both men and women are very much aware of the sexual imagery in this song, as the young bride speaks to the groom (Raheja and Gold, *Listen to the Heron's Words*): "Bridegroom-Prince, your fan from Alwar has a golden stick. / Bridegroom-Prince, in the middle of your cot the fan will spin."

73. See, for example, the album miniature from Kota reproduced in Philip Rawson, *Erotic Art of the East* (New York: Putnam, 1968), p. 62, and a nineteenth-century Kangra miniature (p. 88). So much associated with sexuality are these *bījnās* that I have not seen renderings of these fans in any painting unconnected with such intimacy. There are some paintings, though, in which a female attendant attempts to cool the pain and burning experienced by a woman separated from her lover by waving an embroidered fan. See, for example, M. S. Randhawa, *Kangra Paintings on Love* (New Delhi: The National Museum, 1962), pp. 30–31.

74. See, for example, the drawing "Nala and Damayanti in Three Amorous Scenes" reproduced in Alvan Clark Eastman, *The Nala-Damayanti Drawings* (Boston: Museum of Fine Arts, 1959), plate 26.

75. Das, "Masks and Faces," pp. 6–7.

76. For some examples of how women may practically as well as poetically express such challenges, through the manipulation of gift-giving practices, see chapter 3 of Raheja and Gold, *Listen to the Heron's Words;* see also Das, "Masks and Faces."

77. Trawick Egnor, "Internal Iconicity in Paraiyar Crying Songs," pp. 320–22.

78. Though the practice of cross-cousin marriage frequently, in south India, means that a woman moves at her marriage to a household where she is a known kinswoman, Trawick Egnor finds that many south Indian women's songs, like those in the north, tend to view the husband's house as a foreign place. Thus, the singer's reference to her natal place as a foreign land seems to be an ironic one; she speaks longingly of the place where she was born yet ends by calling it a foreign place, as she juxtaposes words that speak of the "mother who bore me" with words suggesting that her mother's place is a "foreign land" now that she, the singer, has been married. This is the same ironic mode found in the north Indian *bhāt* song discussed earlier in this essay, as well as in chapter 3 of Raheja and Gold, *Listen to the Heron's Words.*

3

The Dilemmas of Domesticity: Possession and Devotional Experience Among Urban Smārta Women

MARY E. HANCOCK

Bhakti *in Social Context*

The introductory essay to this volume suggests that by tracing marriage's margins or boundaries we are enabled to better discern what is central to marriage and, taking this notion a step further, to see that inversions of and resistance to normative versions of marriage may be read as "diagnostic indicators" of the complex relations of knowledge and power that support claims about the meaning of Hindu marriage.[1] In this essay I engage the center–periphery dynamic, and its ambiguities, through a discussion of the interpenetrations of *bhakti* (religious devotion) and spirit possession in several Smārta Brahman households.

Bhakti, an umbrella term for a variety of ecstatic devotional forms dating from the seventh century C.E., has often been viewed as a critique "from below" of the formalism of Hindu orthodoxy and the accompanying structural inequalities of caste.[2] I would like to argue here for a more complicated and nuanced approach to the "resistance" often attributed to *bhakti.* I am particularly interested in female *bhakta*s (devotees), and in the ways that their devotional activities (which included spirit possession and mediumship) were both aligned with and resistant to notions of sexual and domestic order that Smārta Brahmans regard as being grounded by the textual authority of the *smṛti*s. My examination of the social construction of *bhakti* in the context of the Smārta household not only will contribute to our understanding of contemporary devotionalism but also will illuminate how some Smārta women experienced and evaluated marriage.

This essay is based on ethnographic fieldwork conducted in 1987–88 among Smārta Brahmans in Madras City. Many of the women with whom I became acquainted regarded themselves as *bhakta*s, and some were locally renowned as religious virtuosi. While married women's involvement in devotionalism was consistent with many Hindus' emphasis on *bhakti* as an integral part of domestic life and public religious expression, the styles of practice they adopted reflected the curtailments of authority and autonomy that most high-caste women experienced in their homes.[3] I was often told by Smārta men and women that in a well-ordered household women's autonomy should be subject to curtailment by male authority and by the authority of senior females.[4]

In everyday practice these relations of authority are shaped by the composition, size, and socioeconomic status of the household. The women discussed in this essay were members of households of six or fewer persons, headed by middle-class business and professional persons. In such households, which are common among India's urban middle classes, one woman (usually the wife of the head of household) was responsible for cooking, housecleaning, marketing, child care and socialization, entertaining guests, and other forms of housework. In addition, some women were employed on a part- or full-time basis in wage labor. Consequently, while many women professed a desire to engage in devotional practice, those with husbands and unmarried children had limited resources or opportunities for carving out physical or temporal spaces in which to pursue ritual, meditation, or prayer.

Other authors, notably Madan and Ramanujan, have argued that dilemmas such as those faced by the women discussed here are comprehensible in light of the normative values of Hinduism. Madan emphasized *bhakti*'s conformity to this-worldly values of caste and domesticity.[5] His reading of devotion takes account of issues such as those specified earlier, for he noted that the opportunities for involvement in *bhakti* vary according to gender and through the life cycle. This, he argued, is linked to the patriarchal values that underpin Hindu orthopraxy. By implication, women's limited participation in domestic religious practice can be seen as a mechanism that preserves patriarchal domestic order by producing a "muted" female subject.[6] Ramanujan, on the other hand, suggested on the basis of written hagiographies that, for women, *bhakti* entailed a rejection of home and family life.[7] Theirs was a context-specific mode of detachment—a practical, though partial, resolution of what Ramanujan saw as the antinomies of domesticity and renunciation.

My observations, however, raise questions about both models inasmuch as they are predicated on the normative determination of individual subjectivity. Women's devotionalism, including spirit possession, often involved efforts to renegotiate domestic relations of authority while still retaining their patriarchally derived identities as wives and mothers. These religious activities were, moreover, framed and facilitated by the women's class status. For them *bhakti* was a modality that criticized some elements of gender hierarchy, while it preserved other features of class and caste privilege.[8] I argue that this points to *bhakti*'s polyvalence and suggests, contra Madan, that rather than being the overdetermined product of a reified "Hindu" domestic world, *bhakti* is characterized by ambiguity, and that its sociocultural effects can be gauged only with respect to the contexts in which it is expressed.

In this essay I describe the ambiguities of *bhakti*, using the interwoven life experiences of three female devotees. My analysis attends to the ways that it provides a grammar of both resistance to and compliance with the patriarchal norms of Hindu practice. During the period that this essay documents, two of the women discussed were regularly possessed by *ammaṉ*s (goddesses) and acted as mediums while in those states. In one respect their activities were legitimated by the symbolic capital of their esteemed status as *cumaṅkali*s (married women with living husbands).[9] The prestige attached to *cumaṅkali* identity and the capabilities with which it is invested are suggested by the literal meaning of this Sanskrit borrowed word. A *cumaṅkali* is "a most auspicious woman," and is a paradigmatic identity that is associated, in ritual contexts, with *śakti* (Skt., Tamil *cakti*), a term that refers to creative energy, as well as to the female consorts of male deities.

As *cumaṅkali*s the women described here were linked metaphorically and metonymically with feminine forms of divinity, and this association shaped their devotional aspirations. In other, more practical, ways they used the social and material resources of their respective households to facilitate their religious activities. They also attempted to gain wealth and prestige through their devotional practices. On the other hand, their radical appropriation of authority through the avenues of possession and mediumship distanced them from other aspects of domesticity. They captured moral authority by speaking as *ammaṉ*s, and with those voices contested their husbands' and other family members' efforts to control their actions.

In the first place I contemplate the possible reasons that married Smārta women turned to *bhakti* religiosity. In the first section of this essay I deal with some of these issues by recounting the development of three women's devotional interests, using their personal narratives as sources. While I focus mostly on *bhakti*'s implications for gender, I also consider its relevance with respect to caste and class, for the women I discuss are high-caste members of the urban bourgeoisie. These prove to be related issues, because in the same ways that *bhakti* enables them to step into and away from marriage, it provides a means to deny, but also affirm, caste and class distinctions.

I also approach the issue of women's devotionalism contextually in the second section by examining how their devotional activities were situated within the politics and resources of the household. I argue that the case histories reveal that *bhakti* cannot be treated merely as a compensatory safety valve or an interstitial or liminal interlude in an otherwise normatively ordered social existence. *Bhakti,* especially as pursued by *cumaṅkali*s, may be an agency for change in domestic life, whether the *bhakta* is perceived as succeeding or failing in her efforts.

The concluding section includes a discussion of the cultural principles according to which these women evaluated their own histories. This will bring the discussion back around to the issue of marriage. While I will not argue that their actions were those of autonomous, free-willed "individuals," I do maintain that their understandings of the norms of domesticity and detachment, as well as *śakti,* were pivotal in each woman's self-understanding and agency. Specifically, I argue that their understandings of their own histories and desires, their conjugal and familial relations, and their everyday experiences of conflict and moral dilemma guided the ways that they read the aforementioned norms and framed the possibilities for their actions. The three women who are described viewed *bhakti* as the means to attend to a complex web of domestic relations, which included but were not limited to their relations with their husbands. At the same time, *bhakti* was a way to concentrate the creative energy of *śakti* and to transmute it into instrumental power. *Bhakti* enabled them to carve a space in which they could isolate themselves, temporarily, from the demands and desires of family life. It also assisted them in repositioning themselves in the house, thus disrupting the relational nexus that constitutes the primary domestic site of patriarchy. Not only will this material complicate and enrich our understandings of Hindu marriage and female subjectivity in that context, it will also contribute to a more general reframing of current understanding of *bhakti* devotionalism.

The Shape of Bhakti *in Three Lives*

Since the subject of my field research was domestic religious practice, I came to know many persons, male and female, who were regarded by family, friends, and other associates as religious adepts of one sort or another. Among them, a woman named Sunithi was singular. She was a medium for the goddess Karumāriyammaṉ, and as a result she had attracted a following of relatives, friends, and neighbors.[10] Among her followers were the two other women whom I discuss, Saraswati and Minakshi. The relationships among these three women—particularly their interwoven devotional histories—form the core of my essay.

Sunithi, Saraswati, and Minakshi were all Smarta Brahmans, residing in Madras City with their families. Madras City is a regional administrative and commercial center. It is India's fourth-largest metropolitan center with a population (1981 census) of 3,276,622. Its growth during this century has been due largely to in-migration, related to industrial expansion. Tamil Nadu presently ranks among India's most industrialized states.[11]

Though not numerically a large group, Smārtas are among the more prominent Hindu communities in Madras City. They follow the teachings of Śaṅkara, the eighth-century A.D. founder of the monistic philosophical school in Hinduism known as Advaitavedānta. Smārtas distinguish themselves from other Brahman groups (Śrīvaiṣṇava or Aiyyangar Brahmans) on the basis of sectarian affiliation, and they tend to avoid intermarriage. Smārtas trace their origins to Tamil-, Telugu-, and Kannada-speaking regions of south India, though, at present, they are dispersed in cities throughout India and overseas. It is difficult to estimate the community's overall size at present; the 1931 census was the last in which the population was enumerated in terms of caste. At that time Brahmans constituted approximately 3 percent (19,350) of Madras City's total population of 645,000.

Despite their minority status, many Brahmans have experienced significant levels of socioeconomic and political enfranchisement during the past one hundred years: a historical artifact of the city's development in the region.[12] During the colonial period Smārtas were prominent among south India's Western-educated elite; at the turn of the twentieth century they dominated those sections of the provincial civil services and professions open to Indians, making them part of the "large stratum of urban professionals steeped . . . in the values of bourgeois liberalism."[13] Since that time, the organization and political power of the Non-Brahman movement in the south have effectively diminished the political presence of Brahmans at the state level of government. By and large, however, Smārtas have been able to maintain a relatively privileged status through employment in industry, central government service, and white-collar professions. Most of my informants regarded themselves as "middle class," a reflection of income levels (800–2000 rupees per month) and modes of consumption. Their middle-class affiliations were also representative of educational achievements (secondary and postsecondary schooling), occupational status as white-collar professionals, and the pursuit of leisure activities such as performing arts, sports, cinema, and restaurant dining.

The three women on whom I focus most closely in this essay were members of households such as those just described. Each was married and had at least one child. Two (Saraswati and Minakshi) resided in nuclear households during the period when the data were collected, and the third (Sunithi) lived in an extended household that included her widowed mother, her husband, her son, and her daughter-in-law. As is the case with many urban dwellers, each of the three family groups resided in a rented flat. The income levels varied among households, ranging from about 1,500 rupees per month (Saraswati and Minakshi) to 2,500 rupees (Sunithi). Saraswati's household had only one working member, her husband, whereas both Sunithi's and Minakshi's families relied on the earnings of at least two members.

Because Sunithi was the center of this network, I turn to her story first. As I noted, she was a devotee of the goddess Karumāriyammaṉ, and was referred to by her followers as "*ammaṉ*." Sunithi had been made aware of her "powers," which she referred to as *śakti*, through a local Untouchable medium of the goddess Karumāriyammaṉ.[14] Approximately ten years earlier, at the urging of her servant, Sunithi had consulted this woman regarding a gynecologic problem. The problem was resolved following the medium's intervention, and Sunithi remained her client for several years thereafter. After her success in "curing" Sunithi, the medium began to interpret various events, objects, and interactions in Sunithi's life in a way that made these disparate phenomena consistent with the idea that the goddess literally wished to take up residence with Sunithi and her family and to use Sunithi herself as the human vessel through which "she" (Karumāriyammaṉ) could speak to and interact with other devotees.

Sunithi explained that, throughout this period, she encountered the goddess often in the forms of persons, objects, and animals during both waking and sleeping times. She claimed, for example, to have been approached on several occasions by an unkempt woman who asked only for camphor—a substance that is ordinarily lit and offered to the deity during *pūja*.[15] At other times she said that she had witnessed a large snake in her home, and on still other occasions she observed a young girl, unknown to her, in her home. Both snakes and young girls are identified with the goddess in certain contexts. Sunithi came to believe, under the local medium's guidance, that these beings were manifestations of Karumāriyammaṉ, who had taken those forms in order to attract Sunithi's attention.

The most convincing and enduring embodiment of the goddess was a mask (*mukam*) of the goddess Varalakṣmī.[16] These masks are generally composed of silver (or a similar-looking metal) and are used by Smārta women in the celebration of Varalakṣmī *nōṉpu*, an observance for the benefit of husbands undertaken annually during the Tamil month of Āṭi (July–August).[17] Sunithi's mask had been purchased from friends several years earlier and used thereafter for the *nōṉpu*.

After the completion of Varalakṣmī *nōṉpu* one year (and subsequent to the experiences described previously), Sunithi had decided to leave the mask displayed and to decorate it on each subsequent Friday, a day that Hindus normally associate with the goddess. During the weeks that followed she noticed changes in the mask, which she initially attributed to fungus. She no longer patronized the local medium, but her mother and a friend convinced her that the changes were due to the spontaneous presence of sacred ash, sandal paste, and vermilion powder: auspicious embellishments that had appeared at the behest of the deity that they believed to be present in the mask. It was this "miracle" (*aṟputam*), Sunithi stated, that compelled her "surrender" (*caraṇam*) to the goddess. A few months thereafter she first experienced possession, and somewhat later she began acting as a medium and issuing *uttaravu* (predictions, advice, and admonishments regarded as coming from the goddess).

The occasion on which Sunithi identified the initial "coming of the goddess" was during her performance of *apiśekam* (a ritual bathing and anointing of the deity's image, which is part of *pūja*) at home for the family's collection of deity icons. Her special affiliation with the goddess Karumāriyammaṉ, was already recognized at this point and was, in fact, the impetus for that particular *apiśekam*. A neighbor suspected that her son had smallpox and had requested that Sunithi perform the *apiśekam* on his behalf. Sunithi had agreed, though she had professed to being unsure about the formalities of the ritual. She said that once she began the ritual, she involuntarily entered into a trancelike state. Her mother, the neighbor and her husband and son, and two of Sunithi's female friends (also goddess devotees) witnessed Sunithi's performance and described it to her and later to me as having been flawless.

This scenario set a pattern for the events that followed. The performance of *apiśekam* was the trigger for the goddess to emerge, and thereafter it was performed at monthly intervals. Sunithi conducted it in the *ammaṉ* persona, and she remained in that state for a few hours after each performance, at which times she advised and counseled an ever-increasing population of devotees. Over time Sunithi added her own signatory flourishes to the performance, one of which was her use of eight to ten liters of milk for sluicing the small icons during *apiśekam*.

With the institution of the monthly possession–performances, Sunithi claimed that her actions were regulated increasingly by Karumāriyammaṉ. She sought the goddess's permission to attend social functions, and she dressed and groomed herself in accordance with what she perceived to be the *ammaṉ*'s desires. From the first possession experience, for example, she wore her hair loose, allowing it to curl around her face and shoulders in the same way that the hair of the goddess Mariyāmmaṉ was pictured.[18] Most household decisions were made in consultation with the goddess as well. Sunithi, in the *ammaṉ* persona, directed her son's marriage negotiations and made decisions about the family's expenditures, among other things.

I have used the term "persona" to describe the face that Sunithi presented to her audience on these occasions. With this term I wish to call attention to the degree that Sunithi self-consciously incorporated the *ammaṉ* personality into her own social identity. She maintained that her early possession experiences were completely overpowering and that she had no recollection of what she had done on those occasions. She was aware of her actions during the more recent experiences, however. In connection with this, she claimed that her "bond" (*pattam*) with the goddess was stronger and that she was better able to control the goddess. In merging with the goddess Karumāriyammaṉ, Sunithi tried to maintain a placid demeanor. The markers of her *ammaṉ* persona were the singsong manner of speech she adopted at those times, as well as her engagement in activities that her family and friends described as uncharacteristic of the ordinary Sunithi. For example, she requested the rice dishes—yogurt rice and lemon rice—that were popularly thought to be preferred by the goddess.

These aesthetic devices were also ways of identifying herself, her followers, and the performance as Brahman, as opposed to non-Brahman.[19] Her followers maintained that her claims were true because her experiences were *not* comparable with those of other mediums. As an *ammaṉ* Sunithi avoided the typical repertoire of possession behaviors (e.g., frenzied dance and self-mortification) observed among other, mostly non-Brahman and Untouchable, mediums.[20] She and other informants associated the latter actions with non-Brahman and Untouchable underclasses.

Sunithi also established certain creative departures from Brahmanic norms. For example, the ritual impurity (*tīṭṭam*) of menstruation was usually cited by orthoprax Brahmans as the reason for women's subordinate ritual roles. Menstruation was thought to render women unfit to cook, to view the deity's image, and to participate in worship. Sunithi, as *ammaṉ*, turned this rule on its head. She announced that menstrual restrictions did not apply in her house and that women could enter the *pūja* space while menstruating. Women, during their menstrual periods, are euphemistically referred to as being "away from the house" (*vīṭṭukkuttūṟam*) or "not in the house" (*vīṭṭil illai*); nevertheless, they were welcomed to the goddess's house with Sunithi's edict.

In describing her experiences to me, Sunithi emphasized the aforementioned attributes in order to distance herself from other mediums. She also distinguished herself from other mediums on the grounds that they performed and issued predictions for preset fees, whereas she, while accepting gifts and monetary donations, did not specify in advance the amounts to be given. I discuss the economic dimensions of Sunithi's activities in greater detail in the next section.

The network that formed around Sunithi included participants in this ritual as well as individual clients. Though she stated that she did not exclude non-Brahmans and Untouchables from her client population, her own circle of followers consisted predominantly of Smārta Brahmans of class status comparable to her own. They participated in ritual visually, that is, by watching Sunithi's actions and by receiving her *darśan*, a Sanskrit term referring to the "sacred perception" of deities or other eminent persons.[21] By contrast with Sunithi herself, the deity icons for whom the *apiśekam* was performed held little attraction for the audience, although devotees did participate in certain acts of worship—for example, by offering flowers and by consuming *prasādam* (a Sanskrit expression that denotes the food that is distributed among devotees after having been transvalued by means of its offering to the deity).

Among Sunithi's clients were the two other women whose stories I also wish to discuss, though more briefly. Minakshi had become a devoted follower of Sunithi during the time I did fieldwork. She was a close friend of mine, and it was she who had insisted on introducing me to Sunithi. Minakshi was self-employed as a private tutor and was a college graduate. She had learned about Sunithi through one of her (Minakshi's) sisters-in-law who lived in Sunithi's neighborhood and attended Sunithi's performances of *apiśekam*.

Minakshi initially had sought Sunithi's advice with regard to several family problems. These included her husband's ill health, her elder daughter's marriage negotiations, and her other daughter's and son's respective job searches. Minakshi's salary and that of her elder daughter (also employed as a teacher) were the backbone of the family's income, but the family's increasing financial needs had put more pressure on Minakshi to find ways for the household to subsist. This set of issues had been troubling Minakshi for several months, and she had consulted astrologers and other mediums. She had also turned to the marital advertisements in newspapers (for her elder daughter), to allopathic and Ayurvedic physicians (for her husband), and to influential family friends (on the job front). Sunithi's advice to Minakshi was essentially that each person should do as much as possible to help him- or herself and that if they all did their best the goddess would also do her best.

Sunithi's directions to Minakshi did not stop with these comments, however. In the *ammaṉ* persona Sunithi had suggested to Minakshi that she harbored a "hidden power," designated as *śakti*, the emergence of which would coincide with the goddess's "coming to" her in the way she had previously "come to" Sunithi herself. Sunithi, speaking as the *ammaṉ*, had verified that "I [the goddess] am deep in her [Minakshi's] heart," and would emerge at a time of her own choosing. This expectation, as well as her desire to exercise control over this process, bound Minakshi to Sunithi. Her willingness to believe Sunithi was due, in part, to the fact that she had consulted some other mediums at around this same time, and they had also confirmed that this *śakti* was present in her. What distinguished Sunithi from the others were the facts that she was a woman (this made Minakshi more comfortable in spending time alone with her), that her class and caste status were similar to Minakshi's, and that Sunithi provided specific information about how and when the deity would emerge. Sunithi's personal history offered Minakshi the model for her own life, and Minakshi therefore became more and more involved in goddess *bhakti* throughout the time I knew her.

I learned over time that the pattern of Minakshi's involvement was not unique, that other women and some men in Sunithi's circle were initiates, as well as clients, and that several were establishing extensions of that network by developing their own client populations. The third woman I will describe, Saraswati, offered a personal history that had many parallels with that relayed to me by Sunithi.

Prior to her acquaintance with Sunithi, Saraswati had become a devotee of Karumāriyammaṉ and had patronized a goddess temple in the city. She said, however, that her relationship with the goddess had reached a turning point when her infant son was stricken with smallpox. Although she had sought the goddess's help, the baby had died. Thereafter, Saraswati had begun to question the goddess's power.

Despite her mounting cynicism, Saraswati agreed (in December 1985) to accompany her younger sister on a visit to Sunithi. There they asked Sunithi, in the *ammaṉ* persona, about the sister's marriage prospects. Although that particular issue had not been adequately resolved (her sister was still unmarried in 1988), Saraswati said that she felt great peace (*amaiti*) in Sunithi's presence. Subsequently, other things in Saraswati's life had begun to change in ways that, to her, ratified Sunithi's powers. Shortly after her first meeting with Sunithi, Saraswati said that she had encountered the goddess in the form of a small girl. As in Sunithi's case, the initial encounter occurred in the context of domestic ritual activity. Saraswati was at home alone, preparing to perform *pūja,* when she was visited by an unknown girl. In her account, Saraswati indicated that the girl was physically present, but that her modes of arrival and departure were not evident, nor was she seen by anyone else. Similar encounters continued (both within and outside her home), and in a few months, Saraswati acquired the ability to give *uttaravu* (predictions, advice, etc.) in the way that Sunithi did.

The object–embodiment of the *ammaṉ* was a figure of Annapūrṇā, the goddess–protector of Varanasi (Banaras). This deity is important in domestic settings because of her association with rice, the quintessential food for South Asians. It is common for women to receive Annapūrṇā figures as gifts from female friends and relations who make pilgrimages to Varanasi, and Saraswati had received hers from her mother-in-law. Though the icon had not changed in the same manner as Sunithi's mask, it served as a focus for Saraswati's devotions and for those of the clients she later acquired.

Sunithi's role in this paralleled the earlier role that the non-Brahman medium had taken in Sunithi's own life. As the events recounted previously unfolded, Sunithi (in the *amma<u>n</u>* persona) verified that the young girl was indeed a form of the goddess and that she had "come to" Saraswati in the same way she had previously "come to" Sunithi. Saraswati, in turn, continued to attend Sunithi's *apiśekam*s and to regard her as a guru, though she claimed she no longer needed to consult with Sunithi in the *amma<u>n</u>* persona, because the goddess had come to her own house.

Sunithi's involvement with her devotees and initiates revealed her recognition that her claims to *amma<u>n</u>*-hood were not accepted uncritically; she was aware that numerous persons who knew about her considered her a fraud.[22] She was therefore careful to offer her devotees ritual-related experiences that were satisfying in emotional and aesthetic ways. She also understood that her success or failure was linked to the efficacy and success of her initiates' developments as saintly exemplars. Accordingly, she often attempted to exercise control over the conduct of initiates like Saraswati. She did this by offering instructions and criticisms of their presentations of self-as-*amma<u>n</u>* when she herself was in the *amma<u>n</u>* persona. Tensions in their relationship were created by Saraswati's claim of authority, the nature of which I describe in the next section.

The experiences recounted by these women point to the importance of idioms of femininity within the discursive practice of devotion; they also suggest some of the ways that devotional practice both reflects and intervenes in the social organization of gender difference. Devotees of Hindu goddesses include both men and women, and the network of clients and initiates that formed around Sunithi included roughly equal numbers of men and women. Within Madras City there are many such networks of goddess devotees. These groups are found throughout the range of class and caste strata, and some are led by men.[23]

Bhakti's gendered quality is a subject upon which both scholars and religious leaders have commented. Ramanujan associates feminine idioms with devotionalism in general terms.[24] He has noted that the *bhakta*'s identity in connection with the deity is one of relational femininity—of subordination infused with the desire, often framed in erotic terms, for union with the deity. For these reasons he sees *bhakti* as a genre of Hindu practice that offers greater scope to women than other, more orthodox, forms.

This attention to feminine imagery and to women's devotional roles is elaborated, as well, in the teachings of Kancipuram Śaṅkarācaryas, who, as descendants of the line of gurus initiated by Śaṅkara, are the main expositors of the Sanskrit precepts regarded as authoritative by orthodox Smārtas.[25] The Śaṅkarācaryas (all of whom are men) are said to have merged with the goddess. The most recent Śaṅkarācaryas have authored songs, prayers, and a variety of ritual forms in honor of the goddess, and have urged their followers to incorporate these elements into their own practice. During the past few decades they have sought greater publicization of goddess worship—and have made particular appeals to Smārta women to form devotional associations to promote goddess worship and to support existing goddess temples through donations, participation in temple rituals, and improvement of temple sites (including cleaning and renovating existing structures). Since, in Madras, many of these temples are located in lower-class, lower-caste neighborhoods, this amounts to a call for a Brahman colonization of these sites—an issue that is significant in terms of regional politics.[26] In effect, Smārta women are being asked to recreate inequalities through the modality of goddess worship and the ideology of protection.

While Sunithi did not describe her own devotion to the goddess as a response to the Śaṅkarācaryas' directives, their advocacy of goddess worship and their support of women's involvement in it contributed to a climate in which Sunithi's, Saraswati's, and Minakshi's interests and actions made sense to themselves and to others. Their experiences also mirrored the implicit class distinctions of the Śaṅkarācaryas' programs. The terms of these women's relations with the goddess drew on feminine idioms—particularly with reference to sexuality and domesticity—and framed them in accordance with the ideologies of class and caste.

The conduit between any deity (male or female) and medium is described as *śakti,* a term that refers to creative energy as well as to the female consort of male deities. However, the ways that *śakti* is conceptualized and channeled are variable and complex. In the cases outlined here the goddess was thought to exist in both somatic and iconic forms. The ways in which the women clothed and embellished themselves, and in which they arranged and decorated the deity's icons, recorded the shifting relations among them and between them and the goddess. These gestures were also modalities for conceptualizing and controlling the deity's desires and identity.

Sunithi's arrangement of the household's icons in the form of a "family" that included the goddess as wife/mother may be seen as her effort to domesticate a goddess who is conventionally understood as independent (i.e., without male consort). At the same time, Sunithi's adoption of the goddess's loose hairstyle and her reversal of orthopraxy regarding menstrual seclusion symbolically invested her (Sunithi) with the goddess's independence and *śakti*—a volatile combination that, in symbolic terms, results in a surfeit of *śakti*. The other version of the goddess that Sunithi encountered and incorporated in her own *ammaṉ* persona was the goddess as young girl. Here we see another inversion of the *cumaṅkali*—a female who is sexually inactive and who is free of the obligations to husband, children, and in-laws that circumscribe the married woman's life.

These interventions, in effect, invited all women—by virtue of their femininity—into the goddess's presence and illustrate how cultural understandings of femininity provided idioms with which connections among women might be formed. However, the same feminine idioms that were the vehicles for bonds among women also enabled them to articulate differences and inequalities.

The relations between Sunithi and the Untouchable medium who initiated her are also illustrative of the ways that idioms of femininity, mediated by differences of class and caste, may divide as well as unite women. Sunithi claimed to have initially established a close and mutually dependent relationship with the Untouchable medium. By the time I knew her, however, that relationship had dissolved, and Sunithi often criticized the medium for what she regarded as a mercenary attitude.[27] The medium was one of those who treated the goddess's "coming" as a mere job, according to Sunithi, though Sunithi herself accepted donations from clients and was, in effect, in competition with her former adviser.

The differences between her own and the medium's performance styles were consistent with the types of distinctions that members of the middle classes (Smārtas and others) drew between themselves and the urban underclasses. Sunithi, however, infused these class distinctions with cultural values through her ritual style. Several aesthetic markers singularized her performances and accommodated the tastes and sensibilities of the urban Brahman community of which she was a member, thereby distinguishing hers from the styles associated with villagers and the low-caste/Untouchable urban underclasses. Sunithi as *ammaṉ* was soft-spoken and used the version of colloquial Tamil spoken by Smārta Brahmans. She accepted only vegetarian foods. Her ritual improvisations—using large quantities of milk to sluice deities and tossing handfuls of flowers on her audience while offering them to the deity's icon—lent informality and spontaneity to the ritual but did not offend the religious sensibilities of her mostly Brahman audience.

Differences, in terms of status and authority, were also articulated among Sunithi and her Brahman clients and initiates. Sunithi drew on the authority of her *ammaṉ* persona to control the actions, performance styles, and credibility of her initiates.

The foregoing section has treated the question of why these women became *bhakta*s almost exclusively on the basis of their own narratives.

As is evident, their interests and forms of involvement in *bhakti* were underscored by their understandings of femininity, sexual difference, and agency, as well as their respective positioning within the complex and interpenetrating hierarchies of caste, class, and gender. On the one hand, *bhakti*'s saturation with feminine idioms may promote bonds based on notions of shared subjectivity. On the other hand, inasmuch as women's experiences are mediated by the structural inequalities of caste and class, the subjectivities shaped by *bhakti* and its social effects cannot be presumed to be uniform. From the Untouchable medium's perspective, goddess devotion was a means for criticizing the hierarchies of caste and class, but it was also a vehicle for socioeconomic mobility. By contrast, though the Smārta women also sought greater wealth and status, their criticism focused on domestic politics of gender and affirmed caste and class inequalities. In the next section I describe the domestic stages on which subjectivities and structural inequalities were constituted and reworked.

Bhakti *and the Currents of Domestic Life*

The primary vehicle through which Sunithi represented her social identity as an *amman̲* was her regular performance of *apiśekam* in the *amman̲* persona, followed by her consultation sessions. These performances relied on the material infrastructure, including labor, of the household. As focal point for the devotional network, Sunithi, and by extension her family, enjoyed a renown that had gradually exceeded the bounds of the immediate neighborhood. Sunithi's followers were, for the most part, members of the urban middle classes and came from many sections of Madras. Because of these outsiders' perceptions of her powers, it was Sunithi herself who had come to stand for the household; this elevated status outside the family had an impact on the level of authority she wielded within it.

In spatial and material terms, the house offered the space and requisite objects for the performance of and public participation in ritual. The room where *pūja* space was located was a multifunctional area of about twelve-by-fifteen feet in size. It was regularly used during her monthly ritual performances, at which times between forty and sixty people assembled there. Because she also delivered the goddess's *uttaravu* (without *pūja*) on the first Friday of each (English) month, the room served as a gathering place at those times as well. Finally, devotees often came on a less formal basis—to view her and the shrine where the Varalakṣmī mask was displayed and to offer private prayer. In return for Sunithi's blessing, they donated money and valuables to the goddess, such as jewelry and saris.

As Sunithi's renown grew, the household underwent transformations that made it more like a public shrine in appearance and in its accessibility to outsiders. The *pūja* room was moved from the physically recessed area, described earlier, to the parlor, a front room to which the flat's main entrance opened. These changes in the house's spatial organization were accompanied by changes in its social composition due to Sunithi's son's marriage.

Sunithi, in the *ammaṉ* persona, directed the negotiations for the marriage and all of the other changes in the household. In 1987 the wedding was arranged and celebrated, and the son and daughter-in-law were given a separate bedroom in the flat. The newlyweds were given a room that had been Sunithi's and her husband's bedroom, and Sunithi and her husband moved their bed into the room that had been used as a *pūja* room. The ritual paraphernalia in that room was then divided between two different rooms. The Varalakṣmī mask and the other major icons were brought into the parlor, where they were displayed on a north-facing shelf. The other things (mostly pictures) were left in the original *pūja* space. With the principal shrine located in the parlor, more visitors could be accommodated, and the newlyweds could be afforded privacy. The house was thus a text on which the convergence of *bhakti* and domestic organization was written.

The sum of these spatial transformations might be expressed as Sunithi's domestication of a volatile and markedly *un*domestic goddess. Sunithi, moreover, employed Smārta idioms in this process. For example, when speaking about her *ammaṉ* persona and her experiences, Sunithi explicitly equated Karumāriyammaṉ with Pārvatī, the Sanskritic consort of Śiva. Moreover, Varalakṣmī *nōṉpu*, the ritual that precipitated the goddess's physical presence in the house, is part of the Smārta repertoire of domestic ritual. These conventional images were further personalized by Sunithi. Rather than displaying the Varalakṣmī mask only during the *nōṉpu* period, she created a permanent exhibition—placing the mask alongside images of those deities regarded by Smārtas as the goddess's family: her husband, Śiva, and her sons, Murukaṉ and Gaṇeśa.

As a socioeconomic collectivity, the household was the source of material and social capital that supported Sunithi's ritual performances. Fruit, flowers, cooked foods, and other expendables for a single *pūja* cost a minimum of one to two hundred rupees. The coffee and snacks served to guests after the *pūja* was over cost between fifty and seventy-five rupees to prepare. The silk saris that she wore on these occasions cost a minimum of eight hundred rupees each. The preparation of food offerings, cleaning of the house, and decoration of the *pūja* room required the collective labor of family, friends, and servants. Finally, Sunithi's personal devotional activities and her involvement with her clients/devotees limited the time she could spend on ordinary housework and thus imposed additional responsibilities on her mother and daughter-in-law.

While the ritual performances required inputs of time, money, and labor, these events also yielded observable improvements in the family's socioeconomic status. As was noted earlier, though Sunithi made an effort to maintain credibility as an *ammaṉ* by framing her motives as nonmercenary, it is clear that her activities resembled a small business in many respects. In the first place, Sunithi's family's earnings were augmented by her devotees' donations of money and valuables. *Apiśekams* were usually performed at the request of some individual, after the potential sponsor submitted their request to Sunithi in the *ammaṉ* persona. If the goddess, speaking through Sunithi, approved the request, the sponsor provided one hundred rupees toward the cost of the ritual. Persons who came for the goddess's *uttaravu* generally donated cash or valuables.

Sunithi further displaced the question of intent by stating that although "she" (the ordinary Sunithi) did not wish to accept money, she had been instructed by the goddess to do so. In general, devotees' donations were funneled into paying for ritual performances and paraphernalia, though the excess was absorbed by other household expenditures and investments. By being cosharers in the ritual economy, through the offerings of money, jewelry, and clothing, devotees thus contributed to the domestic economy as well. The quasi-familial status of client/devotees was matched by a similar ambiguity in the status of family members who assumed clientlike roles in interacting with Sunithi's *ammaṉ* persona.

Sunithi's control over the disposition of resources and her ability to make and enforce decisions in the household were evidence of the considerable authority (*atikāram*) she wielded within the family. She was a mother with one child, a son; she was also a mother-in-law with a resident daughter-in-law. Her own mother lived with her and her family, and was a source of affection and companionship, of domestic labor (the mother did all of the cooking), and of psychological support. It was her mother who suggested to Sunithi that the goddess had "come to" the house with the transformations of the Varalakṣmī mask.

Sunithi as *ammaṉ* made use of the instrumental power that she derived by virtue of her age and familial relationships. By the same token, however, her authority as *ammaṉ* was not incontestable. Her husband, for example, could have invoked his status as head of the household to forbid Sunithi's performance of *apiśekam*, either for the family or for an audience of devotees. Her daughter-in-law could have withheld her assistance and made it more difficult to stage an *apiśekam*. At the time I conducted my fieldwork, all the family members gave Sunithi a great deal of latitude, though this was the result of delicate negotiations. The consequence was that visitors perceived Sunithi's household as harmonious, an image that was essential to the household's "good name" (*nallapēyar*) and integral to the charisma Sunithi exuded as a goddess oracle. The existence of devotees and the publicization of their success stories furthered the household's prestige. The family's increased affluence and its fame ratified the perception that the goddess was present and fed back into Sunithi's ability to attract devotees and to further improve their financial circumstances.

Both the socioeconomic basis and the consequences of Sunithi's *ammaṉ* persona reveal how transitory and fragile Sunithi's "success" as an *ammaṉ* was. Her capability to become an oracle did not lay merely in her perception of herself as an oracle but was a rhetorical feat. She had to persuade others of her credibility as an *ammaṉ;* among those others were her own family. They not only had to accept her claims, they had to validate them by publicly acceding to her authority in a variety of everyday matters—these were always matters of struggle and continuous negotiation.

Looking at the female *bhakta*'s success or failure over time illuminates the constraints and capabilities provided by the domestic infrastructure. Both Minakshi and Saraswati described their respective households as fraught with tensions about money, employment, health, and other matters. Both were attracted to the "peace" (*amaiti*) they perceived in Sunithi's house. Like many Brahman women, they had turned to astrologers and other specialists besides Sunithi for assistance in diagnosing and resolving the problems that existed, though their strategies were not always supported by their husbands, children, and in-laws.

Minakshi's husband argued that she spent too much time visiting temples and advisers and, as a result, neglected her family. This, he claimed, was the root of the problems she was trying to solve. She, on the other hand, felt that her efforts were necessary to solve the particular troubles she faced. Indeed, in her mind, her husband's attitude was one of the problems that needed resolution. Therefore, despite his disapproval, Minakshi persisted in her consultations. Some of the latitude in action that she had was possible because her children were in their early twenties and did not require continual attention. She herself was in her late forties and was employed as a teacher. The fact that she was employed and her husband was not was a source of financial and emotional strain, but it also assured her of a certain degree of autonomy. She was out of the house on a daily basis because of her job, and so could arrange her trips around the city without having to confront her husband each time she left the house. She could also use her own earnings to finance some of these endeavors.

For Minakshi the darker side of this semiindependence was the existence of sexual and emotional distance between herself and her husband. She had indicated to me that she and her husband had not had a sexual relationship for some years prior to her acquaintance with Sunithi. (While sexual detachment is culturally sanctioned for older couples, it is not always desired by both parties, nor can it be assumed to be prevalent.) While I cannot speculate on the causes of her situation, I do know that Minakshi was troubled by her husband's detachment and saw it as a sign of mental depression. She ascribed his attitude of withdrawal to poor health, and this was one of the problems she tried to solve by consulting astrologers, mediums, and so forth.

Despite the frequency of the previously mentioned consultations, she did not always follow the advice that each gave, nor did she patronize any of them over a long term. In deciding whether to heed their directions, she tended to weigh the practicality of their instructions (expense, time involved, travel, etc.) against the benefits she sought and against the practitioner's credibility and sincerity. Her attraction to Sunithi stemmed from the limited financial commitment that Sunithi expected and from the basis of shared experience that Minakshi assumed existed between her and Sunithi, another Smārta woman.

Minakshi patronized Sunithi for almost a year, and she brought her daughters and neighbors with her to Sunithi's *apiśekams*. She donated a sari, jewels, ritual accoutrements, and money to the goddess, and sponsored two *apiśekams*. Some months after meeting Sunithi, Minakshi obtained a color photo of Sunithi (taken by one of Sunithi's clients during an *apiśekam*) and put it in her own *pūja* room. There, during her own daily *pūja*, she directed her attention not only to Sunithi's picture but to the other deity images (pictures and *vigraham*) she kept there. She did not make any other alterations in her own dwelling or in her daily routine as a result of Sunithi's influence. She did, however, visit Sunithi's home two or three times each month, sometimes with me and at other times alone or with her daughter. She continued to go to temples and to consult other practitioners, as she deemed it necessary. Her husband did not participate with her in these activities, but he did not prevent her from attending them or from consulting Sunithi at other times.

In her conversations with me, Minakshi made reference to the peaceful atmosphere in Sunithi's house and spoke of her desire for the same thing. She felt that the emergence of her own *ammaṉ* persona would bring that about in her own household and therefore turned to Sunithi for more information about her own "hidden power" (her expression) and for interpretations of events that might portend its presence. During the year and a half that Minakshi remained close to Sunithi, she continued to expect that the *ammaṉ* would "come to" her, but this desire was not fulfilled. She never became possessed in the way that Sunithi did, although she has not, to my knowledge, abandoned the hope that this will happen at some future point.

While Minakshi seemed to become more dependent on Sunithi's information and on her goodwill over time, Saraswati moved in the opposite direction, as suggested earlier. Both Saraswati and her husband were devotees of the goddess Karumāriyammaṉ, and Saraswati's initial claim of seeing the goddess in the form of a young girl was accepted by her husband. He became critical of her conduct after she ceased accompanying him on his visits to a local goddess temple and began doing *pūja* only at home.

Saraswati's husband's consternation grew as she began to issue *uttaravu* at the request of neighbors, many of whom were non-Brahman. He complained about the presence of visitors in their home and was incensed because Saraswati seemed to lavish her full attention on them rather than on himself and their son. His brothers and parents echoed his disapproval of her behavior. Saraswati herself noted that her assumption of the *amman̲* persona was accompanied by her retreat from him, emotionally and sexually. She said that she felt less desire (*ācai*) for him and that her attentions had become more diffused as the number of clients seeking her services increased.

Feeling increasingly beleaguered by their criticism, Saraswati turned to Sunithi for support and for assurance that the *amman̲* had, in fact, come to her. She attended Sunithi's *apiśekam*s regularly until she received the *uttaravu* that the goddess was in her own house and that she did not need to go elsewhere to perform devotions. To inaugurate this new phase of her career, she invited Sunithi to come to her home and to perform *apiśekam* there. This was scheduled to take place on the festival marking the birth of the god Gaṇeśa, who is propitiated to ensure auspicious beginnings.

Although the *apiśekam* was performed as planned, Saraswati's husband's displeasure continued. Though she ceased going to Sunithi for *uttaravu*, she still looked to Sunithi's household as a model for her own. The calm environment that she desired was one in which her family approved of her activities and, like Sunithi's family, took on clientlike roles. At the same time, she expected her family to accommodate an expansion in their own ranks—to allow clients to literally come inside the house and to interact with the family as though they were part of it. Saraswati ascribed her husband's reluctance to make these accommodations to his jealousy of her *śakti*. Sunithi supported her in this interpretation but advised her own clients not to consult Saraswati because, she said, Saraswati's husband would insult them.

In time Sunithi became more critical of Saraswati. She suggested that Saraswati's "bond" (*pattam*) with the goddess was weak and that, as a result, Saraswati's *uttaravu* frequently turned out to be incorrect. Replaying the theme that had come up with respect to the Untouchable medium, Sunithi accused Saraswati of using her power for personal gain: for wealth and for fame. According to Sunithi, this misappropriation of power had resulted in the domestic conflicts noted earlier. In the *amman̲* persona, Sunithi claimed that she was testing Saraswati. During the time I knew them, Sunithi became more and more vocal in discouraging devotees from consulting Saraswati and thereby cast doubt on the veracity of Saraswati's claims. Sunithi knew that Saraswati's and her own reputations as oracles were linked and that success in this role depended, in part, on domestic harmony—their glosses as *cumaṅkali*s had to remain intact. She therefore tried to preserve her own reputation by disabling her competitor and by dissociating her *ammaṉ* persona from Saraswati's.

To conclude this section, I need to repeat the question "Why *bhakti?*" by bringing to it this focus on the domestic context of devotionalism. To reiterate points made in my introduction, *bhakti* is within the normative scope of the Brahman householder's (male or female) way of k life. However, women are less autonomous than their husbands, fathers, and brothers in terms of decision making and resource control, and their authority in many domestic spheres is encompassed by men's. Thus, the motives for devotionalism and its impact on marital relations and household organization are both gender-coded and context-dependent.

The Smarta women discussed here saw goddess devotion as a modality with which they might put their households in order, in ways that were simultaneously material and moral. *Bhakti* was perceived as a means of fulfilling one's obligations to kin and of assuring the household's wealth and class status. Her protestations notwithstanding, Sunithi was aware that as an *ammaṉ* she contributed to the household's economy—her concern was to frame this fact in a way that would not detract from her credibility among her followers. *Bhakti* was dependent on the social and material infrastructure of domestic life, even as it transformed it. Household spaces were the settings for individual and group worship; money generated by family members facilitated religious activities and was, itself, one type of transactional medium between deity and devotee. The time that each woman could dedicate to *bhakti* was related to her household's composition and its socioeconomic status, as represented by the presence of servants, subordinate family members, and laborsaving appliances. The woman's age and the affective relations among family members also played constraining or enabling roles.

Sunithi, for example, was relieved of most housework by her mother and her daughter-in-law, and by the maid the family employed; moreover, as *ammaṉ* she sharpened the distinctions of status and authority that existed among them. Her elevated status was most apparent in the context of her possession–performances, when she was treated like a revered guest by her family and by her clients. In fact, it was essential to the success of her *ammaṉ* persona that her family accede to her claims of a superordinate relational status.

For Minakshi and Saraswati the negotiation of *ammaṉ* status in relation to their families and Sunithi was problematic as well. As wives/mothers in nuclear households they possessed an autonomy that was circumscribed, though within it they had opportunities to pursue *bhakti*. They tended to their families' health, finances, and social life with what they perceived as the goddess's assistance. In these capacities they had sought out Sunithi as an adviser/oracle, but under her guidance they had acquired new senses of the possibilities of domestic life based on Sunithi's identification of *amman̲* personas in each of them. It was their efforts to expand their preexisting level of autonomy—by controlling the use of domestic space, by deciding how to use their time, and by transacting with others as *amman̲s*—that intensified intrafamilial conflict. In turn, their relations with Sunithi were subject to periodic strains and required occasional reinterpretation (based on the goddess's *uttaravu*) and renegotiation.

These changes in relations within the families and between Sunithi and her followers were linked to the changes in the uses and meanings of domestic space described previously. In many ways Sunithi's house (and to a lesser extent Saraswati's) straddled what I will call interiority (as a clearly bounded, familial space) and exteriority (as an ambiguously bounded, socially heterogeneous space).[28] Sunithi's house was treated by its residents and her clients like the sites in urban India referred to as "private temples." They are found both in domestic compounds and in public spaces but are "private" in that their management lies outside the control of the state government. They are maintained through the labor and finances of families and voluntary associations, and tend to serve a relatively homogeneous public, in terms of sectarian affiliation, caste, class, and/or residence.

Sunithi's home remained under the legal control of the family but was entered and used by a wider range of people than would ordinarily be the case. Visitors/clients treated it like a temple, performing rituals of deference to Sunithi and to the household's deity icons. They also left gifts for the *amman̲*, and the disposition of these items, once given, was regulated largely by Sunithi, in negotiation with her husband and son. Though likened to a temple, however, the house continued to be treated as a domestic space in other respects. It was treated as a temple only during restricted times, and even then guests were urged to be informal. Also, as was noted earlier, domesticity was one of the qualities with which Sunithi endowed the *amman̲*—the *pūja* room arrangement showed a household in miniature comprising the goddess's family. Finally, the degree of social homogeneity among visitors, clients, and initiates, in terms of class and caste, made it less of a public space and more like a home.

Despite the departures from ordinary domestic life that these women tried to engineer, they cannot be considered "renouncers," like the women saints described by Ramanujan.[29] They did not abandon domestic life or their roles as *cumaṅkali*s but tried instead to reorient themselves and their families to the path dictated by *amman̲*-hood. The threat that this reorientation posed lay in its repudiation of hegemonic norms and of the structure of authority based on those norms from which gender distinctions and female subordination were derived. Despite these threats, however, their households, as material and social units, persisted.

Improvised Lives: Bhakti, *Femininity, and Domesticity*

The successes that Sunithi, Saraswati, and Minakshi enjoyed as *bhaktas* were fragile and transitory. Looking at the *bhakta* as a paradigmatic identity, as both Madan and Ramanujan do, one might be tempted to discount these aspects—though the cost of doing so is illustrated by the following postscript.

Some months after I returned to the United States, I received a letter from Minakshi telling me that Sunithi's daughter-in-law had left her husband and returned to live with her own parents. She indicated that the daughter-in-law had become disenchanted with Sunithi's domination in household matters, and she reported (in English), that the daughter-in-law had begun to "speak ill of the *amman̲*" (i.e., of Sunithi in the *amman̲* persona). Other devotees had become skeptical of Sunithi's powers as a result, and this, Minakshi wrote, had caused the size of Sunithi's following to diminish.

Had I ended my story of Sunithi before her daughter-in-law's departure, she would have looked like a success. With her daughter-in-law's departure we see the structural fragility—the open-endedness and reversibility—of her situation. More generally, this story provides a vantage point from which to reflect upon the place of *bhakti* in the domestic world and to consider its relation to the problem of gendered subjectivity.

Attention to domestic expressions of ritual and belief in Hindu contexts has often sought to illuminate core domestic values. There has been a concern, exemplified by Madan, with the importance of moral values of domesticity in Hindu experience.[30] In such works and in the canonical texts of Sanskritic Hinduism, women's rituals are often dealt with as demonstrations of Hinduism's reliance on the *cumaṅkali* figure as an icon of auspiciousness. The *cumaṅkali* is argued to produce domestic order, prosperity, and, by implication, cosmic order.

While rituals of *cumaṅkali*-hood may be central to the reproduction of hegemonic ideologies of caste and Hinduism, it is difficult to understand the range of women's experiences through its analytic lens. One encounters only a vacuous subjectivity, one that is thoroughly mediated by the norms of orthopraxy. It offers a limited sense of the ambiguities and struggles that are both the grounds and the effects of religious practice. It does not begin to suggest the complexities of how persons' understandings of norms are reached, or of how they resist or assert, question, or affirm those norms. This volume asks that we shift our concerns in the latter directions by examining the edges of marriage—its exit gates and inversions. While some forms of religious action may usher men and women into marriage, other forms distance them from the duties and emotional ties that ordinarily shape their identities as husbands and wives.

This distancing can both reinforce and threaten the ideological scaffolding of marriage. Behaviors glossed under the rubric of "detachment" are normatively sanctioned among both men and women. According to the *Manusmṛti*, Sanskrit texts that many Smārtas regard as foundational, the Brahman man's life is divided into four stages.[31] The bachelor (*brahmacāri*) period is devoted to studentship, and it is followed by a man's assumption of the duties of the householder (*gṛhastha*). Once the latter duties have been discharged, he may assume the state of *vanaprastha*, a condition of partial renunciation. As a *saṃnyāsin*, during the fourth phase of life, he is a total renouncer, severing ties with kin and caste. It was not unusual for people to invoke these norms when describing particular men's life histories.[32]

Women, on the other hand, become *cumaṅkali*s when they marry and a woman only loses that status in the event of divorce or her husband's death (see chapter 6, this volume).[33] To avoid what was viewed as inauspiciousness, Smarta women often made efforts to preserve their identities as *cumaṅkali*s through prayer and sacrifice intended to promote their husbands' longevity and, by implication, to ensure that they would die auspiciously, as *cumaṅkali*s. In these rituals, key idioms recur which draw on broad cultural themes linking gender, sexuality, and the creative energy of *śakti*, and emphasizing the *cumaṅkali*'s auspiciousness (*maṅkalam*). Female sexuality, as articulated in these contexts, is understood as a manifestation of the creative energy of *śakti*, something whose fluidity and volatility are reckoned to be both life-giving and life-destroying.[34] The womanhood that is "produced" by faithful adherence to these programs is one modeled on the goddess Lakṣmī, the idealized *cumaṅkali* whose perfect subordination to her "husband," Viṣṇu, bestows health, prosperity, and domestic tranquillity. The Lakṣmīlike woman is a chaste wife, a desexualized mother—her body bears the diacritics of this status, and, not surprisingly, imagery of tying and binding abounds—her silk sari is carefully tied, she wears a marriage necklace and toe rings, bangles adorn her wrist, her long hair is oiled and plaited or twisted into a bun.

In terms of this logic, the control of female sexuality is the linchpin of the patriarchical institutions of caste and kinship, and in some instances may shore up class privilege by naturalizing class identity.[35] In practice women's sexuality is controlled by subtle and not-so-subtle arrangements of power that are formed and reformed through marriage and subordination to masculine authority, as well as through the complex set of relational obligations to kin that are articulated through life-cycle and calendrical rituals.

The fact that a woman's status as a *cumaṅkali* depends on the maintenance of these relations, particularly conjugal relations, means that having a socially recognized and valued identity is contingent on her acquiescence to these multiple relations of force.[36] While the willing docility of the Lakṣmīlike woman belies the intensity and effectiveness of this force, nonetheless it is its diagnostic indicator. These relations of force have concrete expression in everyday acts of physical and emotional violence and in the threat of such action. Equally diagnostic of the force that sustains *cumaṅkali*-hood are the restrictions on a woman's movements and everyday activities, and the demands that she be unquestioningly responsive to the needs and desires of her family.

This is the juncture at which the women described here were poised. For them *bhakti* stemmed from and intervened in these relations of force. Devotion can be a vehicle for women's resistance to one set of norms (e.g., the husband's authority), though it also entails compliance with other, equally hegemonic, norms (e.g., caste privilege). This points to a broader issue that has received much attention among feminist and subaltern theorists—the fact that acts labeled as forms of resistance and complicity are only such within specific contexts, and that agency can involve different degrees of knowledge and intentionality.[37]

Religious action, pursued under the rubric of *bhakti,* distanced women—provisionally—from those duties and emotional ties that ordinarily shaped their identities as wives, mothers, sisters, and daughters. Although Sunithi's, Saraswati's, and Minakshi's experiences inverted some norms attached to *cumaṅkali* status, their inversions were temporary and were framed by those occasions when, as they put it, "the goddess came." Rather than refusing their social identities as *cumaṅkalis*, they depended on the prestige and particular cultural meanings attributed to this status, though they use their capabilities as *cumaṅkalis* to reorient things in their favor.

In their experiences *śakti* was not only a volatile "power" to be controlled but a means to capture other kinds of power.[38] However, such realignments of power were not achieved without struggle, nor did they bring about the stabilization of domestic relations or female subjectivity. Sunithi was successful in establishing a saintly reputation insofar as she persuaded her family to believe her claims and to accede to the demands of the goddess issued through her. In this case Sunithi's performance of miracles and her *amma<u>n</u>* persona were the tokens on which her claims to authority were founded.

Until her daughter-in-law left the household, no one in Sunithi's family explicitly stated that her autonomy occasioned arguments; they did suggest, however, that her status and her activities provoked domestic conflict. For example, they noted that when disagreements arose, the *amman*, speaking through Sunithi, resolved the issues at hand. At the same time, such disagreements were carefully concealed from clients. Because Sunithi's interest was in presenting herself as a legitimate *amman*, she emphasized both the inevitability of the path that led her to that point and the credibility of her persona. Though Sunithi and her family attempted to downplay criticisms and contestations of her claims, her daughter-in-law's departure was, in itself, evidence that all was not right.

Similar conflicts were present in the other cases. As Saraswati's attention turned more often to her own self-realization as an *amman*, she felt less and less "attachment" (*pācam*) to and less "desire" (*ācai*) for her husband, a development that angered him. As she put it, their emotional ties and sexual interactions had become less important as the goddess's presence in her life had become more dominant. She said that she had received the goddess's *uttaravu* that she and her family would, in time, reside in a large house, one with a separate *pūja* room in which Saraswati would spend most of her time.

Saraswati's disengagement from her husband may or may not have been the product of preexisting sexual and emotional problems. My aim in recounting her story was not to support a psychosexual explanation for spirit possession. What is of interest in this material is the fact that her relationship with the goddess was a vehicle to create sexual distance. Her emphasis on chastity (*karpu*) was consistent with the Hindu view that celibacy is a form of *tapas* (the forms of penance in which seekers of deitylike powers engage) and that it fosters the concentration of *śakti* in both men and women, and thus enlarges a person's capacity for action. In her situation we see appeals to norms of detachment to counter the equally powerful norms of domesticity.

Minakshi was also being initiated to *amman*-hood by Sunithi, though she had not yet had the kinds of visitations by the *amman* that Saraswati claimed. However, paralleling Saraswati's domestic situation, Minakshi used Sunithi's disclosures in an ongoing argument with her husband about domestic obligations versus religious aspirations. Her husband argued that these activities drew her attention away from her domestic tasks and therefore were of no spiritual or practical benefit. To support his position he drew upon the shastric norms for feminine conduct, which sanctioned the *cumaṅkali*'s subordination to her husband and to the demands of the household.[39]

As it has been dealt with by South Asianist scholars, the category of *bhakti* both clarifies and confuses the issues of feminine religiosity that are addressed in this essay; it is possible to rethink these understandings on the basis of observations made here. In essence *bhakti* describes the unmediated relation of love between deity and devotee. The poetry and songs that constitute *bhakti*'s "liturgy" celebrate the devotee's all-encompassing love for the deity. Being a *bhakta* implies a claim of experiential knowledge of divinity, which, in some cases, is predicated on the substantive merging of the human self with a divine person.[40] By definition, each *bhakta*'s particular experience of divinity is considered incommensurate with that of any other.

These principles underscore the *bhakta*'s ambivalence toward societal institutions of caste and household, something that my observations support. Some scholarship, however, has focused on more systematic accounts of *bhakti*, suggesting that regardless of its sociocultural or historical context, *bhakti* relies on a limited set of reversals involving caste, gender, and institutional norms, and that such inversions may appeal to debased persons and groups. Ramanujan writes that "in the lives of *bhakti* saints 'the last shall be first': men wish to renounce their masculinity and to become as women; upper-caste males wish to renounce pride, privilege and wealth, seek dishonor and self-abasement, and learn from the untouchable devotee".[41] This voluntary "lowering" of status is accompanied by an implied upgrading of the status of traditionally disenfranchised groups: women and Untouchables, most notably. *Bhakti* (and allied religious phenomena) has been analyzed in psychological terms and interpreted both as symptomatic of psychosexual conflict and as a coping mechanism.[42] Political and deconstructivist readings of *bhakti* treat this same marginality as enabling the *bhakta* to challenge the prevailing social and political order in certain situations.[43]

The interpretation I advance here takes account of the semiotic instability of *bhakti* and recognizes that its social and political implications are diverse, and in some cases contradictory. In certain historical contexts *bhakta*s have taken pains to distance their practices and lifestyles from the domain of formal ritual (e.g., *pūja*) associated with Sanskritic Hinduism.[44] In other contexts, however, *bhakti* is viewed by its practitioners as a complement to the formalized ritual of orthoprax Hinduism. In these instances, exemplified by the Smārta-dominated *bhajan* (devotional song) groups in Madras, *bhakti*'s focus on the devotee's personal relation with the deity was retained, but its radical critique of inequality and privilege was excised.[45] Indeed, it could be argued that, for Smārta *bhajana*s, devotionalism served as an emblem of group identity that masked their social and material privileges by means of its democratizing language.

In domestic contexts, as we have seen, *bhakti*'s effects were diverse. Sunithi's virtuosity depended on her family's labor and financial resources, though as an *ammaṉ* she enjoyed a liminality that offered some of the autonomy that female saints were accorded by virtue of their renunciative status. Neither Sunithi, Minakshi, nor Saraswati entirely relinquished her domestic identity as a *cumaṅkali*. It was *as* a *cumaṅkali* that each woman formulated a special relationship with the goddess, and it was through the household as a collectivity that this relationship was accorded social value.

Though they advocated a release from worldly and sexual attachments, they represented this state of release not as detachment (*virattam*) but as "weightlessness" (*ilēcu*). They used this term, as well as "peace" (*amaiti*) to describe how they felt in Sunithi's presence. Sunithi herself, when in the *amman̲* persona, described her sensation (*uṇarcci*) similarly; it was, she said, as though she could "fly" (*pa*r̲*a*).

Although their comments referred to sensations that were physically perceptible, these expressions entailed implicit metaphors of release from obligations and bonds that shaped *cumaṅkali* personhood. Rather than a permanent removal from the house, however, "release" could involve an inversion of roles in the house. As an *amman̲* Sunithi temporarily relinquished her duties as wife, mother, and mother-in-law while retaining the privileges and authority of her divine persona.

Their desires for release, however, were carefully hedged. Unlike the goddess Karumāriyamman̲, whose power remained unrestrained and unchanneled (due to the absence of a husband), the women described here were not eager to be similarly independent, apart from the liminal interludes of the goddess's coming. Indeed, as we saw, Sunithi set about redressing the goddess's own independent status by displaying with the Varalakṣmī *mukam*, images of the Śiva, Murukan̲, and Gaṇeśa, the goddess's "family." Autonomy, with its connotations of pride and boldness, was similarly troubling. Minakshi, for example, often stated that she did not wish to become arrogant with the emergence of her "powers." In this light the women's deference to the goddess, incorporated as a facet of their persons, delivered autonomy without arrogance. Because overt expressions of authority were restricted to the occasions when the *amman̲* "came to" them, their personae as *bhakta*s did not necessitate independence (lack of husband and family) and thus did not invite inauspiciousness.

The women about whom I have written pursued *bhakti* with varying degrees of success and consistency. The material and social resources of their households enabled these women to develop reputations as religious virtuosi, but it was the *cumaṅkali*'s likeness to the goddess that engaged their imaginations and gave shape to their aspirations. In this same context, however, each endeavored to use her status as religious adept to undo the moral webbing of *cumaṅkali* identity. Their audiences were their relatives, friends, and neighbors. The "texts" they offered for scrutiny—to be emulated, ignored, or rejected—were not hagiographies but the oral histories of their encounters with divinity as told by themselves and others.

Sunithi, Saraswati, and Minakshi offered to other women and men models for the diverse ways that marriage may be experienced by Tamil Smartas. They show that, besides the boundaries established at the edges—by divorce, death, or single status—there are more subtle and more fluid boundaries within marriage that take shape around religiosity and ritual autonomy. These images of femininity and their ritual realizations are available and intelligible to middle-class Brahman women. They offer modes of self-expression and small spaces of autonomy from which they might resist the authority of fathers, husbands, and other affines, and the demands of children. At the same time, however, these same practices may hold them in suspension within the diffused, and sometimes concealed, patriarchies of caste and class.

NOTES

I wish to thank the editors of this volume and my fellow contributors for their criticisms and suggestions. Draft versions of this essay were delivered at a panel discussion entitled "The Dynamics of Competing Religious Ideologies," held at the annual meeting of the American Anthropological Association in November 1988, and at the Social Anthropology Seminar at the University of Pennsylvania. I am grateful to Arjun Appadurai for his careful and constructive reading of both versions and to Lila Abu-Lughod for her extensive comments on the second version of the present essay. I benefited as well from the questions and comments provided by panel and seminar participants.

Field research conducted in 1987–88, upon which this essay is based, was supported by the American Institute for Indian Studies through a Junior Fellowship. A two-month visit to Madras in 1985 was funded by the department of anthropology of the University of Pennsylvania.

1. See Lila Abu-Lughod, "The Romance of Resistance: Tracing Transformations of Power through Bedouin Women," *American Ethnologist* 17, no. 1 (1990): 41–55.

2. For background information on *bhakti*, see C. J. Fuller, *The Camphor Flame* (Princeton, N.J.: Princeton University Press, 1992), pp. 155–81; John S. Hawley, "Morality Beyond Morality in the Lives of Three Hindu Saints," in *Saints and Virtues*, ed. John S. Hawley, (Berkeley: University of California Press, 1987), pp. 52–72; John S. Hawley and Donna M. Wulff, eds., *The Divine Consort* (Berkeley: Berkeley Religious Studies Series, 1982); A. K. Ramanujan, *Speaking of Śiva* (Harmondsworth, Eng.: Penguin, 1973); Karine Schomer and W. H. McLeod, eds., *The Sants: Studies in a Devotional Tradition of India* (Delhi: Motilal Banarsidass, 1987); Krishna Sharma, *Bhakti and the Bhakti Movement: A New Perspective* (New Delhi: Munshiram Manoharlal, 1987); and Milton Singer, *When a Great Tradition Modernizes* (Chicago: University of Chicago Press, Midway Reprint, 1972).

3. See Lawrence A. Babb, *The Divine Hierarchy* (New York: Columbia University Press, 1975); Lawrence A. Babb, *Redemptive Encounters: Three Modern Styles in the Hindu Tradition* (Berkeley: University of California Press, 1987); Sandria Freitag, ed., *Culture and Power in Banaras: Community, Performance and Environment, 1800–1980* (Berkeley: University of California Press, 1989); T. N.

Madan, *Non-Renunciation: Themes and Interpretations of Hindu Culture* (Delhi: Oxford University Press, 1987); Singer, *When a Great Tradition Modernizes,* pp. 148–98.

4. Women were expected to be responsive to the demands of other family members—for food, emotional attention, and assistance and support in a variety of other areas. These demands and the privileges to which they were entitled changed during a woman's life cycle. Women with adult children often had more latitude for self-directed action than did women with young children. Women with coresident daughters-in-law had structural subordinates and a broader-based domestic authority than did women without daughters-in-law. See Patricia Caplan, *Class and Gender in India* (London: Tavistock, 1985); Hanna Papanek, "Family Status Production: The 'Work' and 'Non-Work' of Women," *Signs* 4, no. 4 (1979): 775–81; Ursula Sharma, *Women's Work, Class and the Urban Household* (London: Tavistock, 1986); Sylvia Vatuk, *Kinship and Urbanization: White-Collar Migrants in North India* (Berkeley: University of California Press, 1972).

5. Madan, *Non-Renunciation,* pp. 37–39.

6. Madan, *Non-Renunciation,* pp. 44–45.

7. A. K. Ramanujan, "On Woman Saints," in Hawley and Wulff, eds., *The Divine Consort,* pp. 316–24.

8. The complexity of spirit possession, in terms of both subjectivity and sociopolitical location, has been addressed frequently in anthropological literature. In framing this essay I have relied especially on the following analyses: Janice Boddy, *Wombs and Alien Spirits: Women, Men and the Zar Cult in Northern Sudan* (Madison: University of Wisconsin Press, 1989); Erika Bourguignon, *Possession* (San Francisco: Chandler and Sharp, 1976); Ione M. Lewis, *Ecstatic Religion: An Anthropological Study of Spirit Possession and Shamanism* (Harmondsworth, Eng.: Penguin, 1971); Ione M. Lewis, *Religion in Context: Cults and Charisma* (Cambridge: Cambridge University Press, 1986).

9. While the category of *cumaṅkali* is recognized across caste and class strata among Hindus, it does have a particular ritual construction and aesthetic marking among Smārta Brahmans.

10. Karumariyamman is a form of the Tamil deity Māriyammaṉ, a goddess known in scholarly literature as a "village goddess." Such goddesses are represented as independent, that is, without male consort, and thus as having unfulfilled sexual desires. They are described as the special guardians of villages, though the faces that they show to their human devotees can be fierce as well as protective. They tend to be associated with measles, smallpox, and other fever diseases, but they are also thought to grant fertility and prosperity. See Richard Brubaker, "The Ambivalent Mistress: A Study of South Indian Village Goddesses and Their Religious Meaning," Ph.D. Diss., University of Chicago, 1978; Hawley and Wulff, eds., *The Divine Consort;* David Kinsley, *Hindu Goddesses: Visions of the Divine Feminine in the Hindu Religious Tradition* (Berkeley: University of California Press, 1986); and Margaret Trawick Egnor, "The Changed Mother, or What the Smallpox Goddess Did When There Was No More Smallpox," *Contributions to Asian Studies* 18 (1982): 24–45.

11. S. Muthiah, ed., *A Social and Economic Atlas of India* (Delhi: Oxford University Press, 1987).

12. See Caplan, *Class and Gender in India*, pp. 21–35; Misra, *The Indian Middle Classes;* Lloyd Rudolph and Susanne Rudolph, *The Modernity of Tradition* (Chicago: University of Chicago Press, 1967); David Washbrook, "Caste, Class and Dominance in Modern Tamil Nadu," in *Dominance and State Power in Modern India*, ed. Francine Frankel and M.S.A. Rao (Delhi: Oxford University Press, 1989), pp. 204–64.

13. Achin Vanaik, "The Rajiv Congress in Search of Stability," *New Left Review* 154 (1985): 62.

14. This woman was still practicing as a medium in a neighborhood near Sunithi's home at the time of my fieldwork. I visited her on several occasions and viewed her performances.

15. *Pūja* refers to the paradigmatic form of Hindu worship, consisting of praise (*stōttiram*), offerings of food (*naivēṭṭiyam*), and the redistribution of the transvalued remains (*prasādam*) of the offering. See Arjun Appadurai and Carol Breckenridge, "The South Indian Temple: Honor, Authority and Redistribution," *Contributions to Indian Sociology* n.s., 10 (1976): 187–211.

16. Varalakṣmī is the form of the goddess Lakṣmī who grants "boons" (*varam*), hence the prefix "vara-".

17. *Nōṉpus* are a category of rituals undertaken by Tamil women to ensure their husbands' longevity and, by implication, to ensure that they themselves die as *cumaṅkalis* rather than as widows. *Nōṉpus* entail fasting and other forms of self-denial and are performed on cyclic bases. (See Holly Baker Reynolds, "The Auspicious Married Woman," in *The Powers of Tamil Women*, ed. Susan Wadley (Syracuse, N.Y.: Maxwell School of Citizenship and Public Affairs, 1982), pp. 35–60.) Varalakṣmī *nōṉpu* is performed primarily by Smārta women.

18. Matted hair (*jaṭa*) is a dramatic visual marker of the ascetic in South Asia. The goddess Pārvatī (Śiva's consort) is so pictured when she is represented in an earthly manifestation, separated from Śiva and performing *tapas* penance in anticipation of their reunion. For a detailed analysis of this subject, see Gananath Obeyesekere, *Medusa's Hair: An Essay on Personal Symbols and Religious Experience* (Chicago: University of Chicago Press, 1981)

19. It is worth noting here that neither Sunithi nor her devotees spoke of her possession using terms such as *āvēcam*, that referred to the more typical manifestations of that state. I was told by one of her clients that Sunithi's experiences could not be described as a general state of being but as a specific, temporary transformation. Thus, it was to the event to which they referred in observing that "the *ammaṉ* has come" (*ammaṉ vantatu*).

20. See Babb, *The Divine Hierarchy;* Peter Claus, "The Siri Myth and Ritual," *Ethnology* 14 (1975): 47–58; Margaret Trawick Egnor, "On the Meaning of *Śakti* to Women in Tamil Nadu," in Wadley, ed., *The Powers of Tamil Women*, 1–34.

21. See Babb, *Redemptive Encounters*, pp. 214–17, and Diana Eck, *Darśan: Seeing the Divine Image in India*, 2nd ed. (Chambersburg, Pa.: Anima Press, 1985).

22. Those of her critics whom I knew fell into two camps. Some simply indicated that they did not believe in the possibility of possession; others conceded that spirit possession was possible but that Sunithi was a fraud. All viewed Sunithi as a charlatan who was simply seeking attention and wealth.

23. I have no quantitative data on this, though I was acquainted with members and/or leaders of five such groups in and around the Mylapore section of Madras City. Lee Weissman (personal communication) suggested that many of these groups were parts of a wider organizational nexus, the informal leaders of which were several elderly men. I was aware, as well, that some of these groups were connected, through ties of patronage, to the Kancipuram *maṭam* (monastery) and thus to the reigning Śaṅkarācarya (Jayendra Saraswati) who is seated there. Other groups were more critical of the Brahman hierarchy. An important, highly organized example of the latter were the devotees of the goddess Ātiparacakti. The group was led by a non-Brahman male oracle, and its core constituency was non-Brahman (though Brahmans participated). Its idioms and iconography derived from Dravidian cultural nationalism—the populist, anti-Brahman movement that originated early in the twentieth century to promote regional autonomy in cultural and political spheres. See Lee Weissman, "Who Is Pankaru?," paper presented at the Conference on Religion in South India, Research Triangle Park, N.C., June 14, 1988.)

24. Ramanujan, "On Woman Saints"; see also Kumkum Sangari, "Mirabai and the Spiritual Economy of *Bhakti*," *Economic and Political Weekly* 25 (1990): 1464–75, 1537–52.

25. William Cenkner, *A Tradition of Teachers: Śaṅkara and the Jagadgurus Today* (Delhi: Motilal Banarsidas, 1983), pp. 109–34.

26. M.S.S. Pandian, "From Exclusion to Inclusion: Brahminism's New Face in Tamilnadu," *Economic and Political Weekly* 25 (1990): 1938–39.

27. Sunithi was vague about the reasons for their estrangement, though the medium indicated that their interactions had ceased when Sunithi turned her away when she sought help for her daughter, who was ill.

28. This distinction is consistent with Ramanujan's differentiation of the categories of *akam* and *puṟam*, as they inform Tamil poetics. *Akam* refers to a relational interior (home, self, mind/heart), while *puṟam* describes a relational exterior. See A. K. Ramanujan, "Afterword," in *Poems of Love and War: From the Eight Anthologies and the Ten Long Poems of Classical Tamil*, ed. and trans. A. K. Ramanujan (Delhi: Oxford University Press, 1985), pp. 229–300.

29. Ramanujan, "On Woman Saints".

30. Madan, *Non-Renunciation*.

31. Georg Bühler, trans. *The Laws of Manu*, Sacred Books of the East, vol. 25 (Delhi: Motilal Banarsidass, 1964).

32. See Mary Hancock, "Saintly Careers among South India's Urban Middle Classes," *Man*, n.s., 25 (1990): 505–20.

33. Barrenness also compromises the *cumaṅkali*'s status, for lack of fertility renders her auspiciousness questionable. See Reynolds, "The Auspicious Married Woman."

34. See Margaret Trawick Egnor, "On the Meaning of *Śakti* to Women in Tamil Nadu," in Wadley, ed., *The Powers of Tamil Women*, pp. 1–34; Fuller, *The Camphor Flame*, pp. 41–48, 199–203; Hancock, "Saintly Careers"; and Susan Wadley, *Shakti: Power in the Conceptual Structure of Karimpur Religion* (Chicago: University of Chicago Department of Anthropology, 1975).

35. See Caplan, *Class and Gender in India*, pp. 186–215; Uma Chakravarti, "Pati-Vratā," *Seminar* 318 (1986): 17–21.

36. My conception of power as having multiple centers and variable effects is derived from Michel Foucault's now classic formulation, articulated most concisely in *The History of Sexuality: An Introduction,* vol 1 (New York: Random House 1978), pp. 92–102.

37. See Judith Butler and Joan Scott, eds., *Feminists Theorize the Political* (New York: Routledge, 1992); Douglas Haynes and Gyan Prakash, eds., *Contesting Power: Resistance and Everyday Social Relations in South Asia* (Berkeley: University of California Press, 1992); and Linda Nicholson, ed., *Feminism/Postmodernism* (New York: Routledge, 1991).

38. On the distinction between power as "puissance" and "pouvoir," see Peter van der Veer, "The Power of Detachment: Disciplines of Body and Mind in the Ramanandi Order," *American Ethnologist* 16, no. 3 (1989): 458–470.

39. The *Laws of Manu* states that a woman "must not seek to separate herself from her father, husband, or sons; by leaving them she would make both [her own and her husband's] families contemptible. She must always be cheerful, clever in [the management of her] household affairs, careful in cleaning her utensils, and economical in expenditure" (V, 149, 150). It also insists that "no sacrifice, no vow, no fast must be performed by women apart [from their husbands]; if a wife obeys her husband, she will for that [reason alone] be exalted in heaven" (V, 155). See *The Laws of Manu,* vol. 25.

40. See Louis Dumont, *Homo Hierarchicus* (Chicago: University of Chicago Press, 1970); A. K. Ramanujan, *Speaking of Śiva* (1973).

41. "On Woman Saints", p. 316.

42. See Vincent Crapanzano and Jane Garrison, eds., *Case Studies in Spirit Possession* (New York: John Wiley, 1977).

43. See Clive Kessler, "Conflict and Sovereignty in Kelatenese Malay Spirit Seances," in Crapanzano and Garrison, eds., *Case Studies,* pp. 295–331; David Lorenzen, "The Kabir-Panth and Social Protest," in Schomer and McLeod, eds., *The Sants,* pp. 281–303; and Sangari, "Mirabai and the Spiritual Economy of *Bhakti*".

44. Dumont, *Homo Hierarchicus;* Hawley, "Introduction: Saints and Virtues," in Hawley, ed., *Saints and Virtues,* pp. xi–xxiv.

45. Singer, *When a Great Tradition Modernizes,* pp. 199–244.

4

No Longer a Wife: Widows in Rural North India

SUSAN S. WADLEY

[The husband] is the main pillar of life. When he dies, then there is nothing for women. Other supports are like the small branches of a tree. These always break at will. But when the main pillar of life falls, then it is most sad.

This comment from Saroj, a Brahman widow in her fifties from the village of Karimpur in north India, captures the views of north Indian Hindu widows: to lose one's husband is to lose one's main support. Yet the branches that Saroj belittles—a woman's other kin, both natal and affinal—must exist for support and be strengthened if the new widow is to prosper. Using case studies from Karimpur, this essay explores why widows find this loss so difficult and hence why marriage is of such major concern to Hindu women. While feminists may decry the *pardā* system and the economic dependence of north Indian women, the lives of widows only reinforce the desirability of marriage for Hindu women themselves.

Widows present both ideological and economic challenges to the Hindu system. Ideologically their femaleness and their sexuality is to be controlled by fathers, husbands, or sons. Economically they are to be supported by male kin, through whom they gain access to resources. Whether the control of women is rooted in ideology or economics, it rests in male hands. Ideally, if a woman is widowed at all, she is widowed in old age, with a son to control and support her. But in fact that ideal is more often challenged by early death, presenting Hindu families with the ultimate paradox: how to provide symbolic control of and economic support to an often young, childless widow.

Understanding how Hindu families approach this paradox requires that we focus on wider kin relationships often obscured by our concern for the institution of marriage per se and the symbolic transfer of a woman from her natal to her affinal family. Further, we must consider the heterogeneity of female roles and statuses within India. There is no homogeneous, essential "Hindu woman"[1] but rather a multiplicity of Hindu women in different socioeconomic classes, life stages, and personal situations. Moreover, each individual woman is herself a multiple person: a daughter, wife or widow, daughter-in-law, sister-in-law, mother, etcetera. These various personae, often demanding contradictory behaviors, become foregrounded in different life contexts, necessitating behaviors and decisions that may be difficult or unwelcome to some other role held by that same woman. The most markedly different personae are those with a patrifocal orientation toward affinal relationships (wife, daughter-in-law) and those with a filiafocal orientation toward consanguineal relationships (sister, daughter).[2] Further, the concerns of a woman's affinal and natal families often come into conflict in decisions about a widow's future. Just as the two families negotiated a marriage, they must now negotiate the forced break in that marriage and agree on the new widow's future. Thus in examining widowhood I highlight not only the importance of marriage but also the immense value placed on relationships with male kin other than the husband.

Privileged Males and Nonprivileged Females

In north India, gender stratification places severe constraints upon the activities and roles of women. It results in male control of females at all ages, the exclusion of women from public venues and places through *pardā* restrictions, and the prohibition of women from participating in income-generating activities, aside from those in which they participate with their husbands or male kin.[3] It is not remarkable, then, that the widow has been considered the "most sinful of all sinful creatures," her widowhood thought to be a result of accumulated *karma,* and her life made miserable by both natal family and affines.

Within this wider picture of female dependence upon males, in a society where alternatives to such dependence are rare, widows have the theoretical potential for becoming female household heads, earning their own livelihoods, and being "independent" women. Further, the life cycle of the Indian female suggests increasing power, authority, and autonomy as a woman ages,[4] creating the possibility of a powerful older female household head. But males' privileged access to productive resources and employment stifles, except in rare cases, this potential for widows.

Moreover, this system of gender stratification interacts with a system of hierarchical relations among men, so that men of high status are able to control the men, and hence the women, of low status. These two systems of gender stratification and social stratification have both a material base by which upper-class men control economic resources, especially land, and an ideological base defining acceptable gender relations and behavior as well as proper caste relations and behavior, respectively.

The critical arena for women's subordination is the family.[5] This subordination is clearly articulated in Hindu law, which has long recognized the threat of the female in a system of ideology giving women great power yet demanding their control by men.[6] Several sections of *The Laws of Manu* are devoted to defining proper behavior for women. A woman must never be autonomous. Rather, the ideal woman, whether young or old, married or widowed, is to be controlled by men. The widow receives special attention:

> A virtuous wife who after the death of her husband constantly remains chaste, reaches heaven, though she have no son, just like those chaste men. But a woman who from a desire to have offspring violates her duty toward her (deceased) husband, brings on herself disgrace in this world, and loses her place with her husband (in heaven).[7]

Hence the ideal widow is chaste and virtuous, and the results of unacceptable behavior are daunting.

There is another model for widows, with variants, less publicized and well known. Found in a variety of law books, it allows remarriage with the husband's (younger) brother. One version, known as a *niyoga,* is found in Manu, among others.[8] *Niyoga* allows a widow to have sexual relations with a husband's brother in order to have sons. It is noteworthy that the law books were especially concerned about the woman who desired offspring, because in a male-dominated society the desire for male offspring is particularly strong; sons are seen as a channel through which women can attain power, authority, and autonomy and, as we shall see, sons do in fact alter the strategies available to widows. Moreover, these codes of conduct (and rules for reproduction) for women are written in law books composed and read by high-caste men who seek control of women.[9]

Yet while the male-authored scriptures and law books of the Brahman elite have gained a hegemonic role in Indian and Western understandings of Indian society, in fact the vast majority of castes allow widow remarriage, as defined by a permanent relationship with a man other than the first husband. The divide in the law, and in actual practice, between those who marry again and those who do not is clear. A caste group in a local area either does or does not allow widow remarriage.[10]

Hindu legal codes not only have mandated male control of women but have denied women access to resources. Even today in rural India, land is the most valuable resource. Until the 1920s, women in north India had few rights of inheritance, and land was a resource held by men and passed from father to son. Legal changes in the 1920s, 1930s, and 1950s gave daughters and widows legal rights of inheritance, in the absence of male heirs.[11] Yet since women can inherit only in the absence of male heirs, and their chances even then of actually gaining control of land are questionable, having sons is the best security.

Thus Hindu law and high-caste ideology have mandated the control of women's sexuality and denied women access to economic resources. These norms are embedded in a hierarchy of caste and class; looking at widows demonstrates the key role of caste and class concerns, as my work in Karimpur shows. Among the upper strata of Hindu society, the ultimate threat to the privileged role of males is the woman who moves into male realms, an action most probable for women who are widows.[12]

The Intersection of Gender and Class in Karimpur

Karimpur is a village located 150 miles southeast of New Delhi. In 1984 it was an agricultural community of 327 families (2,048 individuals) divided among twenty-three castes. Although Brahmans owned nearly 60 percent of the land in 1984, a second large caste of Farmers (*Kachi*)[13] owned another 17 percent. The Brahmans have one of the highest educational levels in the village and have maintained political control for several centuries.

Although some families of Karimpur are wealthy, the village is not well off. Many families in the village live on the equivalent of less than fifty cents per day. Indebtedness affects all but a few large landowners, and increasing dowry demands affect all sections of the community. Karimpur is, however, better off than in previous years: bicycles, brick houses, and synthetic saris are seen in many parts of the village. Better crops and increased irrigation have been important to its general rise in prosperity.

Brahman political and economic superiority is reflected in social superiority: village standards for proper behavior are set by the Brahman community. Social standards for women include a rigorous seclusion of young wives, a ban on women's participation in field work, and a dislike of having one's teenage daughters traveling to high school in the nearby town. Upper-caste women maintain strict *pardā;* they remain inside their family compounds while young and stay carefully veiled before a husband's older male relatives. Gradually some restrictions are eased, so that a woman in her midthirties can leave the courtyard to fetch water, make cow-dung cakes, or process grain on a veranda. Female household work is thus defined by age, with the mother-in-law having to do outside jobs, while her young daughters-in-law cook, grind, and work inside the courtyard. All these restrictions are lessened as economic status decreases. The young poor Washerwoman, for example, will have to move about the village to collect clothes from her patrons.

Working in agriculture is a male activity. While women of some groups help their male kin plant certain crops (e.g., garlic), weed, harvest, or irrigate, women do not plow or prepare fields or work, with rare exceptions, for cash wages (when women earn, they earn less than men). Some income-producing activities, defined by caste and the *jajmānī* system of hereditary patron–client relationships, are solely or mainly female: sweeping houses and cleaning "latrines" (*Bhaṅgī*), serving as midwives (*Dhānuk, Bhaṅgī*), preparing flowers for rituals (*Mālī*), carrying water and cleaning utensils (*Kahār*), washing clothes (*Dhobī*). But income and opportunity for these jobs are sporadic, and no family can afford to rely on them for its livelihood. Women also can earn by making and selling cow-dung cakes (five cents per one hundred cakes), raising cattle and selling milk (which may involve obtaining grass daily for fodder), or, less rarely, raising chickens. Only one woman (a Brahman) in Karimpur has a regular income: in her fifties, she has been a schoolteacher for over thirty years.

The poor and landless have increasingly moved out of agricultural pursuits. Since the 1970s there has been an expansion in the incidence of nontraditional and extravillage sources of income, especially for the poor. These men drive rickshas, carry bags of grain for mills, load brick kilns, unload trucks, work in construction, or do any other of the many labor-intensive jobs that one finds in India. As men have moved out of agriculture, women's work opportunities, given the ban on female participation in agriculture unless accompanied by male kin, have declined. Moreover, the decline of the traditional *jajmānī* system has further eliminated female employment opportunities. These changes in access to employment limit the possibilities for maintaining a livelihood for widows.

The subordination of women within the family is best seen by examining the life cycle, for the roles of women within the family in north India change as women age. In addition, a fundamental distinction must be made between richer, higher-status families, which tend to remain joint and have land, and poor, lower-status landless families, which tend to be nuclear. Class itself is fundamentally gendered, and the maintenance of social classes is built upon distinctive household roles for lower-caste/class and upper-caste/class women and men,[14] and it is the patterns of the upper-caste/class that are closest to those in Manu and other texts, and that are often emulated by the poor.

The native terminology for female life cycles in north India corresponds to the categories derived from Manu: *bacpan* (childhood; also *mā kā rāj* [mother's kingdom]), *sās kā rāj* (the mother-in-law's kingdom), and *bahū kā rāj* (the kingdom of the daughter-in-law).[15]

In childhood the girl, whose birth is rarely celebrated and whose survival chances are not equal to those of her brothers, grows under her mother's care. If wealthy or high-caste, she may attend school for five to eight years. The most important ritual for unmarried girls is *bhaiyā dūj*, Brother's Second, a day on which women worship their brothers and seek the protection that brothers are obliged to give throughout their lives. As a girl develops, her family voices continual concern about her marriage and may spend much time and money seeking the best possible husband for her, given the constraints of its ability to pay a dowry (often equivalent to the household's yearly income, an enormous sum for both the poor and the not-so-poor peasant farmer).[16] The period of marriage ceremonies is fraught with tension, as the groom's family may not accept the proffered dowry or may make other unexpected demands.

Fortunately for most girls, the transition to the groom's house is slow: five or six days at the time of the wedding (*śadī*), then a month or so when the marriage is consummated (*gaunā*), often two or three years later, and finally "the time of crying" (*ronā*), the more permanent move to the groom's house some weeks or months after the consummation.[17] As her parents are unable to accept hospitality in her affinal village, her brothers become her main links to her natal community.[18] Women's folk songs speak of the father who forced a girl out of her home and of the brother who comes yearly to take her to visit to her parents.

The toe rings put on a woman during the marriage ceremony symbolize her dual foci on natal and affinal homes, highlighting her dual status as sister and wife. Karimpur women wear two sets of toe rings on each foot, "one for the husband and one for the brother." When either a husband or a brother dies, one set is removed. Some Brahman women wear neither set if they are widowed, but poor women remove the second pair only when husband *and* brother are dead (and often not even then). If the husband's protection, symbolically and economically, is lost, then a brother's protection should replace it.[19]

Fathers seeking husbands for their daughters want a family which will not abuse the girl, in which the potential for employment and economic security is good, and in which educational and medical facilities are not too remote. Affines desire a hardworking, childbearing, "productive" daughter-in-law. Barrenness, a husband incapable of feeding his family, and widowhood are the primary threats that may send a woman back to her brother's house. Although a woman has the moral right to demand that her natal family care for her, her family's goal is to prevent her from exercising it. Folktales tell of the widowed sister who returns to her brother's house, to be welcomed by him but mistreated by her sister-in-law. It is the "unproductive" widow without a son who highlights the conflict between her two homes, as affines are unwilling to provide for her and brothers see her as an unwelcome burden. Rituals mark these two foci, as women seek their husband's long life and the protection of their brothers in several annual cycle rituals.[20]

Once married to the person of her parents' choice, a woman of a high-status family is raised by her mother-in-law in what is almost always a joint family for at least some years after marriage. The new bride is the lowest-ranking member of the family. In landowning families the woman gradually gains seniority over yet younger wives and, critically, as she gives birth to sons, her status increases. A woman with no sons is taunted, and threats, often acted on, of a second marriage for her husband are common.

The rural landowner's wife reaches her maximum potential as a matriarch of a joint household (she gains control of the house and its environs, not of family estates or public activities), where she can exercise authority over sons, daughters-in-law, and grandchildren. By now her own mother-in-law is dead or feeble, and she has separated from her husband's brothers' families.[21] It is as senior female of a joint family that the Hindu woman attains her greatest power, authority, and autonomy. Daily household decisions are hers: what minor purchases to make, what and how much to cook, whether to send a child to the doctor, and so forth. Moreover, she is rightfully invested with the authority to make these decisions. I have seen older women asked how to cook such and such a dish, not because the younger women did not know but because the olders' authority to know and to tell must be acknowledged. Younger women sometimes wield power in joint families but are also criticized for doing so.

If belonging to a landed or farming family, lower-caste women may join their husbands in planting or weeding fields. In all cases this work is done in conjunction with male household members. *Khetī kā kām* (field work) is considered degrading, and women in the wealthier or Brahman families will not do it. Yet even high-caste richer women are significant contributors to household activities involving the production of agricultural goods, especially postharvest processing such as winnowing and threshing lentils or fennel. These are labeled *ghar kā kām*, (household work), however, and take place on verandas or hidden by the walls of their courtyards.

Older women, preferably past menopause, of all social groups have autonomy. The older woman need not ask others for permission to visit neighbors, to go to town, or to stay with relatives. With age comes a lessening of *pardā* restrictions. Most upper-caste village women retain the outer symbols such as a sari pulled over the head and a shawl when outside the house—but their faces are mostly uncovered and their mobility less restricted. This status and authority come with motherhood—having sons and daughters-in-law to dominate. Being a wife does not give status: the older barren wife may well share in decision making with her husband, but she has no one over whom she has authority. The woman, then, from ages forty to sixty, after which old age begins to take its toll and daughters-in-law gain power, is often a significant authority figure in her household.

The north Indian widow is no longer barred from auspicious religious ceremonies. Head shaving has rarely existed in the north. But the widow should wear white, break her glass bangles that symbolize auspicious marital status, and remove her toe rings, given in the marriage ceremony itself.[22] She should lead a simple life, one of chaste asceticism and religious devotion. But this ideal is seldom achieved, as women struggle to feed their families, find money for children's schooling, repair a house, or negotiate children's marriages with the aid of more distant male kin. Further, this is the time of the *bahū kā rāj* (the rule of the daughter-in-law), as the widow is unable to retain the power that she had while her husband lived.[23]

Several features of this familial picture need elaborating. First, it is critical that there are no options: rural women are expected to marry,.to bear children, to aid in household production, and to become mothers-in-law. Given the lack of alternatives, women benefit by adhering to the norms defined by the male-dominated system. If wealthy, they will eventually attain the rewards of the authority and autonomy of the mother-in-law. Second, the powers and autonomy of the north Indian wife are less than those of women elsewhere in India.[24] The north Indian wife rarely retains control of her dowry: she does control household decisions, but these are often trite, with husbands making the major purchases. A women can only hope to influence decisions about educating children,[25] marriages, fields, and so forth.

Third, the situation of poor women in north India is fundamentally different from that of wealthier women. The poorer woman has little hope of ever attaining the power that comes with ruling a joint household. She is married earlier and has little or no education. Often separated from her in-laws by the time of her first child, she will have a daughter-in-law for an equally short period of time.[26] Though family ties remain very close in separated families, the constant struggle for survival forces each family unit to be self-sufficient, especially if no land or agricultural implements are shared. Without a mother-in-law a woman quickly achieves power over her own family (children), authority, and autonomy. But domestic power is of a different order of meaning when defined not by "How much must I cook?" but by "Do I have enough food to cook today?," not by "Shall I take my baby to the doctor?" but by "We have no money. He/she will have to stay sick." Poor women of any age may have domestic power, but they lack the access to resources to utilize this power. Suffering from their low rank in both gender and class systems of stratification, poor women are doubly burdened.

Poor women are unable to keep strict *pardā*, lacking the means to enclose a courtyard and by necessity having to move in public space.[27] The poor woman may be involved with her husband in *jajmānī* duties or agriculture. The widows wear whatever clothes they can get, while never removing their bangles and toe rings. This denial of the outward attributes of widowhood reflects their vulnerability as poor women without male support: if no "widow" signs are given, they have a greater chance of avoiding abuse. Those forced to be economically independent must leave *pardā*, and the protection of male kin, to work as laborers with strangers.

Karimpur Widows: Caste, Sons, Land, and Survival

Let me now examine the life situations of widows in Karimpur.[28] Given the diverse roles of women, we must seek to understand which become dominant when the role of wife is lost. Some widows are seen as primarily daughters or sisters; others as mothers or sisters-in-law. Caste, age, economic class, and sons are key components in the decision about the widow's future role, as is the personality of the individual woman. Male kin play critical roles: as affines or parents they decide on new marriage partners; as sons they determine the likelihood of remarriage; and as close relatives, they can help the widow survive by acting for her in public places. Often the desires of natal and affinal kin are in conflict and must be negotiated. The upper-class widow who is able to retain the power, authority, and autonomy that she may have gained as the senior female in a joint household is rare. Instead, widowhood marks the transference of that power to a new generation. The poor, often younger, widow becomes the female head of a subnuclear household where resources are minimal and survival dependent upon her ability to feed herself. Independence is not valued, and women state a clear preference to be a subordinate wife in a joint household.

Let us look first at a Brahman widow. Jiya, as she is called by her family, is the widow of Prakash, a wealthy Brahman landowner. Prakash died in 1976, when Jiya was sixty-six years old. Jiya and Prakash were then living with the youngest son, as is the norm for most lineal joint families. Although his four sons lived in separate households within a large compound, until his death Prakash retained control of most of the family lands. Upon a man's death, his lands are split evenly among his sons, and household authority is transferred to the sons as heads of household.

At the time that Prakash died, Jiya was a major voice in her sons' families and participated in major decisions affecting all four families. But with his death her authority slowly diminished. Moreover, as old age and cataracts began to weaken her, her primary role in the family became child care: watching infants and providing a focal point where the young girls of the family and neighborhood cluster to chat and gossip. Jiya's brothers are both dead, and while she sometimes receives visits from her brothers' sons, contacts with her natal home are rare. She does, however, spend some time with her younger daughter, deserted by her husband and making her way in a nearby town. While Jiya is fed and cared for by two of her sons' families, her presence creates tension because she is an economic burden. Thus no one is willing to provide funds for a cataract operation. One grandson, now head of her eldest son's household, claims that women should have land in their own names so that they don't end up begging from their sons as Jiya does. But while people may grumble about food and clothing, Jiya is only rarely the target of harsh words. Her best friend, an equally aged Bard (*Rāy*) widow, is supposedly mistreated by her son's wife. Both these widows represent new stress in Indian families as the aged population increases.

Yet Jiya remains a key actor in all four sons' families. Her advice is sought in all major decisions. She remains the ritual head for all four families and has played the role of senior woman in any birth or marriage ceremonies they have had. Until 1984 she did all ritual visiting for the family, marking their unity, despite the separate enclosures, for the rest of the village. When a great-grandson was born the family celebrated his birth with a songfest and ceremony in which Jiya was presented with a tiny golden ladder "to take her to heaven," for, they say, if you live to have a great-grandson, entrance to heaven is assured and you can die a happy death. Reaching down and putting the tiny ladder under her foot, Jiya then raised her fist high, a large grin on her face. Once Jiya told me that her community could sing at her death, not ban singing for a month as is required when there is a death in the village, for her death would be joyous.

Brahman women widowed with younger sons are more likely to retain their authority for some time. One Brahman woman, Saroj,[29] took advantage of her widowhood to move into male spheres of activity normally closed to women in Karimpur. Moreover, she relied heavily on her filialocal relations for support and aid. There is no doubt, too, that Saroj's temperament contributed to her lifestyle. Her intelligence and wit, combined with a fierce determination to do her best for her family, led her to village and district politics, as well as making her clearly the head of her household.

Saroj's husband, Ram, was a Brahman landlord of Karimpur. He died very suddenly about age fifty-two. Saroj was about fifty at the time of her husband's death, but their sons were still young, as no children had survived until Saroj was in her late twenties. At the time of Ram's death, the joint household contained three unmarried daughters, aged seven, thirteen, and sixteen; a son, aged twenty-one, and his wife; and a son around nine years of age. The oldest son had completed tenth class and, like many educated Brahman boys, had resisted working in the fields with his father. His father's death changed that, but the shift was slow. Initially, Saroj took over responsibility for the fields, turning them over to sharecroppers. The land in the younger son's name is still sharecropped. For some years Saroj was the sole leader in their house: she married off two daughters, arranged the marriage of the second son, organized the fields, supervised the sharecroppers, etcetera. Outside of her sons, Saroj had no close male kin in Karimpur who could act on her behalf because the land and house had been inherited by her husband's mother, who had had no brothers. She also had no brothers, but her sisters' families provided material and emotional support when her children were married, marking very strong filialocal ties. Since Saroj had been married at nine and started living with Ram shortly thereafter, her continuing tie to her sisters was remarkable, especially since they had no common natal home to visit. Clearly, natal kin are more important to women than is generally acknowledged.

Eventually the older son, abetted by his wife, separated his small family, which contained a young daughter. The reason for his move was partially financial: his brother and sister both had to be married, presenting a major drain on the family resources. By separating he no longer had any responsibility for these marriages. The move was precipitated by a personality clash: both Saroj and her son's wife are articulate, forceful women. Their feuding continues, but often silently, as the two women refuse to speak to one another for long periods of time.

With the separation of her older son, Saroj lost some of her authority, as only her other son and her youngest daughter remained with her. But widowhood also meant a drastic increase in other kinds of authority. She had fields to supervise. There was a tractor to sell, as it was not a viable investment with the fields being sharecropped. There were potatoes to store in the cold plant, and daughters to be married. Saroj quickly moved into spaces and activities that are almost solely male. Moreover, she added politics to an otherwise busy life, becoming leader of the local women's nonformal education group and later joining the Congress party, as a member of which she campaigned actively for Indira Gandhi, being rewarded with trips to Lucknow and Delhi to meet national leaders, including Mrs. Gandhi herself. By 1984 she was known as "the village Indira," an appellation given her, so some said, because she stuck her nose in other people's business and acted like a man, as they thought Indira Gandhi did. Saroj forcefully claims that her political activities would not have occurred if her husband had lived. Until his death she was a proper Brahman housewife, living a rather secluded life and ruling over her family. And while she relishes her many political activities, she claims that the life of a widow is a sad one and that she would gladly return to being a wife with a living husband.

When Ram was alive, he and his wife shared a considerable amount of household authority. They were married when he was fourteen and she nine, and she began living in his family at age ten. The household consisted of three persons—the very young couple and Ram's mother, herself a widow. Despite owning considerable land, this small female-headed household was extremely impoverished for some years. As Ram matured he slowly began to farm his fields, sharing much of the decision making with his wife. She says that they both worked very hard to gain the prosperity that the family had at his death. Clearly, too, they shared in this work. Moreover, the lack of living children for so many years gave them time to build a base of financial prosperity often denied to those hit earlier by dowries. At Ram's death the household was prosperous and respected.

The initial lack of management after Ram's death (household management is in any case difficult for any woman to achieve), allied with marriages (and their substantial dowry requirements) for two daughters, eroded the family's financial base. To some extent this financial loss has diminished Saroj's power. But she gained power and authority over other villagers through her control of the women's nonformal education group and the Congress party. Without a husband and with mild-mannered sons, Saroj has almost total autonomy. This independence is critical to her continuing movement into spheres of activity normally forbidden to rural women in this part of north India.

In the cases of both Jiya and Saroj, their roles as mothers dominated decisions about their future when widowed. Their caste, age, children, and the prosperity of their families left little to be decided. Yet even Saroj, with her active "public" life, considers a husband to be the "pillar of life" and continually bemoans the fate (*karma*) that left her a widow with children to raise. Despite her successes there is little doubt that the family would be better off if her husband had lived.

Jiya and Saroj, like all Brahman widows, cannot remarry. In Karimpur only Brahmans, Bards, and Accountants (*Kāyastha*) forbid widow remarriage (see table 4.1). These three castes are landowning and relatively well off. Among the remaining castes, four are landowning or better off, while the remainder, averaging less than two acres per household, are poor. Land ownership and economic status are related to the treatment of widows. Those castes not allowing remarriage have the highest percent of widows in the adult female population: 37 percent in 1952 and 16 percent in 1984. Those with land, but allowing remarriage, had 28 percent widows in 1925 and 15 percent in 1984,

Table 4.1 Karimpur Widows by Caste and Economic Status, 1925 and 1984

	1925			*1984*			
Caste	*Total Families*	*Widows*	*Percent Adult Females Widowed*	*Total Families*	*Widows*	*Percent Adult Females Widowed*	*Average Land (Acres/Family)*
Wealthy/No Remarriage							
Brahman (Priest)	41	21	40	62	22	17	9*
Kāyastha (Accountant)	1	1	50	3	0	0	2.5†
Rāy (Bard)	2	0	0	2	1	25	5
Landowner/Remarriage							
Banyā (Shopkeeper)	3	0	0	5	1	14	8‡
Kāchi (Farmer)	26	14	33	59	16	14	2.8
Lodhī (Farmer)	1	0	0	2	1	33	5
Sūnar (Goldsmith)	2	0	0	—	—	—	—
Poor/Remarriage							
Baṛhāī (Carpenter)	8	4	31	11	1	6	1.3
Bhaṅgī (Sweeper)	8	2	20	19	3	10	.18
Bhurjī (Grain Parcher)	1	2	100	4	0	0	1.4
Camār (Leatherworker)	8	3	33	16	0	0	.8
Darzī (Tailor)	5	2	25	4	0	0	.75
Dhānuk (Midwife/Matmakers)	7	2	22	30	6	20	1.4
Dhobī (Washerman)	1	0	0	3	0	0	0
Dhunā (Cottoncarder)	1	1	25	5	0	0	.6
Faqīr (Beggar)	8	1	17	13	3	19	.01
Gaḍariyā (Shepherd)	6	1	17	20	5	16	1.2
Kahār (Watercarrier)	19	9	30	45	8	13	1
Kumhār (Potter)	3	0	0	3	1	50	17
Mālī (Flowergrower)	1	4	50	3	1	17	1.8
Manihār (Bangle Seller)	2	1	33	5	0	0	0
Nāī (Barber)	1	0	0	—	—	—	—

Table 4.1

	1925			1984			
Caste	Total Families	Widows	Percent Adult Females Widowed	Total Families	Widows	Percent Adult Females Widowed	Average Land (Acres/ Family)
Nat (Acrobat)	—	—	—	1	0	0	0
Tawaif (Dancing Girls)	2	0	0	0	—	—	—
Telī (Oilpresser)	4	0	0	11	0	0	.98
Ṭhākur (Farmer)	—	—	—	1	0	0	1
TOTAL	161	68	—	327	69	—	—

Note: Three castes present in 1925 were gone by 1984, while two others had migrated into Karimpur.
*This figure was 17.6 in 1925.
†As accountants, this caste in Karimpur has always been well off, having access to outside employment.
‡This figure was .09 in 1925.

while among the adult female population of the poor, 28 percent were widows in 1925 and 11 percent in 1984. The high percentage of wealthy widows is due to the lack of an option: they cannot remarry. On the other hand, the women of minor landowners, while permitted remarriage, often will not remarry if they have a son and/or land. Those with significant land holdings can afford widows, in that they have the material resources to care for an unproductive woman (especially one not producing children). The widow's claim to material resources more "properly" belonging to the larger family is dealt with either by retaining the widow in the joint family or by illegally stripping her of her land.[30]

High-caste widows like Jiya and Saroj are mostly older and in joint or supplemented nuclear families. Because they are older widows, their affinal ties are stronger than their natal ones; only rarely does an older widow leave her husband's village. (Some poor widows will leave to live with a daughter if they have neither sons nor land.)

Widow's living situations must be understood in the broader context of change in Karimpur family types. The increased longevity of all Karimpur residents has altered the distribution of family types and thus changed the likelihood of a widow's being economically independent. As table 4.2 shows, in the 1920s the dominant family type in Karimpur was supplemented nuclear; in 1984 it was nuclear.[31] The proportions

Table 4.2 Family Types in Karimpur, 1925 and 1984

	Number (Percent) of Families						
Year	*Single Person*	*Nuclear**	*Subnuclear*	*Nuclear*	*Supplemented (Lineal)*	*Joint (Other)*	*Total*
1925	13 (8)	33 (20)	36 (22)	42 (26)	25 (16)	12 (8)	161
1984	7 (2)	26 (8)	143 (43)	58 (18)	91 (29)	2 (.6)	327

*Subnuclear includes supplemented subnuclear families.

of both nuclear and joint families increased between 1925 and 1984 (from 22 percent to 43 percent for nuclear and from 16 percent to 29 percent for joint) as life expectancy rose and families were not continually threatened by the early deaths of adults.[32] In addition, poor families are likely to be nuclear (over 50 percent), while rich families are most likely to be joint (over 38 percent). Over time the family types in which widows are found shift from predominantly subnuclear, other, and single-person households (58.8 percent in 1925)[33] to joint and supplemented nuclear households (67 percent in 1984) (see table 4.3).

Widows like Jiya and Saroj who live in joint or supplemented nuclear households are older than those in subnuclear households (see the stories of Jiji and Caci that follow). Subnuclear households are frequently female-headed, containing a young widow and her small children or an unmarried but adult son and his mother or siblings. (Exactly when these cease to be female-headed is difficult to pinpoint, as Caci's story will illustrate.)[34] The average age of widows in subnuclear houses remained constant over time (44–45 years). However, the average age of widows in supplemented nuclear and joint households increased from fifty years in 1925 to sixty-eight years in 1984. It is these latter family organizations that have absorbed the older widows. Another shift is notable: in 1925 only thirty-six widows lived with a child or children, while twenty-seven lived with collaterals or parents. By 1984 fifty-eight lived with children and only eight with collaterals. Widows in single-person households were old (late fifties) in both time periods and often

Table 4.3 Widows, Average Age, and Family Types in Karimpur, 1925 and 1984 (by number and age)

Year	*Single*	*Subnuclear*	*Supplemented Nuclear*	*Joint*	*Other*
1925	3 (60)	22 (44)	18 (50)	17 (51)	8 (44)
1984	3 (56)	18 (48)	25 (67)	21 (69)	2 (44)

were women who were barren or had no living children and today have no living relatives. In 1984 all three owned or had owned land.

Brahman widows, with one exception, all live in economically secure households. The exception is a childless woman who inherited her husband's land, only to have it slowly stolen by his relatives, who could manipulate land records and courts while she watched helplessly. Now in her seventies, she lives alone in a mud hut; she begs from neighbors and curses her husband's nearby relatives. This woman became impoverished because her natal kin did not protect her land or offer her a home.

Other Brahman widows without sons have been more fortunate. One lived for thirty years with her husband's brothers and their families in the largest joint household in Karimpur. Her twelve acres remain in her name and will be passed to a nephew who now lives with her. Another Brahman woman, widowed in the 1930s, was economically secure only because her relatives guarded her interests and fought a court case for her young daughter. The family not only saved the land for the widow and daughter but educated the girl so that today she is the only educated working woman in the village. Both Brahman and low-caste women are vulnerable if they do not have male kin in their natal households to protect their interests.

Because they cannot remarry, Brahman, Bard, and Accountant widows are most likely to be childless, although no married male under age forty from these groups has died since the early 1960s, so there are no young widows in wealthy families in Karimpur today. In 1984 there were no widowed Brahman daughters living in Karimpur, whereas in 1925 there were three—young, childless, and living with the brothers' families. The increasing life span and economic security enjoyed by Brahman families in the area, for example, have worked to decrease the chances of Brahman families having to bear the burden of a widowed daughter and the relative size of that burden. Moreover, these families are most able and ready to fight the necessary court cases to ensure their daughters' rights to the property of their deceased husbands.[35]

The lower-caste widow with sons and no land is in a particularly serious predicament. If she has a son, she may not remarry, but whether her life will be even moderately free of hunger and dismal living conditions is questionable. About half these women remarry.

The stories of two Watercarrier widows illustrate these issues, as well as highlight the importance of patrilocal and filialocal ties. Jiji, literally "older sister," is considered by many the poorest person in the village, and her story illustrates a woman's difficulties in earning a livelihood for herself and her children. Jiji's own mother was widowed young and remarried after five or six years. Jiji lived mostly at her maternal grandparents' home, where her mother had returned after her husband died.

She was married young—at eleven or twelve—in a simple ceremony in 1962. Her marriage was consummated a year later, and she had her first child within a few years. From her six pregnancies, two children lived.

Within two years of her moving to Karimpur, Jiji was kicked out of her in-laws' house: she says that her husband took her to bathe at the Ganges and her mother-in-law had not given her approval, so a separation took place. Meanwhile, her husband started to gamble, as had his father. Jiji was soon forced to be concerned about feeding her small family. Her husband shared one acre of land with his father and two brothers, but there was little food from this and he took whatever household money there was for gambling. He also beat her regularly. She says, "I did not know the love of my husband. All I knew was that God has given me two hands and I have to work with them to earn a living." When asked how she felt about her husband's death she replied, "Sister, what can I tell you about my sadness. I had problems from the start." She started making cow-dung cakes to earn enough to feed her children, but her husband would search the house and find the hidden money. Somehow they managed until her husband's death in 1982. Six months earlier their one daughter was married. Although they were poor, they borrowed nine hundred rupees to pay for the wedding. Now the daughter lives with her husband in Panjab, where he does field labor.

Her husband's brothers and father also died about 1982, leaving the three young widows alone. One has since married a distant relative from Karimpur and gone to live in the nearby town; the other returned to her parents. Only Jiji remains in the village, with no affines to aid her. A critical move was her reestablishing connections with her brother, whom she had not seen in years: her mother was dead, and this one brother is her only potential source of aid. For a while her son lived with his uncle, but Jiji missed him dreadfully and brought him back to the village, despite problems in feeding and clothing him, as well as not being able to supervise him while she worked.

Unlike most village women, Jiji had earned trifling sums before her husband's death, as she tried to protect (and feed) her family while he gambled. But even though she had been earning, widowhood forced her into new income-generating activities. She could no longer survive by making and selling cow-dung cakes, a woman's activity that is often expanded for income. She has therefore taken up other employment of various sorts. Changes in Karimpur have denied her the traditional work of widows fifty years ago: then most grain was ground on large grinding stones in each house, often requiring hours of female labor per day. With the advent of grinding machines, most richer families no longer grind their own flour, and poor women are denied a source of acceptable employment. For a year Jiji worked in the nearby district town; she earned her food and two to three dollars a month washing utensils or storing garlic. But this work was poorly paid, and she didn't have her son, so she returned to Karimpur after a year. Now she raises two goats, given by her brother, does field labor during the harvest and planting seasons, and works cleaning pots and carrying water for Brahman families at ritual occasions. For this she earns enough for a kilo or two of wheat. Altogether she works three to four months a year on a regular basis. Seldom does she earn more than what is needed to eat that day, so she must stretch her money. Her clothes are torn and filthy. Her few cooking pots are worn. Her house has only one cot and a torn quilt for the winter.

Jiji is known throughout the village as being honorable, as hardworking, and as doing her best. People respect her efforts to help herself and her son. But she leads a hard life. Even though she comes from a caste where the women traditionally work in others' homes and where *pardā* restrictions are minimal, she is working harder than almost any woman in the village and at jobs not normally held by women. Her labor comes cheaper than men's, and with no one to argue for her, landlords regularly take six months to pay her.

Jiji's story reflects why a widow would want to remarry: a woman with no land and with a small child has few job opportunities, and those that do exist are laborious and poorly paid. Although she now values her filialocal ties, she refused to have her son live with her brother anymore, saying, "I brought him back here because of the festival. I had celebrated Holi and Divali alone, but my affection for my son started growing. So I have brought him because of Holi. I could not celebrate Holi nor even eat if I was alone."

To Jiji the dual roles of mother and sister have been key to her strategies as a widow. With a son, she is not interested in remarriage. Her brother has provided a small amount of intermittent support as she struggles to subsist. While she is a female household head, she has little meaningful power and authority since she is a female household head in a socioeconomic group at the bottom of a rigidly male-dominated hierarchical society.

Caci, Ashok's widow, is also a female household head and a Watercarrier by caste. She has used her affinal links as a daughter-in-law to provide for her family. She was widowed in her early forties and has three sons and one daughter. Her husband's father had a small parcel of land, but her share is minuscule. He wasn't the best of men: Ashok did work, but he loved to sing and dance and to sit with the women. However, he did work regularly, and until his death his wife didn't have to work outside the house except for *jajmānī* duties. Yet when he died, his brothers had to pay the funeral expenses and the children were hungry. As his wife told me, "His dead body was in the house and they were asking for bread." Ashok was one of four brothers who shared a large compound for many years; even today with the compound broken into pieces and walled into sections, the kin ties are strong. There is also a wealthy sister who periodically aids one or more of her brothers. These close affinal kin put Caci and family in a situation quite different from Jiji's. Whenever she needs help, she gets it. Like Jiji, she first turned to selling cow-dung cakes. Her daughter would go to the fields and pull weeds that were edible and carry them to Brahman houses to trade for bread. But eventually her nephew loaned her money to buy a water buffalo, whose milk she sells daily. Her sons' parcel of land gives the family food for up to three months a year. And she has traditional *jajmānī* ties as a Watercarrier with Brahman houses in the village and is able to work in the few weeks a year that Brahman families now ask of their hereditary servants. Caci feels that she wouldn't work if her husband were alive. Moreover, she has an active affinal kin support system. Although she could claim full power and authority over her sons, she does not, preferring to rely on her male affines to make final decisions. Her fate has not left her totally bereft of male kin, a decided advantage in this community.

Whereas Jiya and Saroj depended most on their children when widowed, there was a difference. Jija relied on her relatives in Karimpur for support. Saroj turned to her natal family—her sister and sister's husband—and to her daughters and their husbands for support. Jiji, like Saroj, lacking close kin in Karimpur, reestablished ties with her brother, even leaving her small son with him initially. Caci, though living separately, was able to draw on the resources of her husband's large kin group for aid and support. From the marginality of widowhood, kinship ties other than one's husband and children become crucial.

Although Jiji and Caci did not remarry, many widows from the low castes do remarry, and they and their families face different choices than do Brahman, Rāy, and Kāyastha families. Further, the youth of some of these widows makes the decisions harder. In 1984 in addition to sixty-nine widows living in Karimpur, there were ten widows who had remarried. Three other widows whose husbands had died recently were living with their parents. Other young widows have dropped from memory as they returned to their fathers' houses or remarried out of the village. Table 4.4 provides information on this population.

It is immediately evident that women widowed in their teens have a secondary marriage if possible: the only widows who lost their husbands while teenagers and did not remarry are Brahman (excluding one Shepherd girl who was only eighteen in 1984 and a candidate for remarriage). I cannot identify all these youthful "remarried" widows since they have left the village. However, I do know of one childless Farmer girl who lost her husband and remarried elsewhere, while two other teenage women widowed in 1984 stayed with their parents, who hoped to arrange second marriages. For such

Table 4.4 Karimpur Widows, Remarriage, and Economic Status, 1984

	Number Current Widows	*Number Without Child*	*Number Moved Out*	*Age of Widowhood*							*Economic Status*		
				11–20	*21–30*	*31–40*	*41–50*	*51–60*	*60+*	*Old****	*O.K.*	*Subsistence*	*Poor*
Cannot remarry	23	4		4	3	1	4	3	2	5	22		1
Did not remarry	46	2	3*	1	3	7	10	11	6	8	12	12	22
Did remarry	11	1	1**		5	2	2	1		1	2	1	8

*one aged 21–30, two aged 30–40.
**aged 20–30.
***elderly people of undetermined age.

teenage widows, filialocal ties are key as they first return home to be remarried with the aid of parents and brothers. The roles of daughter and sister dominate.

Most of the non-Brahman women widowed in their twenties remarried (five out of seven). However, these older remarriages occur mostly within the husband's village. These older widows also have children, and their roles as sisters-in-law and mothers dominate those of daughter and sister. Of the ten widows who were residing in Karimpur after having a second marriage, nine married a relative of their husbands' while one is a widow who moved to Karimpur after her second marriage.

Among the landed, levirate is likely. Three of these second husbands are the first husband's younger brother(s): all three marriages are polygynous—two added as a second wife, one as the first. The latter case is interesting: the young widow, who was able to claim her husband's land, was remarried to her husband's younger brother, and when she remained childless he married again and had a large family by his second wife. With his brother's land in the first wife's name, he could not throw her out, but he mistreats her. Clothed in rags, she is often beaten. As in one of the other levirate marriages, when the older brother's widow has a right to land, "marrying" her alleviates potential disputes (see "Economic Status O.K." column in table 4.4).

Two recent cases further highlight the role of sons and land in remarriages. A young Kāchi man of a landowning family died of cholera in 1984, leaving a teenage wife. Both the girl's family and the village community felt that the family should marry her to the younger brother, but her in-laws refused, despite a caste *panchayat*'s approval. His family felt that it could get a large dowry for the younger son if a new bride was sought, and they returned the widow to her natal home. In 1986 a twenty-five-year-old Watercarrier (Kahār) from a minor landowning family died of tuberculosis, leaving a wife and son. This widow remains in her husband's household as a daughter-in-law/mother. Her son's claim to land and the family's ability to care for her have been crucial in this decision.

As table 4.4 suggests, women without land remarry to avoid the dire poverty of a landless "single" woman, and will do so even at older ages. While most widows who remain unmarried (fifty-three) live with their sons, whether adult or juvenile, some are forced into other choices. Widows without children, those with only daughters, or those with only young children have the most difficulty. Childless widows present special problems. Two live with their husbands' brothers or the families of their husbands' brothers. One, a blind and childless Shepherd widow, was her husband's second wife: he had agreed to take her as a second wife (she was his first wife's younger sister) because otherwise, being blind, she would have remained unmarried, which he felt was an untenable state for a Hindu woman. When he died in 1984, there was some discussion about whether she would be allowed to inherit his land: if the villagers claimed that it was not really a second marriage, they could deny her the land and put it in the name of her sister's daughter, which eventually they did. Meanwhile, the blind woman began to live with her dead husband's elder brother, who was himself a widower.

Women with only daughters also often face difficulties, especially if their daughters are young and there are no sons-in-law to provide assistance, whether legal, financial, or physical. In the absence of aid from her husband's lineage, one Farmer wife with a daughter of about ten moved in with her neighbors. Her husband had owed them a considerable sum, so in exchange for his remaining land, they cared for the woman and arranged her daughter's marriage. With the land now gone, she is totally dependent upon her neighbors' generosity. A Muslim widow with two young daughters survives by begging. Two or three times a week she makes the rounds of Karimpur and nearby hamlets; she gets enough handfuls here and there to feed her small family for the next few days. This household lacks a cot to sleep on or a quilt for the winter cold. Her older daughter was eventually married, and twenty or so Hindu villagers contributed food and goods for the ceremony and necessary (but small) feast. This family survives, but barely.

Landless women with small children often return to their parents. Those widows with children and some land will remain in Karimpur, for their claim to land would undoubtedly be challenged if they left. One Farmer woman with two children owns one and one-half acres, but since her son is only ten, the land must be let on shares. The 50 percent (or less) that she receives leaves her family in dire poverty, even though the young son tries to help by selling vegetables in the village. Yet a woman with sons and land thinks carefully before remarrying, for a second marriage might be detrimental to her son's inheritance: if the land is sufficient to allow her to struggle through until her son reaches an age when he can earn, she can survive unmarried.

No Longer a Wife

Structurally, being a wife is the least problematic role for Hindu women. With the loss of that role, a woman and her affinal and natal families make a series of decisions about which of her many kin roles will dominate and which will be renegotiated. If a woman is a mother, that role will most likely take precedence, as with Jiya and Saroj, though among the poor remarriage to become again a wife is common. Other women must reestablish moribund kin ties, as Jiji did in seeking her brother's aid. Caci forged new ties as a daughter-in-law/sister-in-law in order to gain support from her husband's brothers.

This examination of widows provides insight into the system of male privilege as it affects marriage in north India. Further, this gender system operates within a hierarchical class and caste system, so that widows of different social groups face different strategies for survival. Widows, as potential inheritors of land thought rightfully to belong to their husbands' male kin, are the biggest threat to landed families. Affinal relatives contain the threat by controlling widows and their lands. Few high-caste or wealthy widows become female household heads. This concern for controlling the material resources of women is manifested in caste rules that prohibit remarriage or lead to levirate, if it is allowed. It is also obvious that the only economic security of importance to women is land. Land, however, is the material resource most fully controlled by men and least likely to be accessible to women.

A widow's circumstances also depend on her having produced sons. If land provides economic security, sons, with their access to land and to employment, provide another kind of physical insurance, usually a place to live and food to eat, as well as some insurance against mistreatment by affines and natal family. The importance of sons in women's lives further reinforces the system of male privilege, but having sons is the only strategy likely to relieve the double burdens of class and gender hierarchies suffered by the poor widow.

This importance of sons and brothers, in addition to the husband, as seen through the lens of widowhood, reinforces earlier statements about the north Indian woman's ritual focus on husbands, brothers, and sons. Most women perform yearly rites to gain sons and to ensure both their brothers' and their husbands' long lives. Women's ritual behavior reinforces the ideology of the male-dominated system and reproduces it in the next generation as women teach their daughters and daughters-in-law.

Widowhood forces some women without adult sons or other male relatives to act on their behalf in relation to the community, or to go "public"—they must enter spheres of activity normally reserved for males. As Sharma has shown,[36] *pardā* acts to cut women off from those who have power in a community: widowhood may force women to enter these public spheres of activity and seek aid from those who have power or other resources. Jiji was forced to work as a day laborer, while Saroj had to supervise fields and sharecroppers. Widowhood permits a woman a physical mobility otherwise denied to her, but it is a mobility not sought by "proper" women, and Jiya and Caci have rarely used it.

In sum, viewing marriage from the position of widows emphasizes the importance of a woman's links to kin other than the husband. While the husband may indeed be the trunk of the tree, the branches that are her other kin and caste-mates become vitally important to the widow. As Jiji's reunion with her brother and Saroj's connection with her sisters show, a woman relies on others. The giving and receiving (see Raheja, chapter 2, this volume) that have endured from the initiation of her marriage help to maintain the ties that are called upon when disaster strikes. The woman's sometimes extended visits to her natal home contribute to the emotional bonding necessary to obtain financial and moral support from her natal family. It is not surprising, then, that many older women feel that their daughters have greater love for them than their sons: the daughter seeks to maintain her natal links as a form of insurance. One thing is clear: a woman cannot make it alone.

NOTES

1. For a discussion of the inessential woman, see Elizabeth V. Spellman, *The Inessential Woman: Problems of Exclusion in Feminist Thought* (Boston: Beacon Press, 1988).

2. See Lynn Bennett, *Dangerous Wives and Sacred Sisters: Social and Symbolic Roles of High-Caste Women in Nepal* (New York: Columbia University Press, 1983).

3. Unlike south Indian women, those residing in the Gangetic plain are not regularly hired as independent agricultural laborers, instead working most often with husbands on their own or sharecropped fields. (See Jean Dreze, "Social Insecurity in India," paper presented at the Workshop on Social Insecurity in Developing Countries, London School of Economics, 1988). Women whose families worked in traditional *jajmānī* service occupations also share chores with their husbands but are not considered as contributing to family income. "North" and "northern" are used in this essay to mean the Gangetic plain, the largely Hindi-speaking area of northern India.

4. See Sylvia Vatuk, "The Aging Woman in India: Self-Perceptions and Changing Roles," in *Women in Contemporary India and South Asia,* ed. A. de-Souza (New Delhi: Manohar Books, 1980), pp. 287–309.

5. Gail Omvedt's work on female subordination is critical here. See especially "Patriarchy: The Analysis of Women's Oppression," *Insurgent Sociologist* 13 (1986): 30–50.

6. My earlier article on women and Hinduism considers this point in detail. See Susan S. Wadley, "Women and the Hindu Tradition," in *Women in India: Two Perspectives,* Susan S. Wadley and Doranne Jacobson (New Delhi: Manohar Books, 1977, pp. 111–36.

7. *The Laws of Manu* (1886), trans. Georg Bühler: Sacred Books of the East, vol. 25 (Delhi: Motilal Banarsidass, 1964), pp. 160–65.

8. Ibid., Book IX:190. See also Doniger, chapter 7, this volume.

9. In joint families in north India, a woman's reproduction is often controlled by the mother-in-law, who arranges sleeping quarters, watches after her son's health, and verbally condemns unapproved behavior. For a discussion

of patriarchy and fertility, see Michael A. Koenig and Gillian H. C. Foo, "Patriarchy and High Fertility in Rural North India," paper presented at the Rockefeller Foundation Workshop on Women's Status and Fertility, Mt. Kisco, N.Y., June 1985. These law books are minimally concerned with the behavior of poor, low-caste widows, and specific prescriptions are directed at the higher castes only.

10. Pauline Kolenda vividly demonstrated the actuality of widow remarriage among Sweepers in a village north of Delhi. She also found a series of caste rules about better or worse remarriage options. See her "Widowhood Among 'Untouchable' Chuhras," in *Concepts of Person: Kinship, Caste and Marriage in India*, ed. A. Östör, Lina Fruzetti, and Steve Barnett (Cambridge, Mass.: Harvard University Press, 1982), 172–220. N. K. Walli has data showing a switch in caste codes in Maharashtra from allowing remarriage to forbidding it in the early years of British rule (personal communication).

11. Bina Agrawal, "Women, Poverty and Agricultural Growth in India," *Journal of Peasant Studies* 13 (1986): 165–220.

12. Hancock (chapter 3, this volume) illuminates the threat of economic independence on male kin.

13. Except for Brahmans, I have translated caste names, giving the Hindi at the first occurrence. Caste names in English are marked by a capital letter (as in Farmer).

14. See Rayna Rapp, "Family and Class in Contemporary America: Notes Toward an Understanding of Ideology," in *Rethinking the Family: Some Feminist Questions*, ed. Barrie Thorne with Marilyn Yalom (New York: Longman, 1982), pp. 168–87.

15. Note that here the control is seen as coming from other women, not from men.

16. Hindu families in most of India look for a husband for their daughters: to have to seek a bride for a son brings much dishonor to the family.

17. As the average age of marriage has increased from eleven to sixteen, these periods have been condensed, and for brides over fifteen, *gaunā* may occur at the time of the *śādī*, although the visit is still short.

18. Upper-caste families are particularly strict, and parents are forbidden even water in their daughter's married village. These strictures ease as caste and class status lessens.

19. Bennett reports that a widow should receive her saris from her brother, again marking the importance of this key natal relative (*Dangerous Wives and Sacred Sisters*, p. 244).

20. For more details on the worship of male kin, see Susan S. Wadley, "Brothers, Husbands and Sometimes Sons: Kinsmen in North Indian Ritual," *Eastern Anthropologist* 29 (1976): 149–70.

21. My understanding of separation is defined by the Hindi term current in Karimpur—*nyāre. Nyāre* means, in practice, separate eating and cooking facilities and, when possible, separate living quarters. Most families prefer separate farming as well. In reality, separation is a drawn-out process, with the separation of farming, religious activities, and decision making not occurring for years in some instances.

22. Recently, even the white sari and no-bangle rules are easily broken: even

Brahman widows regularly wear plastic bangles (giving the appearance of glass), and only the oldest widows wear white.

23. In one joint household the father has essentially deserted his family, though he sometimes lives with them. His oldest son is the effective head of household, and his mother has far less voice than his wife in household decisions.

24. Tim Dyson and Mick Moore, "On Kinship Structure, Female Autonomy, and Demographic Behavior in India," *Population and Development Review* 9 (1983): 35–60.

25. Women whose desires with regard to the education of children are thwarted by their husbands will often turn to their own natal families for aid, and it is not unusual to learn of a son studying at his mother's natal village.

26. See table 4.2 for figures on family types in Karimpur. David Mandelbaum documents a series of cases where lower-caste and/or nonlandowning castes had larger percentages of nuclear families. See David Mandelbaum, *Society in India: Continuity and Change* (Berkeley: University of California Press, 1970). In Karimpur 38 percent of rich families are nuclear and 38 percent are joint (with the remainder primarily in supplemented nuclear households). Among the poorest, 60 percent are nuclear and 10 percent are joint, with the remainder evenly split between subnuclear and supplemented nuclear households. See Susan S. Wadley and Bruce W. Derr, "Karimpur Families over 60 Years," *South Asian Anthropologist* 9 (1988): 119–32.

27. Women who are poor do not threaten male privilege by being in public spaces because, like poor men, they already lack access to economic and political power.

28. Data from 1925 derive from the census records collected by William Wiser. Later data were collected by William Wiser. Later data were collected during three research periods in Karimpur: in 1967–69 with funding from the National Science Foundation; in 1974–75 with funding from the American Institute of Indian Studies; and in 1983–84 with funding from Faculty Research Abroad, U.S. Dept. of Education and the Smithsonian Institution. Bruce W. Derr is due many thanks for aiding in collecting these data and for the analysis of census data. This paper is in memory of Ant Ram Kahar, who painstakingly transcribed pages of life histories and whose widow provides data for this analysis.

29. For a fuller discussion of Saroj's life and role as as Brahman woman active in politics, see Susan S. Wadley, "The 'Village Indira': A Brahman Widow and Political Action in Rural North India," in *Balancing Acts: Women and the Process of Social Change,* ed. Patricia Lyons Johnson (Boulder, Colo.: Westview Press, 1992), pp. 65–87. Parts of this story are also found in Charlotte Wiser, William Wiser, and Susan S. Wadley, *Behind Mud Walls,* rev. ed. (Berkeley: University of California Press, 1989). Saroj also appears in Susan S. Wadley, *Struggling with Destiny in Karimpur, 1925–1984* (Berkeley: University of California Press, 1994).

30. Little is known about the life circumstances of rural widows even today in India, let alone historically. In the early part of this century, life expectancy for women was under twenty-five (William Wiser, "Social Institutions of a Hindu Village in North India," Ph.D. diss. Cornell University, 1933, p. 104), ep-

idemics were common, malaria was uncontrolled, and famine and drought were regular occurrences. Data on widows show markedly different situations in recent versus earlier times. In 1925 widows in Karimpur constituted 30.4 percent of the adult female population, while in 1984 they represented merely 13 percent. Moreover, widows aged considerably: in 1925, the average age of a Karimpur widow was 47 years; in 1984 it was 61 years. However, the actual number of widows in 1925 and 1984 was almost the same (68 in 1925; 69 in 1984), facilitating comparison. As table 4.1 shows, there is little difference in the distribution of widows by caste in 1925 and 1984, with the two largest castes, Brahman and Farmer, having similar numbers in both years.

31. Family types as used here follow Pauline Kolenda, "Region, Caste and Family Structure: A Comparative Study of the Indian 'Joint' Family," in *Structure and Change in Indian Society*, ed. Milton Singer and Barnard Cohn (Chicago: Aldine, 1968), pp. 339–96. Joint includes lineal, collateral, and supplemented joint families.

32. Because of the larger populations per household, the percentage of the total population in joint families was always higher than that in any other family type: 28.0 percent in 1925 and 41.8 percent in 1984.

33. Thirty-six percent of Karimpur households in 1925 were fragmented types (i.e., did not contain a married couple). In 1984 this figure was 10.7 percent.

34. Pravin Visaria and Leela Visaria, "Indian Households with Female Heads: Their Incidence, Characteristics and Level of Living," in *Tyranny of the Household: Investigative Essays on Women's Work*, ed. D. Jain and N. Banerjee (New Delhi: Shakti Books, 1985), pp. 50–83.

35. While not all Brahman families in the area are wealthy, the relative prosperity of Karimpur's landowning Brahmans means that their daughters are marrying into equally prosperous landowning families.

36. Ursula Sharma, "Women and Their Affines: The Veil as a Symbol of Separation," *Man*, n.s., 13 (1978): 218–33; and idem, "Purdah and Public Space," in *Women in Contemporary India and South Asia: Traditional Images and Changing Roles*, ed. A. de Souza, (New Delhi: Manohar Books, 1980), pp. 213–39.

5

The "Jungli Rani" and Other Troubled Wives in Rajasthani Oral Traditions

ANN GRODZINS GOLD

Introduction: Clever Bride or Lady Magician?

Women's oral traditions often express immediate, daily concerns that are both practical and moral.[1] Those stories that women tell as an integral part of domestic rituals, although filled with unlikely events and supernatural interventions, realistically portray household roles and relationships. They also articulate the conflicts and anxieties entailed by those roles and relationships. The persons, both male and female, who populate these stories are almost never named but rather are referred to by kin categories ("there were seven sons' wives"; "there was a sister's brother"; "there was a Brahman's daughter"). Some stories focus on relationships in a woman's natal home, where she is daughter or sister, others on her married roles, most often as a brother's or son's wife. In several stories a transition from one setting to the other is central; these begin with a daughter and end with a wife. Although the new bride arrives in her husband's home as a distrusted stranger, she will eventually—especially with the onset of motherhood—come to feel and act as an integral family member. However, this personal passage and transformation is not always a smooth one.

As told in one Rajasthan village, the story of the "jungli rani" contains a daughter to wife transformation that is exceptionally problematic. *Janglī rānī* in Hindi and Rajasthani could translate as "queen from the jungle" or by strong implication "uncivilized queen." Throughout this chapter I persist in using the Anglicized spelling "jungli"—which is not an accurate transliteration—because I wish to sustain in English the same evocative powers the word *janglī* has in the original. An examination of this story and its meanings offers some insights into female identity, not only in relation to particular kinship roles but well beyond these always partial facets of a woman's total career. By way of introduction I shall briefly place my reading of the jungli rani's story in the context of some broader perspectives—my own and those of other scholars—on women in South Asian thought.

For several years now I have been writing about women's self-images, finding my inspiration and substance in oral traditions—both stories and songs—recorded in and around a single Rajasthan village.[2] Mustering the persuasive evidence available in these rich texts, I have attempted to revise, in part, the common characterization of Hindu female nature (both divine and mortal) as split between two ideal types.[3] In the split image paradigm, to oversimplify heuristically, one sort of female is tame, paired, fertile, nonerotic, and beneficent; one is wild, unpaired (or adulterous), infertile, sexual, and dangerous. Such contrasts have been sketched by male and female scholars of various disciplines and draw both on myth (Sītā versus Kālī) and on kin roles. In the latter field of discourse, the split comes down in various ways: wives and mothers are safe and good while courtesans are dangerous if attractive; or sisters are asexual and good while wives are sexual and thus untrustworthy; or wives are controlled and docile while mothers are controlling and thus terrifying.[4]

Underlying all these varied schematizations is the notion that females are dangerous when their power, often defined as sexual or at least as sexually charged, is not contained, channeled, harnessed, or directed by males.[5] Whether the focus is on goddesses or mortals, these various split images—I have argued—are projected by men, although they may well be shared at times by women. Mythological split images come from texts authored or at least written down by literate, high-caste men. Domestic split images explicitly define women as the sisters, daughters, wives, and mothers of men.

In Rajasthani women's songs and stories I have found lore whose creative inspiration can be attributed with some conviction to women, that does not perpetrate such radically split identities. Women's folklore reveals more unified feminine images, although recognizing externally imposed splits. Strikingly, women portray themselves as sexually alluring and simultaneously motherly; indeed, the erotic roots of motherhood are obvious to mothers. The "jungli rani" eluded my earlier analyses, which concentrated on the sexy mother, because her story's concern is neither sex nor fertility. Even though, as we will soon see, the king marries her because her food is so delicious—an attribute perhaps equatable with sexual attractions—and even though she bears him a son in just nine months, these matters are peripheral. The source of the jungli rani's problems is more basic still: the people around her assume that female virtuosity cannot coexist with female virtues, at least not without a supporting male lineage.

As first conceived, this chapter's title was "Clever Bride or Lady Magician? Balancing Acts of the 'Jungli Rani' and Other Troubled Wives." I sought with such a cumbersome phrase to reflect on the split-image perspective, adding a female response. The first half highlights an important dichotomy between approved womanly skills and disapproved black magic: clever brides improve their marital homes but magicians threaten them. Its second half implies a self-conscious resolution of that split characterization as a balancing act: clever brides perform wonders without drawing accusations of performing magic. Together these terms imply an externally imposed, judgmental dichotomy straddled by a female person self-consciously trying to sustain her integrity. If issues of erotic and reproductive capacities are secondary here, the idea that an independent, powerful woman is intrinsically dangerous certainly looms large. It looms, however—and this is the crux of my argument—not as cosmic reality but as human obtuseness. The jungli rani's power acquired through proper worshipful acts is *mistaken* for black magic or witchcraft. It is thus externally imposed and false assumptions about female nature that threaten her life more than once.

Also at stake in the jungli rani's tale, only somewhat more submerged, are questions about what constitutes marriage, and how it transforms a woman's body and character. As the story goes, when a king happens upon a girl living in a hollow pipal tree, he marries her by what the storyteller euphemistically describes as a *dharma* marriage. The authors of treatises on *dharma* would, however, probably classify this union as a "gandharva type," one of the "disapproved forms" recognized in ancient texts.[6] It is most definitely not a "gift of a virgin" or *kanyā dān*[7] (see Nicholas, chapter 6, this volume; Inden and Nicholas 1977), the most valued kind of marriage in ancient law books as well as in modern Rajasthan. There is no dowry and no transforming Sanskrit ritual.

Since all approved forms of Hindu marriage involve negotiations between families, the girl in the pipal tree who lacks a family could not participate in one. The disapproved quality of her marriage clearly contributes to her problems in "adjusting" to the role of wife or, more accurately, in being adjusted to by those with whom she lives—cowives and husband.[8] Thus they call her a "jungli rani"—an improperly married queen of questionable origins. Eventually her patron the Sun God provides her with a chimerical father's house complete with appropriate songs and all-important gifts. This is his attempt to remedy the difficult situation in which his devotee's unswerving worship habits, and her consequently unorthodox marriage, have placed her. Significantly enough, the attempt fails. Not even divine intervention can bestow what she lacks: a proper natal home, and a properly arranged and enacted affinal relationship.

The jungli rani is a favorite among village women. Her story, told in the context of worship, is received with more animation than many other rote-told tales. Her situation—especially her lack of natal kin and besiegement by antipathetic cowives—inspires sympathy. Her world, however weird the events which take place in it, is not perceived as remote. Parochial as she appears, emerging from her hollow pipal tree, there is something elementary and moving in the jungli rani's story. And that something reflects on the nature of female identity, which in turn helps clarify what marriage means to Hindu women.

To study the jungli rani's tale should help us understand how women respond to the predicament of being *perceived* as split when they are really whole, and of being perceived as threatening when they are only acting according to moral and devotional convictions. This understanding includes the obvious but elusive fact that, although marriage changes a woman's life in many ways, her identity as a person is continuous from girlhood into the marital state. The jungli rani always refers to herself as a "brahman's daughter." It is her cowives and the residents of her husband's kingdom who dub her "jungli rani" in a distinctly negative tone. But the storyteller and her female audience use the same rubric with sympathetic affection. As we listen to or read the story it is clear that, despite the very different connotations in Hindu society of "brahman's daughter" and "uncivilized queen" they are incontrovertibly a single human being.

Without much further preamble, I give the jungli rani's story. I then draw some comparisons and contrasts between it and a few others of the same genre—women's worship tales—where approved, clever-bride heroines predominate. I also briefly examine the lady magicians who appear in the epic tale of King Gopī Cand as sung and explicated by a male bard of the Nāth caste in the same village where the jungli rani's story is told. These villainous females have genuinely nefarious goals and questionable characters. I hope, then, effectively to contrast the way that women may sympathetically portray unsupported women as viewed with unjust suspicion by men and by women aligned with men with the way that men zestfully describe amoral, independent, saucy, "bad" women whose rebellion is enjoyable because it inevitably ends in defeat. In conclusion I will suggest some connections, posed by these oral traditions, among women's worship, women's magic, and wom-

Figure 5.1 Shobhag Kanvar tells the "Jung Rani" story. Photograph by Ann Gold.

en's power, and will try to summarize what these connections contribute to our understanding of Hindu marriage.

The Jungli Rani's Tale

Although everyone calls the tale in question the story of the "jungli rani," according to villagers' usual classification system by performance context it is a "story of the Sun God" (*Suryā Rāj kī kahānī*) and is told on the first Sunday after Holi as part of a fast for that divinity.[9] As described in the story, a cow-dung worship space, raw whole grains, and *roṭ*—thick, unsalted bread prepared for offerings to the gods—compose the simple ritual paraphernalia.

I give here a composite of two tellings of the jungli rani's tale, recorded from the same Rajput teller—a grandmother in her fifties whose repertoire of religious stories was the largest in the village. One version I recorded on March 2, 1980, a year in which the Sunday following Holi happened to be the very day after Holi, a ritually busy one for village women even when not a Sunday.[10] Miller's recorded text of the jungli rani's story, made the previous year before my arrival in the village, supplied some details lacking in mine. Perhaps because the storyteller had so much ritual work to accomplish the year I recorded the tale, she abridged it somewhat.

The Jungli Rani: A Story of the Sun God

There were two, a mother and a daughter. They both said, "Yesterday was Holi," and so prepared a cow-dung worship place: "We will tell the Sun God's story." On that Sunday after Holi mother and daughter plastered the courtyard with cow dung. And then the mother said to the daughter: "Daughter I am going to bathe and you roll out the bread."

So the mother went to bathe and the daughter was making bread. First she rolled a bread made of one and one-quarter seers [of flour]. Then the Sun God arrived, disguised as a holy man. He said to her, "Give me a small piece of that first bread you have made, as alms."

She said, "Great King, this bread is reserved for my mother. You can take some alms of raw grain, or whatever you want to take, but the first bread is reserved."

"Give me some of it."

"O, Great King, it belongs to my mother. You can't have that bread."

"I'll have the first bread; I'll take some of it, or else there will be trouble. If you don't give it to me I'll curse you."

"So take it," and she quickly tore up the bread and gave one-fourth of it to the holy man. That's what happened. Then her mother came, and said to her, "Daughter, bring the bread, bring yours and bring mine too. And light the lamp on the cow-dung square and put some whole grains down there and then tell the story."

At once, she did all these things.

"But Daughter, what happened? My bread, why did you break it? Why is it broken?"

"Mother, a holy man came and asked me for alms and I said, 'Great King, I'll bring grain.' Then he said, 'What need do I have for grain? That first bread you are making, that first bread, give it to me.'

" 'So, Great King, feast on my bread; that one is my mother's.'

" 'But I want you to give me some of your mother's. I will take some of the first bread, and if you don't do as I say then I'll curse you.'

"So I tore your bread and gave him one-quarter of it."

The Mother began to scream like a crazy person, "Give me my whole bread!"

She screamed, *"Dhī roṭo da roṭā māṭī kor da, dī roṭo da roṭā māṭī kor da."*[11]

When her mother began carrying on in this way, the daughter became deeply disturbed. "And now what will I do?"

Because of her mother she went wandering this way and that in the forest. Then she came to a *beṛ* tree and step-well and nearby was a pipal tree[12] with a hollow niche in it. She climbed into the hollow and there she sat and sat and the Sun God gave her his grace. He gave her nine kinds of treats, thirty-six sauces, and thirty-two treats and in a small clay pot he gave her good water. Who? The Sun God, he gave his grace. So there she sat and ate bread and drank water. Right there in the hollow tree she lived. Twelve months passed.

Now a king was out hunting in this forest, accompanied by his barber. But he got lost. Coming upon the step-well and the *beṛ* tree, he went there and lay down. He went to sleep and his mouth fell open in his sleep. A crumb fell into his mouth from one of her nine kinds of treats. He had never tasted such food, the kind of food that if you eat one crumb your soul is utterly satisfied.

The king thought, "I have never tasted such delicious food. I am a king, but I have never eaten anything like it." The king was astonished. How could there be food this good in the jungle? Then another crumb fell. And she was drinking water and a drop fell into his mouth and he said, "O, I was so thirsty and with one drop my thirst was extinguished." And another fell and his soul was satiated.

So he told his companion, the barber, "Climb that pipal tree and see who is there, who is there that has such food as I've never tasted and such water as I've never drunk."

When the barber climbed he looked everywhere but found nothing.

Then the king himself climbed up and looked in every direction carefully, but he saw nothing. Just as he was descending he glimpsed [the girl], and he understood [where the food had come from]. "Oh ho ho, who is this? Brother, is it a witch, is it a ghost, is it a deceptive illusion or a spirit-seductress?"

"Who are you? Explain this mystery."

"I am not . . . not . . . I am not a witch, not a ghost, not a deceptive illusion, not any kind of spirit-seductress at all." [She narrates all that has happened up to now.]

She was talking to the king.

"God has had such grace on me that every day I receive all kinds of good cooked foods and today I was eating and one piece slipped from my hand and fell in your mouth. In this way, from this sign, you have found me."

The king said, "If you are a Brahman's daughter then I will marry you." In that jungle the king made a *dharma* marriage with her. The king already had six queens. And she became the seventh. When the king arrived in his kingdom, then the news spread everywhere: "The king has married a seventh queen, a jungli one."

People said: "Oh, the king has married a jungli rani. Oh, he has married a jungli rani, he has married one more queen and brought her here." She began to live in the palace, and after just nine months she had a son, and the Sunday after Holi came. The seventh queen prepared for worship; she plastered the courtyard with cow dung, she made a cow-dung worship space with a thousand rays, and kept the fast of the Sun God and began to tell his story. Then the other queens, seeing this queen's method, began to say, "This jungli rani is doing some kind of magic on the king."

Another queen said to the king, "That queen is a magician [*kāmaṇ gārī*], a magic-knower [*jāṇ jugār*], a magician doing magic on you."

The king said, "Oh, you're just talking."

"This jungli rani is doing magic on you."

The king said, "You're just saying this."

"Every day, sir, what does she do? She lights a lamp and sets it in a cow-dung worship space, and sprinkles around golden grains, and she also places bread, one and one-quarter seers of it, and tells the story. The other queens say that she is completing her magic on you today. So go, you had better go and see what she is doing."

The king went to the place. Just as he came, the jungli rani covered up the bread and she also covered up the offering flowers. At that time the king had a sword in his hand. The king lifted the cover and looked beneath it. The bread was of gold and the flowers were diamonds and pearls. Seeing this, the king raised his sword and confronted her: "Queen, what are you doing?"

"King, from where did you bring me? I tell the Sun God's story and then I will eat bread. From where did you bring me?"

The king said to the queen, "We will go to your mother's home."

The queen said, "Hey, Mahārāj, I am the daughter of a poor house, a starving natal home."

"But I want to see it."

"I am from a starving natal home and lineage, such a starving natal home."

"I too will see it, whatever kind of a starving natal home it is."

At this the queen became angry and went to bed. She didn't eat food or drink water. In the morning her crazy mother came from somewhere, selling grain sifters. The jungli rani thought, "We should buy one for ourselves," so she went out from the palace. As soon as she went out, her gaze fell on her mother. The mother also recognized her. The mother, recognizing her daughter, began calling for that same bread. All these things the other queens were watching, and the queens began to say, "The jungli one has called her mother here too." The jungli queen heard this and the jungli one shut her mother up inside the house. Having shut up her mother, her mother became a golden icon. Those other queens told the king about it. "This queen isn't good. She is a witch, a magician. A woman came, and this jungli rani ate her." At this the king became angry.

That jungli rani went to bed. She was very worried. When midnight came, the Sun God arrived, "You're awake, you're not sleeping, what's the matter?"

Then she said, "Great Lord, I'm not awake and I'm not asleep and I'm very worried."

"Go, I will give you a natal family and home for three hours, over there by the *beṛ* tree and the step-well. Go over there."

"Great." So she said [to the king the next day], "Yes, let's go sir, let's go sir to my natal home, if you desire it, let's go." So they went; they took a chariot with horses and they went.

They took their baby boy and they took the barber with them too. They went there and found a nine-story mansion, and in it were aunts and uncles, mother and father, brothers and brothers' wives and all. And when they got there these relations sang son-in-law songs for the king and they seated them.

They served them nine kinds of festive food. An entire, populated city appeared there. But the three hours were over and the jungli rani's soul was sorrowful. Then she pinched her little son very hard [so he started howling] and said, "Let's go!" She said to the king, "The child is sick, we ought to return." The king agreed.

To the jungli rani her brother and father's brother gave many things of gold and silver. All three then set off to return to their kingdom. On the way the barber said, "I left my riding crop behind."

The king said, "We have much gold and silver, we will have another made." But the barber insisted on going back to get his whip. When the barber reached the pipal tree place, he saw that there was nothing, no castle and no garden. All that met his gaze was a desolate jungle.

The barber took his whip and came to the king and said, "Hey king, this queen is a very big magic worker. Everything over there was the play of her illusional art. I have just seen it. Over there now is neither castle nor family."

At this the king took out his sword and prepared to kill the queen. And he said, "What is all this? First you made bread into gold. Then you made a woman into a golden icon. Then in this way you made a castle and a family. Reveal the full mystery; if not I am going to kill you."

The queen said, "Hey Mahārāj, don't ask me this mystery, because you took me from a hollow pipal tree. I am a poor Brahman's daughter. In this world I had nothing but my mother. But I worshiped the Sun God, I kept his fast, and this is the miracle. All this work was done by the Sun God. For this reason, he gave me both wealth and a natal home."

Hey Sun God, if it's a little short, then complete it; if it's complete, witness it. Four names short or four names too many, hey Grain-Giver, hey Sun God, as you gave to her so give to the whole of *saṃsāra*!

The Jungli Rani's Troubles

The same storyteller from whom I learned the jungli rani's tale had a number of others in her repertoire concerning resourceful brides who, against all odds, triumph over adversity in their husbands' houses. But in no tale, with half an exception, does this adversity include suspicion of practicing magical arts (*jādū, kāmaṇ*). Rather, most of the other stories are about young women who overcome poverty, unkind in-laws, and so forth through a combination of a chosen deity's blessings, native intelligence, and good fate—in proportions that vary from case to case. Their success is more often praised by kin and neighbors than subject to hostility and disapprobation.

For example: There is a Brahman's daughter who, married off (by a cruel stepmother) to one among five ill-mannered, bachelor brothers, effectively brings order and religion to their chaotic household through her own unstinting labors and by enlisting the sympathy of neighbor women. Eventually she devises a foolproof plan to coerce the goddess into granting them infinite prosperity. Public opinion dubs this clever bride not "magician" but "Lakṣmī"—goddess of auspiciousness and wealth.[13]

There is also the story of a sister who renounces her own hearth and home to save her brother's life. The peculiar actions she must perform to achieve this end lead others to judge her mad for a time. But she is never maligned for evil intentions or threatened physically, even though she pronounces vile curses on her brother.[14]

In another narrative a girl tricked into marrying a sword becomes pregnant (the goddess having miraculously produced a husband–prince for her in a secret room); although there is some scandalmongering about her condition, there is certainly no talk of black magic. In the end her mother-in-law touches her feet and praises her for the good fate that granted existence to a long-desired son.[15]

Besides the jungli rani's tale, only one other women's story that I know from my area includes the motif (expressed far more obliquely than in the jungli rani's case) of suspected magic. That is the story of King Nal, told on the last day of worship of Dasā Mātā, the Mother of Well-Being.[16] Nal notices a cotton string on his queen's neck. The implications of their interchange about this string are that he finds her wearing such a thing, among her golden necklaces, suspicious as well as ugly. She forthrightly informs him: "This is my special women's power." The string represents, indeed is, the Goddess of Well-Being. But the king, because he doesn't like its looks, rashly and brutally destroys it, bringing endless misfortune upon himself and his wife. Only her return to the goddess's grace, when the annual worship comes round again, restores their former prosperity and undoes all the disasters that have dogged both king and queen since his violent folly.

Why, when the majority of worship stories show women's power, acquired through devotion, accepted without question as an indication of great virtue, do a few describe such power as attracting violent suspicions? The jungli rani acts only according to moral precepts, both in her mother's house when she gives the bread to the holy man and in her husband's palace when she worships the Sun God. Yet she incurs abuse, distrust, and accusations of magical practice.

Before speculating on the reasons for the jungli rani's troubles, let me introduce another set of females of a very different type from those portrayed in women's worship stories. This group is composed of low-caste artisans and traders rather than Brahman's daughters or queens. It includes a female yogi, a potter, an oil presser, a wineseller, a laundress, and their ilk. These are the lady magicians of Bengal as presented in the Rajasthani folk epic of King Gopī Cand. They are "spicy" characters; indeed, the yogi Carpaṭ Nāth refers to the guru of them all, Behrī Yogin, as "a bag of hot chilis."

These ladies have husbands, and they make some pretense of performing women's typical domestic chores when there is nothing more interesting to occupy their attention, but such drudgery is not their true avocation. Thus, although we meet them on their way to fetch water—the paradigmatic female task—the first to note the presence of a yogi near the water place exclaims: "Burn up all other matters and listen to me. . . . Many days have gone by since we've played a contest, but today's our lucky day. So burn up all other matters and let's hurry to the waterside, for today we'll have a contest with this yogi." They quickly abandon their unfilled pots and surround the hapless yogi and former king, Gopī Cand.

The tale presents this readiness to drop household chores—whether filling water jugs, nursing babies, or making bread—as a dangerously contagious one. For although only the seven magicians themselves go to play with (and easily to best) Gopī Cand, when the first rescue team of fourteen hundred yogis arrives in search of the lost disciple, each of the seven lady magicians brings seven hundred more ordinary women to the contest. The bard describes this antagonistic mob as "like clouds mounting" in the rainy season. And, hearing about the grand female victory that concludes *this* encounter, all the rest of the city's women clamorously beg: "Take me with you next time, take me with you. Next time, sister-in-law, don't leave me behind."

The low-caste lady magicians of Bengal seek their own pleasure and power and appear to be without loyalties, whether to gods, husbands, or one another (for they blatantly lie to each other in competing over who should possess their victim). Even though Behrī Yogin is repeatedly described as the guru of the other six, they are quite capable of attempting to lie to her too, demonstrating an amorality truly beyond the Hindu pale. Although a few of their husbands are mentioned, Behrī Yogin is the only one of the seven actually portrayed interacting with her husband, Asmāl Yogī; her demeanor on this occasion is certainly not that of an ideal wife. She hopes to impress him with her accomplishment of transforming Gopī Cand into a parrot. But her husband chides her for playing an ill-advised, foolhardy prank, warning her of its potentially dire consequences should Gopī Cand's guru, Jalīndar, come to save him. Instead of accepting criticism or advice, she defies Asmāl boldly and insultingly. Her parting lines as she stalks away are: "My pockets are filled with many such as Jalīndar Bābā. I keep them in my pockets." The husband, not insignificantly, has the last word, calling after her: "Ho, lady-yogi, one day your pockets will split and Jalīndar Bābā will emerge. Your pockets will burst, and on that day, I won't come to help you."

Behrī enjoys some sweet moments of triumph until Śiva's own disciple, Jalīndar Nāth himself, does indeed arrive in Bengal and, as predicted by Asmāl, takes the wind out of her sails. Jalīndar Nāth sends all the Bengali women, transformed into braying she-asses, into the wilderness, where they starve pathetically because the yogis they have previously turned into donkeys and camels have already stripped the terrain of edible plant life. For all their impudence, independence, and irresponsibility toward hearth and home, it is the wife and mother role which saves them by making their absence difficult to endure: bread burns, babies howl. Accordingly, their husbands miss them, and eventually the king is persuaded to control the magicians and restore normalcy to society.[17]

How might this excursion into a male oral tradition help to illuminate the questions raised by the women's tale of the jungli rani? In both genres indigenous distinctions are made between magical arts (*jādū, kāmaṇ*) and religious practices: yogis' meditations in the male epic, devotion (*bhakti*), and the habits of worship (*niyam*) in women's tales. In the Rajasthani view, magic—a manipulation of deliberately cultivated power for selfish or destructive purposes—is threatening and dangerous to particular victims and, when it gets out of hand, to the social order. *Dharma*—acting according to biomoral duties which, in relation to a grace-granting divinity, can bring special powers and boons—is by contrast beneficent and helpful, not just to the actor but to community and cosmos.

The chief characteristic of the lady magicians in Gopī Cand's tale would seem to be their selfishness. They have no higher purpose in life than the dubious aim of playing power contests for fun. To enjoy this sport they drop all pretense of serving domestic needs. A suggestive if undeveloped antipathy emerges here between women ready to abandon hearth and home for the selfish motivations of exercising power, and male yogis who also leave their families for the (perhaps equally selfish) cause of spiritual development. Such social irresponsibility, the tradition implies, is fine for male devotees, but female adepts are "sluts" (*rāṇḍ*). A familiar double standard is at work here.

Aloof, independent, and uncompromising, the jungli rani clearly values her relationship with the Sun God above all human connections, much as the Bengali magicians value their magical sport. The transformation of the crazed mother into a golden icon speaks quite strongly for the priority of devotion, or *bhakti*, over kinship, as does her giving the fatal bread in the first place. The Bengali magicians and their female followers abandon their babies when an opportunity to joust magically with yogis presents itself; the jungli rani does not mind pinching her baby hard in order to get her husband to leave the illusory natal home before the time allotted by the Sun God's grace expires. Those attributes that the jungli rani has in common with the lady magicians may reveal why her devotion is perceived as dangerous. It fosters independence from, rather than submission to, familial demands—whether natal or marital.

The clever bride who manages the five bachelors puts her energies not into worship but into cooking and cleaning. The sister totally dedicated to her brother's well-being averts fate itself without evident recourse to a deity.[18] The wife of the sword–husband misbehaves a bit in her daughter-in-law role (snitching the keys to the inner room when her mother-in-law is dozing) but only toward the approved end of perfected wifehood. But the jungli rani's devotion to God overrides her domestic attachments. It appears to be selfishly inspired and thus is perceived as magic, not religion. This is the main source of her troubles. If all women's worship stories have a foundation of devotional emotion and action, the jungli rani's is unusual in giving these concrete priority over the family (although that of King Nal's wife being well justified in spoiling the looks of her golden ornaments with the goddess's white string might also be said to do this).

Connected to the public misperception of the jungli rani's character is the ambiguity attached, in her case, to both daughterly and wifely roles—an ambiguity deriving from her devotional prowess. Such indeterminacy in one woman's identity has no place in Gopī Cand's epic. Where split images prevail it is never hard to decide what kind of woman you are dealing with. The females connected to Gopī Cand by kinship may be loving impediments to his renunciation but are of unassailable virtue; the rest—dangerous, defiant "bags of hot chilis"—threaten his life and passage and insult his person. All the latter types, including servant girls and slaves as well as the magicians and their followers, are often referred to by the male bard as "sluts." The jungli rani is never called a slut, but for her to be called a lady magician means that her devotion and character have been misunderstood, if not without cause.

Whenever she is accused of magical practices by her husband, the jungli rani responds, "From where did you bring me?" as if demanding that the king himself acknowledge her as a jungli rani. She, however, consistently describes herself as a Brahman's daughter—that is, as high-caste and part of a family. Others dub her "jungli," with its implications of tribal castelessness and uncivilized kinship patterns. In fact, her daughterhood is quite problematic. She has no brothers or father. When the story opens she has a mother. (Indeed, the tale begins: "*Do māṅ beṭyā hī* . . . There were two, a mother and a daughter. . . ") But the initial episode concerns her total rejection by that mother, and soon enough there is only one, the daughter, alone in the jungle. After she becomes the king's wife—one of seven—she is still isolated, bearing the stigma of her jungli origins and her improper marriage.

I began by noting a prevailing dichotomized view of Hindu women as tamed, paired, matched, motherly, and safe; or else untamed, single, unmatched, unmotherly, and dangerous. In the case of the jungli rani and in a few other worship stories a homologous opposition between women's miraculous manifestations of power as divinely bestowed or acquired through black magic seems to exist. But, I hope I have shown, women's tales define such splits as externally imposed and work against acceptance of their validity. The jungli rani's troubles come from false, externally imposed splits that are magnified and exacerbated by her lack of a family, especially her lack of male kin. In reality, the barbaric "jungli rani" and the innocent "Brahman's daughter" are one. Village women speak the words "jungli rani" with fond approval rather than insultingly, as do the citizens of the story kingdom.

Definitions of the self in women's lore are in part responses to externally imposed labels and in part expressions of self-knowledge. In examining the jungli rani's tale, we have seen some interplay between these two modes—an interplay reflecting something of the ambivalence aroused in the Hindu world by manifestations of women's power when divine gifts are not immediately channeled into domestic bliss. Presumably, as the story ends, the king lowers his sword and takes his seventh queen home vindicated, but his recognition of her innocence is never verbalized. It would be easy to imagine her troubles continuing, yet the closing prayer, a standard one, brings the jungli rani's somewhat odd gifts within the circle of blessings sought after by all women. After all, through the Sun God's grace, she has a wealthy husband, a palatial home, and a son, and this is far more than a virtual orphan, from a starving kind of natal home, could reasonably expect.

The jungli rani is not afraid to remind the king that, although she is a Brahman's daughter, he took her out of a tree. In doing so she also acknowledges that her marriage is of a "disapproved" type, her body untransformed by refining rituals. All these factors determine that she maintain her integrity as devotee first; as daughter, wife, and mother second. The Sun God blesses her for this determination to put his worship before all other ties, to put devotional love, or *bhakti*, before family love. But the blessings she receives are in the form of family. While the natal kin the Sun God provides may be illusory and temporary, the husband and child seem real enough. Perhaps the implicit happy end-ing to the jungli rani's tale gives expression to women's visions of themselves as persons empowered by divine beneficence as well as maintaining familial bonds—stretched, but not split, by dualistic characterizations of female nature.

NOTES

Susan Wadley's invitation to participate in a panel on women's oral traditions at the 1987 annual meeting of the Association for Asian Studies gave me the impetus to write this essay, whose seeds had long lain dormant. She has also helped me directly with her informal comments and indirectly with her many published insights into the relationship between women's lore and women's lives in India. My most enormous debt is to Shobhag Kanvar Cauhan (Bhabhasa) of Ghatiyali, who told me the jungli rani's story and whose unwavering self-esteem and independent actions gave me cause to ponder the social relevance of folk heroines. Another version of this essay recently appeared in *Listen to the Heron's Words: Reimagining Gender and Kinship in North India,* ed. Gloria Goodwin Raheja and Ann Grodzins Gold. (Berkeley: University of California Press, 1994).

1. For other discussions and examples of religious and social content in South Asian women's lore, see Margaret Trawick Egnor, "Internal Iconicity in Paraiyar Crying Songs," in *Another Harmony: Essays on the Folklore of India,* ed. Stuart Blackburn and A. K. Ramanujan (Berkeley: University of California Press, 1986), pp. 294–344; idem, "Spirits and Voices in Tamil Songs," *American Ethnologist* 15 (1988): 193–213. See also Susan Snow Wadley, *Shakti: Power in the Conceptual Structure of Karimpur Religion,* Dept. of Anthropology Series in Social, Cultural and Linguistic Anthropology, no. 2 (Chicago: University of Chicago Press, 1975); idem, "Texts in Contexts: Oral Traditions and the Study of Religion in Karimpur," in *American Studies in the Anthropology of India,* ed. Sylvia Vatuk (New Delhi: Manohar Books, 1978), pp. 309–41; idem, *Struggling with Destiny in Karimpur* (Berkeley: University of California Press, 1994).

2. All the materials I consider here and elsewhere were recorded in the village of Ghatiyali between 1978 and 1981 by me and my colleague, folklorist Joseph Miller, whom I thank for generous access to his extensive collections. My own sojourn in this large Rajasthani village extended from September 1979 through March 1981, with brief revisits in 1987 and 1991. For various aspects of women's traditions there, see Ann Grodzins Gold, *Village Families in Story and Song: An Approach Through Women's Oral Tradition in Rajasthan,* Indiakit Series, Outreach Educational Project, South Asia Language and Area Center (Chicago: University of Chicago, 1982); idem, *Fruitful Journeys: The Ways of Rajasthani Pilgrims* (Berkeley: University of California Press, 1988); idem, "Mother Ten's Stories," in *Religions of India in Practice,* ed. Donald S. Lopez, Jr. (Princeton, N. J.: Princeton University Press, forthcoming); and Gloria Goodwin Raheja and Ann Grodzins Gold, *Listen to the Heron's Words: Reimagining Gender and Kinship in*

North India (Berkeley: University of California Press, 1994).

3. See Ann Grodzins Gold, "Sexuality Fertility and Erotic Imagination in Rajasthani Women's Songs," in *Listen to the Heron's Words: Reimagining Gender and Kinship in North India*, pp. 30–72.

4. A few key examples of the split-image approach I have synthesized here are found in Lynn Bennett, *Dangerous Wives and Sacred Sisters: Social and Symbolic Roles of High-Caste Women in Nepal* (New York: Columbia University Press, 1983); Paul Hershman, "Virgin and Mother," in *Symbols and Sentiments: Cross-cultural Studies in Symbolism*, ed. I. M. Lewis (London: Academic Press, 1977) pp. 269–92; Sudhir Kakar, *The Inner World: A Psycho-Analytic Study of Childhood and Society in India* (Delhi: Oxford University Press, 1978); Wendy Doniger O'Flaherty, *Women, Androgynes, and Other Mythical Beasts* (Chicago: University of Chicago Press, 1980); Ved Prakash Vatuk and Sylvia Vatuk, "The Lustful Stepmother in the Folklore of Northwestern India," in *Studies in Indian Folk Traditions*, ed. Ved Prakash Vatuk (New Delhi: Manohar, 1979), pp. 190–221; and Susan Snow Wadley, "Women and the Hindu Tradition," in *Women in India: Two Perspectives*, ed. Susan S. Wadley and Doranne Jacobson (New Delhi: Manohar Books, 1977), pp. 111–36.

5. For the notorious, most frequently quoted passage from Hindu classical texts describing the necessity of, and prescribing precise modes for, the subordination of women, see Georg Bühler, trans., *The Laws of Manu*, Sacred Books of the East, vol. 25 (Delhi: Motilal Banrasidass, 1964), pp. 195–97.

6. See Raj Bali Pandey, *Hindu Saṃskāras* (Delhi: Motilal Banarsidass, 1976), pp. 158–64 for the six kinds of marriage, three approved and three disapproved. Gandharva marriage is described as a form where it was "not the parents of the girl who settled the marriage, but the bride and the bridegroom arranged it among themselves out of sensual inclination" (p. 162). Some modern Indians claim this form as an ancient precursor to the now fashionable, if still disapproved, "love marriage."

7. See chapter 6, this volume; see also Ronald Inden and Ralph Nicholas, *Kinship in Bengali Culture* (Chicago: University of Chicago Press, 1977).

8. Although it is not made explicit, the jungli rani's marriage is probably intercaste: she is a Brahman and the king would be a Rajput. As such it would be doubly disapproved—marriage "against the hair"—because she belongs to a higher *varṇa* than the king.

9. Sūrya Rāj is also worshiped, and a different story of his told, on Makar Sankranti, the day celebrating the winter solstice (for that story see Gold, *Village Families*, pp. 58–61). His vow, or *vrat*, may be performed by devotees on any Sunday, but the published story (*vrat kathā*) that accompanies that undertaking is not the jungli rani's. In a Marwari manual of "the festivals of twelve months," a very truncated fragment entitled "Story of the Sun God's bread" (*Suraj roṭ kī kahāṇī*) is included as part of a Sunday vow falling within the major festival of Gangaur (see Campadevi Rajgarhiya, *Bārah mahīno kā tyauhār* [Calcutta: Hari Arts Press, n.d.], pp. 174–75).

10. It is the prescribed occasion for the worship and story of Brother's Second and for the first of the ten-day series of Dasā Mātā's worship, as well as an auspicious time for various life-cycle rituals. For the story of Brother's Second, see A. K. Ramanujan, *Folktales from India* (New York: Pantheon Books, 1991),

pp. 62–69; for the worship of Dasā Mātā—a form of Lakṣmī—see Gold, "Mother Ten's Stories." In the household where I was living, on this particular second day of Holi, a *ḍhūṇḍanā*, or protective ritual for a first son, was also performed and celebrated.

11 This mad cry is not readily translatable. Its rhythmic nonsensicality indicates that the mother has become irrationally upset about her broken bread.

12. Pipal trees are proverbially famous for offering shelter to small animals in danger; they are also personified at times as female, and their weddings may be performed by those inclined to religious actions (see Gold, *Fruitful Journeys*, pp. 248–50).

13. Gold, "Mother Ten's Stories."

14. Ramanujan, *Folktales*, pp. 62–69.

15. Gold, "Mother Ten's Stories."

16. Gold, *Village Families*, pp. 15–23.

17. Ann Grodzins Gold, *A Carnival of Parting: The Tales of King Gopi Chand and King Bharthari as Sung and Told by Madhu Natisar Nath of Ghatiyali, Rajasthan, India* (Berkeley: University of California Press, 1992), pp. 219–64. For a more extensive discussion of women in the Gopī Cand epic, see Ann Grodzins Gold, "Gender and Illusion in a Rajasthani Yogic Tradition," in *Gender, Genre, and Power in South Asian Expressive Traditions*, ed. Arjun Appadurai, Frank Korom, and Margaret Mills (Philadelphia: University of Pennsylvania Press, 1991), pp. 102–35.

18. On Brother's Second, it is said, the brother is the deity.

6

The Effectiveness of the Hindu Sacrament *(Saṃskāra)*: Caste, Marriage, and Divorce in Bengali Culture

RALPH W. NICHOLAS

In *Kinship in Bengali Culture* Ronald Inden and I analyzed the symbolic constitution and meaning of kinship in Bengal at a level of generality that we think is shared by most Bengali Hindus.[1] Our most significant discoveries concern how relatives are categorized, the love relationships among them, and the existence of alternative dominant and subordinate patterns of classifying kin together with corresponding alternatives for the proper display of love. The general importance of this portion of the analysis lies in our demonstration that, rather than separating relatives into two opposed categories, as consanguines and affines, the Bengali system classifies them into two overlapping categories. Although these are matters of intense interest to students of kinship, they are not important to most people, and they are not the subjects of this essay.

Marriage seems to be more intrinsically interesting than the classification of kin, and it seems to be a universal practice. In *Kinship in Bengali Culture* our analysis of Hindu marriage, both as a rite and as a relationship, focused on the forms of solidarity it creates and sustains among people as kin. We did not deal with failures of solidarity, which led some readers to think we idealize Hindu marriage, or are biased toward a Brahmanic view of Bengali culture at the expense of a putative lower-caste culture. In this paper, therefore, I consider some facts about divorce as I encountered them in fieldwork in rural Bengal to see if these alter our analysis of marriage in some way. Since divorce is very differently distributed among castes, I also discuss how Bengali Hindus think about differences among castes. Much of the Bengali theory about castes, their various capacities, and their distinguishing characteristics is contained in a version of the myth of the wicked King Veṇa and his virtuous son Pṛthu. I discuss the Bengali variant of this myth, which relates the origin of the Bengali castes and of their qualities. Before doing so, however, I review briefly the conception of the *saṃskāra* rites, and particularly the *saṃskāra* of marriage in Bengali culture. Although we have discussed these rites at some length, we did not say much about variety in the practice of the *saṃskāras* among Bengali Hindus, simply noting that "in our view, one of the most important sources of variation [in the practice of these rites] has been caste, with the *saṃskāras* of higher-caste people being more elaborate and regarded as more efficacious than those of lower-caste people."[2]

The Saṃskāra *Rites*

Although we followed the general practice in anthropology since the publication of van Gennep's *Rites of Passage* in referring to the *saṃskāras* as "life-cycle rites," in fact the implications of the term *saṃskāra* are somewhat different:

> The word *saṃskāra* means to "complete," "prepare," "make over," "fully form," and above all, to "purify" (*śuddhi*). Every *saṃskāra* is regarded as a transformative action that "refines" and "purifies" the living body, initiating it into new statuses and relationships by giving it a new birth. A *saṃskāra* removes "defects" (*doṣa*) from the body, such as those inherited "from the seed" (*baijika*) and "from the womb" (*gārbhika*), and infuses "qualities" (*guṇa*) into it. These goals are accomplished by immersion, aspersion, or sprinkling, by touching various parts of the body, by donning new clothes, by anointing and feeding with special substances, and by the recitation of special words into the ear. Each *saṃskāra* in the sequence prepares the person for the next; all of them cumulatively prepare him for the penultimate goal of attaining "heaven" (*svarga*), "rebirth" (*punar-janma*) in a higher caste, or becoming a proper "ancestor" (*pitṛ*), *in preparation for the ultimate goalof "release" (mukti, mokṣa)* from the cycle of birth and "life in the world" (*saṃsāra*) by the separation of the person's *ātman* from his body and its union with *brahman*.[3]

Bengalis conventionally say that there are ten of these rites (*daśa-saṃskāra*) and that they are to be performed upon a person in a fixed sequence at particular times of life. Observation and analysis reveal that each of the *saṃskāras* initiates a person into a new status and a new set of relationships by means of the symbols of rebirth. At the same time, observation also reveals that very few persons receive ten *saṃskāras*: women and Śūdras—that is to say, the great majority of Bengali Hindus—are considered ineligible for some of these rites, and most Brahman males do not receive a complete sequence. Moreover, certain rites are often done together rather than at discrete stages of life. For example, the famous *upanayana*, or "initiation into Vedic learning," in which Brahman boys are said to become "twice born" (*dvija*) and in which they are first invested with the sacrificial thread, is often done in a severely truncated form as a preliminary rite just before the marriage. Facts such as these may make it appear that we rested entirely too much weight on the rich symbolism of the *saṃskāras* at the expense of contemporary reality. Bengalis who are much better aware of the facts about their contemporary practices than I am have not, however, quit talking about the ten life-cycle rites as if they were matters of some importance. And at least one of them—marriage—remains very nearly universal.

Various explanations are offered for failure to observe rites that are considered important. Poor people blame poverty, and there is no doubt that paying for food and shelter often takes precedence over ceremonial expenses—often, but not always. Western-style education is sometimes blamed for creating an outlook on life that disvalues ritual. But some of the most elaborate ritual observances of all kinds, including the *saṃskāras*, take place in households of very well-educated people. Perhaps the most generally invoked of all explanations for inobservance is a rather vague statement about the condition of the "contemporary age" (*vartamāna kāla*). On first inspection this looks like a Bengali version of what might be called "explanation by modernization": as a society becomes more "modern," people become more enlightened and rational; ceremonies seem increasingly mystical and the importance given to the supernatural declines. The image of "modern society" held by most Bengalis—particularly in rural areas—is, however, quite different from this: the modern age is the Kali *yuga*, in which morality declines and disorder increases, in which the qualities of persons that are sought to be refined and purified in the *saṃskāras* are inferior. There is, in this explanation, a reference to a distinctively Hindu conception of cyclic time, to which I shall return. However, insofar as it implies the existence of a golden age in the past, this form of explanation is familiar from other cultures. And, in this respect, Bengalis show themselves to be no better historians than most of the anthropologists of modernization.

Since practically nothing is known about the rates of performance of the various *saṃskāra*s today, much less in the past, it does little good to speculate about a decline (or an increase) in them. And since little is known about the popular, nontextual customs associated with—or standing in place of—the *saṃskāra*s as they were formerly practiced, there is little ground for saying that the forms of the contemporary rites have been degraded or corrupted. The only datum available is the widespread perception that the life-cycle rites are not sufficiently and/or properly performed in the contemporary period. This is significant because it means that the *saṃskāra*s are not disvalued or considered a quaint archaism; if this were so they would likely be ignored or discussed merely for their curiosity. An additional piece of information is afforded in the very nearly universal unwillingness of Bengalis to neglect the *saṃskāra* of marriage, which gives it a place of particular importance in the cycle.

Marriage

Marriage (*vivāha*) is the final *saṃskāra* of a living body; it effects profound transformations of persons by permanently joining together into a single body what were previously two separate bodies. Marriage is said to complete the body of a male and thereby to lift him into the status (*āśrama*) of householder (*gṛhastha*). A man without a wife is not considered capable of making offerings to the gods, so little good can come of his life. The transformation for a woman is even more profound: she is made over from a person of her father's family and clan into a person of her husband's family and clan, and she is thought to become the "half body" of her husband. Such a change requires the transformation of the substances of her body, so that when the marriage is completed—and some say that this is not until the birth of her first son—she is fully a person of her husband's clan and family, a closer bodily relative to them than to her own father, mother, brothers, and so forth. At the most generally shared level of Bengali Hindu culture, the marital transformation is considered irreversible. However, it is also asymmetrical: a woman cannot be made into the half body of a man for a second time, while a man may take additional wives.

Such far-reaching transformations in persons—altering their natural and moral qualities, their qualifications for action, and their standing in society—are not easily made. The marriage rites that Inden and I describe (pp. 39–51) extend over a minimum of five days, most of which are filled with intensive ritual work. The external and internal bodily parts of the bride and groom, and the gross and subtle substances of which they are made, are operated on with a kind of energetic activity that is difficult for persons from Christian cultures to imagine. They are purified and protected by bathing and anointment, sprinkled with powerful fluids, and made to fast so that their bodies will be more susceptible to auspicious influences. The father or other male master of the bride (*kanyā*) should make a selfless "gift of the bride" (*kanyā dān*) to the groom with no expectation of return. The groom accepts this "complete gift" (*sampradāna*) by taking the bride's hand, and their garments are tied together, all under the influence of powerful Vedic *mantras*. The rites of the first day are repeated in synoptic form on the second day so as to ensure that nothing went amiss. The principal rites of the second and subsequent days, done in the groom's house, are longer than those of the first day and heighten the intensity of the ceremony, concentrating even more heavily on forming a perfect bodily union between the bride and groom. I shall not say any more about the ritual details here since we have given an account of them in *Kinship in Bengali* Culture*. I merely want to emphasize that the Hindu marriage in Bengal involves a great deal of demanding ritual work and engages a great deal of power in order to bring about the indissoluble unity of husband and wife.

The nature of Hindu marriage and the assumptions on which it is based would appear to make divorce impossible if not altogether unthinkable. And yet, in my own fieldwork in rural Bengal, I have encountered divorces and other irregularities in marital unions that would seem to be culturally precluded. Such empirical facts appear to vitiate our analysis and to open us to charges of idealism.

A cultural or symbolic analysis of the content of kinship cannot explain a rate of divorce or a percentage or frequency of anything else. In *Kinship in Bengali Culture* we attempted to discover the assumptions on which relationships among "one's own people" (*ātmīya-svajana*) are based. On these assumptions is elaborated a consistent and intelligible conceptual universe—a "folk theory" of kinship, if you wish—that we refer to as "the domain of kinship in Bengali culture." The symbols of which this domain is constituted are symbols of solidarity—various complementary forms of love, notions about binding together, and a natural pull or attraction that persons who share the same body feel toward one another. In Bengali culture a phenomenon like divorce cannot be explained by a theory about solidarity, although such a theory may do so elsewhere.

Divorce is a regularly constituted procedure in Bengali Muslim culture, where it is based on Islamic law and on the premise that marriage is a legal or moral relationship. But the Hindu conception of marriage is different; the marriage rites create a moral relationship between bride and groom, but they also equally create a natural relationship in which the bride shares asymmetrically in the physical body of her husband and in which the two of them together are seen as making up a single body. There is no ritual procedure for reversing a transformation brought about by a *saṃskāra*, and the Hindu "code books" (*dharmaśāstra*), extraordinarily detailed on the subject of marriage, are silent on divorce. Divorces are rare among the highest castes of Bengal, and, until the recent rise of civil marriage ceremonies, divorce was almost unknown in the Calcutta middle class, except as a foreign social problem. Divorce seems to many people to be simply impossible for Hindus and to be symptomatic of the poor moral condition of a country where it is commonly practiced.

The Bengali conception of the moral condition of a country is premised on cosmological ideas about time, order, and entropy. Time (*kāla*) is an ever-present dimension of existence; this time is not simply duration but an active, destructive element that increases its activity and decreases order as the universe becomes older. The time in which the universe exists is a single unit of "four ages" (*caturyuga*). Astrologers have calculated the length of this unit as 4,320,000 solar years. Time is the force of entropy, registered in and characterized by the continuous weakening of *dharma* through the ages. *Dharma* is the universal code for conduct that both supports (*dhāraṇa*) everything and is supported by all actions that are right and orderly. In some texts *dharma* is visualized as a bull. In the first of the four ages, the Kṛta ("four-spot"on a die) or Satya ("good") *yuga, dharma* is said to have stood firmly on four legs. When it was deprived of one leg, the Treta ("three-spot") age began; it was only three-fourths the length of the Kṛta age. In the succeeding Dvāpara ("two-spot") age, *dharma* stood on two legs, and the age was two-thirds the duration of its predecessor. On a full-moon day in the month of Māgha (equivalent to February 18, 3102 B.C.E., according to astrological calculation), *dharma* was deprived of yet another leg and the present Kali ("one-spot") *yuga* began; it will endure only half as long as the Dvāpara age. When *dharma* can no longer stand at all, there will be complete disorder, entropy will prevail, and there will be a total dissolution (*pralaya*) of the universe, initiating another cycle of existence in another Kṛta age.

People in rural Bengal frequently refer to the degraded condition of the Kali age in discussing the bad moral condition of their country and themselves. There are numerous folk sayings that characterize the weakened *dharma* of this age and the disorder that prevails everywhere. The Purāṇas contain extensive descriptions of the qualities of the ages, with particular attention to the miserable character of the present one. The *Matsya Purāṇa*, in a passage dated by Hazra[4] to the sixth or seventh century A.D., describes it thus:

> During the Kali age, people indulge in Hiṃsā, theft, falsehood, deceit, vanity, etc., and delusion, hypocrisy and vanity overshadow the people. And Dharma becomes very weak in the Kali age, and people commit sin in mind, speech, and actions. And works done with the whole heart and body sometimes become accomplished and sometimes not.[5]

The account goes on at great length, but I pause after the sentence last quoted because in it what might appear to be "a Hindu theory of divorce" is implicitly enunciated. "Works done with the whole heart and body sometimes become accomplished and sometimes not" might be understood as saying that in the Kali age you can boil a pot of rice and it may cook properly, but then again, it may not. A work done with the whole heart and body is, of course, something done with a more profound intention than cooking rice: the works referred to here are such things as worshiping the gods and performing the *saṃskāras*. In the Kali age a ritual may be done with the best of intentions and with all the proper form yet fail to achieve its intended results. This is precisely what is thought to be the case with Hindu marriages that end in divorce in rural Bengal—the rites failed to accomplish the results that were intended, the bride was not effectively united with her husband and transformed into a person of his family and clan, as evidenced in the disunity that led to their separation. Although the language they use to speak about divorce—*biye-kāṭā* or *vivāha-viccheda*—suggests "cutting the marriage," or "putting it asunder," what is done more nearly resembles annulment than divorce. It is not the termination of a marriage, in fact, but a public statement that it never happened in the first place.

In the disorder of the Kali *yuga*, any cause-and-effect relationship might become disconnected, so, although general blame for the failure of human action is often laid upon the age, explanation for the success of some marriages and not others cannot be found there. In particular, the Kali age cannot explain why the marriages of the highest castes are so regularly accomplished while those of lower castes are not.

The most complete marriages reiterate, over a period of several days and in a large variety of ritual words and gestures, the union of bride and groom, so that sheer redundancy may guarantee against ineffective ritual work. If the elaborateness and duration of the rites are important determinants of the success of a marriage, then it is surprising that at least a few upper-caste unions do not fail. The entire ritual extending over five or more days is not often carried out for persons of any caste. It is true that the most complete form of the marriage is rarely done by persons of any but the highest castes and that there is a rough relationship between lower-caste standing and the extent to which ceremonies are abbreviated. But there are more than enough instances of severely shortened marriage rites among the highest castes to expect some instances of divorce if ritual insufficiency is responsible.

The form of marriage involving the unreciprocated *kanyā dān*, in which the bride, ornamented with golden jewelry and accompanied by costly gifts, is freely given by her father to the groom, is generally agreed to be the best. The opposite form, involving *kanyā-paṇa* (bride-price), in which the bride is given in exchange for money, is generally condemned and is referred to in the *dharmaśāstra*s as the āsura, or "antigods," rite. In rural Bengal, until the middle of the present century, the practice of giving bride-price was generally followed only among the lower castes, while among the higher castes the practice of giving a dowry (*yautuka,* or *vara-paṇa,* "groom-price") was—and is—nearly universal. Some changes in these practices have taken place in recent years: almost all the marriages that I studied, among castes above the lowest category, were done with at least the form of the unreciprocated gift of the bride accompanied by a dowry. Some well-educated families of the highest castes have discontinued offering very lavish dowries (usually on grounds that it is undignified to "purchase a good bridegroom" for a daughter whose qualities merit such a husband in their own right). Even these changes, however, have not secured lower-caste marriage against breakup, nor have they undermined the stability of the higher-caste marriages. The unreciprocated gift of the bride does not guarantee the success of marriage among lower castes, and marriage done without the gift of a large dowry does not cause the failure of marriages among the higher castes. Moreover, marriages among the lower castes, where bride-price (which is given credit, in much utilitarian anthropological literature, for securing marital stability) is still usually paid, end in divorce more commonly than those of any other castes.

Most people of all castes give their children the best marriages possible within the limits of their capacities (*yathā-śakti*). There appear to be some intrinsic differences in the capacities of persons of different castes to effect permanent marital unions. To understand what these differences of capacity are thought to be and how they came about, I have examined a Bengali myth relating the origin of the castes.

The Myth of Veṇa and Pṛthu

The *Bṛhaddharma Purāṇa,* although not among the most eminent texts of its class, is an important document in the cultural history of Bengal.[6] It was composed in Bengal, probably in the late thirteenth or early fourteenth century.[7] At this time Bengal had come under Muslim overlordship and, although there were many small Hindu kingdoms throughout the region, there was no central Hindu kingdom to encompass them. The shape of Hindu society was profoundly affected by this change, and the *Bṛhaddharma Purāṇa* seems to register this new configuration in a reworking of an ancient narrative about a good and a bad king. This myth observes the convention, still current in Hindu Bengal, of designating all the castes apart from the Brahmans as the "thirty-six castes," and it explains their origin in a way that sheds light on the differential effectiveness of the *saṃskāra*s and on a good deal more as well.[8] There follows a summary of the myth.

The Episode of Veṇa

Even as a child, Veṇa, son of King Aṅga, was fond of cruel sports. The king was so distressed at reports of his son's evil conduct that he abandoned his kingdom to dwell in the forest. Without a king, anarchy prevailed, and at last some Brahman sages (*muni*) were obliged to make Veṇa king in hopes of restoring order. Veṇa's first royal action was a total prohibition of the practice of *varṇāśramadharma*, including marriages between persons of the same *varṇa*. The sages approached Veṇa with a warning about the evils that would befall his kingdom if he encouraged the spread of anti-*dharma*, but he would not accept their advice. He forced Brahmans to cohabit with Kṣatriya, Vaiśya, and Śūdra women; Kṣatriyas with Vaiśya and Śūdra women; and Vaiśyas with Śūdra women.[9] He also compelled Kṣatriyas, Vaiśyas, and Śūdras to cohabit with Brahman women, and Vaiśyas and Śūdras with Kṣatriya women.[10] He forced men sprung from the first set of mixed unions to cohabit with Vaiśya and Śūdra women, producing still further mixed offspring. Then he compelled men born of these further mixed unions to cohabit with women of the first mixed group, as well as with Vaiśya and Śūdra women.

[The mixed castes created by Veṇa are listed in table 6.1.]

These were declared to be the thirty-six castes with a few more.[11] The first twenty had Śrotriya (Vedic) Brahmans as their priests, while the lowborn castes were declared to be outside of *varṇāśramadharma*. The mixed castes originating from the four original *varṇa*s were classed as high mixed castes; those created by men of the high mixed castes on women of other castes were classed as medial mixed castes; those created by men of medial mixed castes on women of other castes were classed as inferior mixed castes.[12]

The Devala (Image-worshiper) who came from Śākadvīpa became famous as the Śākadvīpī Brahman, from whose union with a Vaiśya woman were born the Gaṇaka (Astrologer) and Vādaka (Instrumental Musician). From Veṇa's own body was born the son Mleccha (Non-Hindu), who in turn begot various Mleccha tribes, including the Muslims. When they saw the ruinous conduct of the Mlecchas, the outraged Brahman sages killed Veṇa by shouting *mantra*s at him. They rubbed together the hands of the dead Veṇa and produced from them the son Pṛthu together with his wife.

Table 6.1

Name	*Bengali Name*	*Product of*
High Mixed Castes (uttama saḳara jātī)[a]		
Karaṇa	Kāyastha	V + s
Ambaṣṭha	Vaidya	B + v
Gāndhikavaṇik	Gandhavaṇik	B + v
Kaṃsakāra	Kaṃsakār	B + v
Śaṅkhakāra	Śaṅkhakār	B + v
Ugra	Āguri	K + v[b]
Rājputra	Rājpūt	K + v
Kumbhakāra	Kumbhakār	B + k
Tantuvāya	Tantuvāy	B + k
Karmakāra	Karmakār	S[c] + k[d]
Dāsa	—	S[c] + k[d]
Māgadha	—	V + k
Gopa	Gop	V + k
Nāpita	Nāpit	K + s
Modaka	Modak	K + s
Vārajīvī	Vārajīvī	B + s
Sūta	Sūtradhar	K + b
Mālākāra	Mālākār	K + b
Tāmbūlī	Tāmbūlī	V + b[e]
Taulika[f]	Tilī	V + b[e]
Medial Mixed Castes (madhyama saṃkara jātī)		
Takṣā	—	Karaṇa (V+s) + v
Rajaka	Rajak	Karaṇa (V+s) + v
Svarṇakāra	Svarṇakār	Ambaṣṭha (B+v) + v
Svarṇavaṇik	Suvarṇavaṇik	Ambaṣṭha (B+v) + v
Ābhīra	Goālā	Gopa (V+k) + v
Tailakāra	Teli	Gopa (V+k) + v
Dhīvara	Dhīvar	Gopa (V+k) + s
Śauṇḍika	Śuṇḍī	Gopa (V+k) + s
Naṭa	—	Mālākāra (K+b) + s
Śāvaka	—	Mālākāra (K+b) + s
Śekhara	—	Māgadha (V+k) + s
Jālika	Jālī	Māgadha (V+k) + s
Low-born (antyaja) *or Inferior Mixed Castes* (adhama saṃkara jātī)		
Gṛhi (Grahi)	—	Svarṇakāra ([B+v]+v) + Vaidya (B+v)
Kuḍava	—	Svarṇavaṇik ([B+v]+v) + Vaidya (B+v)
Cāṇḍāla	Cāṇḍāl	S + b[g]

Name	*Bengali Name*	*Product of*
Varuḍa	—	Ābhīra ([V+k]+v) + Gopa (V+k)
Carmakāra	Muci	Takṣa ([V+s]+v) + v
Ghaṭṭajīvī	Pāṭanī ?	Rajaka ([V+s]+v) + v
Dolāvāhī	Dule	Tailakāra ([V+k]+v) + v
Malla	Mālo ?	Dhīvara ([V+k]+s) + s

B = Brahman, K = Kṣatriya, V = Vaiśya, S = Śūdra. Uppercase letters/left-hand elements = males; lowercase letters/right-hand elements = females; + = union.

[a]The order and orthography provided by Hazra, *Studies in the Upapurāṇas*, pp. 437–39, are followed here. I have supplied a currently used Bengali name for each caste that is identifiable with one of those listed in the text. See Majumdar, *History of Bengal*, pp. 567–70, and Raya, *Bāṃalī hindur varṇa-bheda*, pp. 89–94.

[b]Banerji, *Bṛhad-dharma Purāṇa*, p. 207, says Śūdra.

[c]Banerji says Brahman.

[d]Banerji says Śūdra.

[e]Banerji, *The Bṛhad-dharma Purāṇa*, p. 208, says Śūdra, which is in agreement with the Vaṇgavāsī ed. and a manuscript source cited by (Hazra, *Studies in the Upapurāṇas*, p. 437n).

[f]Or Tailika according to some sources.

[g]See endnote 11.

The Episode of Pṛthu

The sages made Pṛthu king, and he ruled with ability, but he could not find peace of mind and his subjects began to suffer from lack of food. He called the Brahmans to his court and consulted them about the source of the distress in his kingdom. They told him that the country was suffering because of the mixed castes, who were born of anti-*dharma* (*adharma-saṃbhava*) at his father's command, and who were making still further mixed unions. Pṛthu said that he could not bear to kill these poor wretches, although they were a permanent threat to the well-being of his country; he asked the Brahmans what he should do. They advised him to put a stop to any further mixed unions and to divide those already created into distinct castes with fixed occupations, chastising the defiant ones.

Accordingly, Pṛthu summoned the mixed castes before him and asked them why they were so deformed and ill dressed. They replied to the king that they were strong and handsome, with fair complexions and well-formed bodies, and dressed in fine clothing. They accused him of having lost his vision and told him that, since they had been created and cared for by Veṇa, they should be respected like him; they were in no way inferior to Brahmā, Viṣṇu, and the other gods. The Brahmans merely laughed at the vain words of the mixed castes, but Pṛthu was angry and ordered them bound hand and foot. They immediately revealed that they were cowards by crying aloud for mercy and promising complete obedience to the king. Then he requested the Brahmans to determine their castes (*varṇa*) and occupations (*vṛtti*).

The Brahmans declared the thirty-six castes (*ṣaṭtriṃsa jāti*) to have been born as Śūdras and asked them what occupations they wished to follow in accordance with their own intrinsic capacities (*svaśakti*), telling them that they would be named by their occupations. The Karaṇas came forward first and said to the Brahmans: "We are ignorant, devoid of caste (*jāti-hīna*), and especially devoid of wisdom. You are all-knowing; make us what we should be." The Brahmans found them to be of humble conduct and knowledgeable in statecraft, so they classed them as good Śūdras (*sat-śūdra*), advised them to avoid enviousness (*mātsarya*), and to pursue the work of the state and of scribes.

The Ambaṣṭhas got their name because they had created mixed castes (Svarṇakāra and Svarṇavaṇika) upon (*stha*) women of the same caste as their mothers (*ambā*), for which they were condemned as great sinners.[13] In order to purify them of this sin, they were given the *saṃskāra* of second birth (*vipra-janma*, "Brahman birth"), thus making them almost like Brahmans. The Brahmans told the Ambaṣṭhas they would be Vaidyas (physicians), and while they should follow the Śūdra code for conduct (*dharma*), they should also follow the Vaiśya occupation (*vṛtti*) of making and distributing medicine, and they should study the *Āyurveda* (Veda of long life) but not other Sanskrit texts.

The Brahmans asked the Ugras (whose name means "violent" or "cruel"), who were physically strong (*balavat*) and brave, to follow the occupation of Kṣatriyas in warfare. The Māgadhas, who were unwilling to fight because of the necessity of killing (*hiṃsā*), were asked to be bards (*vandī*) to Brahmans and Kṣatriyas, to carry messages, and to study the Kṣatraveda (Sanskrit works on warfare). The other castes were given the following occupations:

Tantuvāya—making cloth
Vaṇik [= Gāndhikavaṇik]—selling scents
Nāpita—shaving and dressing of hair
Gopa—writing
Karmakāra—working with iron
Taulika—selling areca nuts
Tāmbūlī—selling betel leaves
Kumbhakāra—making earthenware
Kaṃsakāra—working with copper, brass, etc.

Śaṇkhika [= Śaṇkhakāra]—making conch-shell ornaments
Dāsa—agriculture
Sūta—helping Dāsas in agriculture
Modaka—making sweets with molasses
Mālākāra—supplying flowers for the worship of deities
Svarṇakāra—making gold and silver ornaments
Kānakavaṇik [= Svarṇavaṇik]—testing the purity of gold and silver

The Brahmans gave the Sanskrit texts on astronomy and astrology to the Gaṇakas and made them the "Brahmans of the heavenly bodies" (*graha-vipra*). The mixed castes asked the Brahmans for priests to perform their rites. The Brahmans declared that they, the Śrotriya Brahmans, were the priests of the first twenty castes. The priests of the second twelve castes were "fallen" (*patita*) Brahmans, who would be equal to those castes and known as the "friends of Brahmans" (*brahma-bandhu*). Thus Pṛthu put an end to the further mixing of castes, and the world obtained propriety and well-being.

Analysis

Even excluding numerous other features that identify the *Bṛhaddharma Purāṇa* as a Bengali work, this discussion of the castes leaves no doubt that it is speaking about Bengal. Six centuries later most of the caste names still appear in Bengal—and not elsewhere in India—little modified from those given in the text. The places of the Karaṇas (Kāyasthas) and Ambaṣṭhas (Vaidyas) above the other Śūdras are quite evident in contemporary Bengali society. And the high-ranking Brahmans' provision of priests for the high Śūdras, while "fallen" Brahmans provide them for others, is a characteristic pattern today. However, there are respects in which this myth is an all-India one, such as the relationship between kings and Brahmans it illustrates.

The kings employ the distinctive royal power of coercive force (*daṇḍa*). The evil Veṇa uses it to compel the unions of persons of different castes, and the good Pṛthu uses it to chasten the mixed castes and make them obedient to his commands. The Brahman sages possess a power that is different from and superior to the coercive force of the king, and this power is demonstrated in four different forms: (1) the Brahmans control the words and other actions necessary to make or install a king; (2) their words have the power to kill a king; (3) they have the power to produce a king (from the body of a king, not from their own bodies); and (4) they possess the mental power of wisdom, discernment, or discrimination. Even the evil Veṇa does not attempt to use coercive force on the Brahman sages, and the good Pṛthu calls on them in situations requiring wisdom or discernment. The mixed castes show themselves to have neither coercive force nor wisdom, thus establishing a tripartite distinction among the king, the Brahmans, and the mixed castes.

The mixed castes are classified twice in the myth, once in each episode. In the episode of Veṇa, the principle on which they are classified is that the quality of the less-mixed castes is superior to the quality of those that are more mixed. Thus, the high mixed castes are produced from a single mixture, the medial ones from a double mixture, and the inferior ones from quadruple and further mixtures. This is an example of what Tambiah describes as a "key" classification, in which the categories are produced by the overlap of classes.[14] However, unlike the examples Tambiah discusses, which are drawn from the early *dharmaśāstras*, this is a very gross key in which only the number of overlapping classes and not the ranked standings of those classes nor the propriety of the unions (*anuloma* versus *pratiloma*) represented by their overlaps is made to count. Even unions between males of one *varṇa* and females of another (e.g., Brahman men and Vaiśya women) do not always produce the same mixed caste, although a thoroughgoing key classification would seem to call for consistency in this respect. Thus, unlike the caste hierarchy described in the *Mānavadharmaśāstra*, the key classification employed in the episode of Veṇa is based only on the "principle of compounded degradation" and generates only three ranks. The fact that there are *anuloma* (hypergamous) as well as *pratiloma* (hypogamous) unions is mentioned, but no use is made of this distinction in classifying the castes.[15]

There is considerable redundancy between the first and second episodes of the myth. The occupational names given to the mixed castes by the Brahmans in the second episode have been previously announced in the first. The assignment of the Vedic Brahmans to be priests for the high mixed castes is made in both episodes. And the threefold distinction among the mixed castes, which is pronounced ex cathedra in the episode of Veṇa, is reestablished under Pṛthu. However, the distinctions that are made in the first episode are carried further and refined in the second, and there is a significant change in the principle on which the classification of castes is based.

In the episode of Pṛthu, the mixed castes of all categories reveal themselves—in their vainglorious boasting, deluded self-perception, and display of cowardice—to have something in common with one another. What they display overtly in their conduct is seen by the Brahmans to be an outward manifestation of their inborn Śūdra character. But, while they are all Śūdras, the very discerning Brahmans are also able to discover many further distinctions among them, based, it is said, on individual innate capacities (*svaśakti*). Not only are there caste differences between the products of different mixtures, but there are even different castes whose *varṇa* ancestries are identical.

The Karaṇas are identified by the humility of their conduct, their knowledge of statecraft, literacy, and, perhaps, a propensity to enviousness as well. The Ambaṣṭhas are identified in quite a different way: because of their sinful character, they are marked by a *saṃskāra* of rebirth and thus become somewhat like their twice-born Brahman fathers; at the same time, although they have the *dharma* of Śūdras, some characteristics of their Vaiśya mothers are also present in them. The Karaṇas and the Ambaṣṭhas are marked out in the myth in two ways: they stand at the top of the rosters of high mixed castes in both episodes of classification (which otherwise present different orders of castes), and there is a detailed discussion of the qualities only of these two castes. The modern representatives of these castes, the Kāyasthas and Vaidyas, stand at the top of the Śūdra category in Bengali society, in several respects much "closer" to Brahmans than to other Śūdras.

The next pair of castes picked out for special distinction in the myth, the Ugras and the Māgadhas, are identified by still different features. The Ugras, whose fathers were Kṣatriyas and whose name identifies them as "violent," are suited by their physical strength to that portion of the Ksatriya occupation involving warfare. The Māgadhas, by contrast, whose mothers were Kṣatriyas but who appear to have inherited a propensity to nonviolence from their Vaiśya fathers, are seen as qualified to be bards who sing the praises of Brahmans and Kṣatriyas, to serve as their messengers, and to engage in the literary study of warfare.

The Brahmans do not go into much detail concerning the distinctive qualities of the remaining high mixed castes, simply identifying the various occupations for which they are qualified. However, they perform two operations that are of interest. The list of high mixed castes given in the first episode is now rearranged so that, with the exception of the closely allied occupations of selling areca nuts and selling betel leaves, mixed castes of common ancestry are now no longer adjacent to one another. It is not said that this order represents any conception of ranked precedence, and I do not think that is what is intended. I think that the significance of the second order of presentation is to say that neither *varṇa* ancestry nor the hypergamous or hypogamous direction of the union that produced a particular caste determines its standing in relation to the others. It is their intrinsic qualities or capacities that are important in this respect. Second, in the episode of Pṛthu, two of the high mixed castes mentioned in the first list—Rājputra and Vārajīvī[16]—are passed over in silence, while two of the medial categories are taken up. Although the reason for the exclusion is unclear, the inclusion of two castes from the medial category sharply distinguishes them from the others of their category. These two—the Svarṇakāra, or Goldsmith, and the Svarṇavaṇik, or Gold-seller (here called Kānakavaṇik, which means the same thing, but which is given the occupation of assaying silver and gold)—were earlier identified as the products of the especially sinful connection of Ambaṣṭhas with women of their own mothers' *varṇa*.

It is not easy to understand why the Svarṇakāra and the Svarṇavaṇik should receive this "promotion" without examining the overall structure of castes created by the second classification. By declaring all of the mixed castes to be Śūdras, the Brahmans eliminated Kṙsatriyas and Vaiśyas from the society (and, with a few exceptions of recent origin, it is still a premise of their culture that all Bengalis are either Brahmans or Śūdras). However, the features that they found characteristic of Karaṇas and Ambaṣṭhas, and the occupations they assigned to them, are "Brahman-like." Similarly, the Ugras and the Māgadhas have some of the features of Kṣatriyas, and they are assigned fragments of the Kṣatriya occupation. In other words, it appears that the myth recreates a classical set of *varṇa*s in ranked order within the Śūdra category. Thus, the third class to be created would be the Vaiśya, a name that, in ancient India, denoted an "increaser" or "producer from the soil" but which by the thirteenth or fourteenth century in Bengal usually meant a person who brought about increase through trade—a merchant. Most of the high mixed castes remaining after the removal of the first four are groups that get their livelihoods either directly through trade or by selling the specialized products of their occupations. The absence from this list of the castes who make and sell things made of gold, and their presence in the medial category, are striking anomalies that are rectified in part by the designation of their occupations among the high mixed castes, although they are not moved into this category so far as I can tell.

Allowing that there was some ambiguity in the standing of the Svarṇakāra and the Svarṇavaṇik (an ambiguity that persists in contemporary Bengali society), the medial mixed castes appear within this reconstituted caste order as the "Śūdras of the Śūdras." They are the Takṣa (a kind of carpenter), Rajaka (Washerman), Ābhīra (Cowherd), Tailakāra (Oilpresser), Dhīvara (Fisherman), Śauṇḍika (Distiller), Naṭa (Actor), Śavaka (?), Śekhara (?), and Jālika ("Netter," another kind of fisherman). They receive priestly services from fallen Brahmans whose ranks are the same as theirs. The inferior mixed castes are left outside the four *varṇa*s in the reconstituted system.

The pattern of classification that is employed in the second episode of the myth is not the "key" system based on the overlapping of categories used in the first episode. Rather, the Brahmans identify groups of characteristics shared by the persons of a caste to define that caste. These characteristics seem to be quite heterogeneous—humility, specialized knowledge, receipt of a particular *saṃskāra* rite, bodily strength, and so on—and no single one serves alone to distinguish one caste from another or one caste from all others. This seems to be an ethnosociological example of what Needham had identified as "polythetic classification."[17] A polythetically defined class is one in which all members have a majority of stated characteristics in common. No single one of these characteristics is necessary or sufficient to define the class. Thus, some members of a polythetically defined class may lack some of the characteristics in the defining set, and some elements that are not members of the class may possess some of the defining characteristics, although not a majority of them.

The polythetic approach to classification is, in my experience, a much more common form of discourse about castes in Bengali society than is the approach through a key based on the systematic mixing of categories. When they want to explain why castes stand in a particular relationship to one another, Bengalis most often adduce an apparently heterogeneous list of characteristics for one caste to be compared with a different heterogeneous list relating to another caste. There are disagreements about the relative importance of various characteristics and about the valuation of them, which leads to ambiguity in rankings and to the existence of fairly large groups of castes of more or less equal rank. Putative origin from a mixing of *varṇa*s may be included in such a list, but it is only one characteristic and not an essential one. Victorian ethnographers collected many such lists, which explains the extraordinary length of many of the *Tribes and Castes of*. . . compilations. Later analysts experienced much frustration with these lists because it looked as if we were being asked to compare mangoes with lemons. It is not my purpose here to explore the consequences of a polythetic classification of the castes of Bengal, although such an exploration appears likely to open a new door to caste systems (or, rather, reopen an old one). The purpose of analyzing the myth of the origin of the Bengali castes is to understand why the *saṃskāra* rites—particularly marriage—are less effective for some castes than for others. What a grasp of the polythetic system of categorizing castes contributes to this understanding is an orientation toward the large and seemingly heterogeneous lists of "qualities" (often spoken of as *guṇa* in Bengal) that may be used to characterize a caste.

Caste and the Saṃskāra *Rites*

Among the myths of the origins of things that anthropologists study, the myth of Veṇa and Pṛthu ought to hold a place of particular interest. Far from concerning itself with a primal act of incest necessary for the multiplication of living beings, it deals with numerous latter-day acts of the opposite type (which David Mandelbaum called "excest"), pointing to the Hindu consideration of miscegenation as anathema. The incestlike relationship between the virtuous Pṛthu and his queen, both born from the body of Veṇa, is created by the wise Brahmans. It is the disastrous products of excessively heterogeneous unions that are the source of all the world's evils. In the case of incest, it is a particular sexual union that is abominated. But in the case of the mixed castes, it is a particular kind of *birth* that is held responsible for the misfortunes of humanity; as the Brahmans told Pṛthu, the mixed castes were "born of anti-*dharma*."

Inden and I argued at some length that birth is the central symbolic act of kinship in Bengali culture, and I cannot reproduce all of that argument here. Briefly, a person is said to "receive" or "accept birth" (*janma grahaṇa karā*) from its parents, who together give it birth (*janma dāna karā*). Specifically, what a child receives at birth is its body (*deha, śarīra*), which is thought to be made up of the different but complementary substances of the bodies of its mother and father. Those substances, the semen (*śukra*) of the father and the uterine blood (*ārtava*) of the mother, respectively, provide the hard but inert structuring parts of the body and the soft but energetic parts. Rather than semen and uterine blood, Bengalis usually refer to the "seed" (*bīja*) and the "field" (*kṣetra*); the father plants the seed, which is nourished and grown in the field of the mother. As is the case in agriculture, seed and field must be closely matched to one another. The seed of rainy season rice sown on a low-lying field suitable for winter rice will produce a very poor crop. The qualities of seed and field—of the bodily substances of husband and wife—that match them to one another are not only "natural" qualities, as we think of "nature" in Western cultures, but are at the same time "moral" qualities.

There are many ways of illustrating the postulate of Hindu cultures that both the "natural" and the "moral" qualities of a person—indeed of anything—are coextensive with one another and are intrinsic in the substance of that person or thing. Analysis of the Hindu conception of *dharma* provides only one such illustration, but it is a particularly important one, since *dharma* is, among other things, the highest of the goals attainable by a person living a life in this world. Earlier I said that *dharma* is the universal code for conduct that both supports everything and is supported by all right and orderly action. Each person, each thing, each genus of things, has its own code for conduct (*svadharma*); its contribution to universal order. The *dharma* of a rice seed is to sprout a stalk, flower, and bear an ear of grain for the nourishment of gods and humans. In doing so, the rice seed accomplishes its *dharma* and realizes its own cause for existing. An unplanted seed cannot accomplish its *dharma;* a seed planted in an improper field produces improper fruit bearing defective seed. It is just the same with human seed and human field. Properly planted in a correctly matched field, a human seed is nurtured into a product that has the same substances and *dharma* as its parents. But planted in a mismatched field, that seed produces a child lacking in the qualities and *dharma* of either parent. It is this deficiency in the offspring of caste miscegenation that the Brahmans point to when they say that the mixed castes are born of anti-*dharma*.

All of the *saṃskāra* rites are based upon the latent paradigm of birth as it is culturally defined in Bengal. They transform the natural and moral qualities of a person by refining and purifying the substances of which the body is made in an action that is symbolic of rebirth. A *saṃskāra* is an antientropic act that "completes" a person by moving that person bodily toward the most organized, self-controlled condition he or she is capable of achieving. However, there are limits on the maximum state of organization and self-control that any human being can attain, and these limits are defined by the qualities of the body that person received at birth. Thus, a person born as a female is considered always to have a more limited capacity for refinement than a male; her interior organization and self-control are inherently of limited perfectibility. She will always lack the qualification to receive a complete set of ten *saṃskāra*s, and is expected to live her life always under the control of a male. Similarly, a person born as a Śūdra remains intrinsically limited by the natural and moral qualities of his body and, even though a male, is never qualified to receive the *upanayana saṃskāra* that is said to give second birth to a Brahman. Moreover, what any of the applicable *saṃskāra*s can achieve in the purification, refinement, and completion of a body possessing chaotic qualities is severely restricted by its limited inherent capacity. Further ritual work after that potential ofperfectibility has been achieved is, at best, wasted and, at worst, productive of results opposite those sought because of its inappropriateness.

In Bengal, marriage is an extremely important *saṃskāra*, and all aspects of it, from the selection of the spouse through the completion of the rites and the birth of a child to the new couple, are undertaken with profound seriousness by everyone involved, whether rich or poor and regardless of caste. This seriousness necessarily includes a self-assessment of the capacities of those undertaking the marriage, a making of allowances for what they can expect of themselves, which is usually in fairly close agreement with what others expect of them. Bengalis of all castes with whom I am acquainted seem determined to make the best marriages they can—permanent, productive, harmonious unions of grooms and brides whose qualities are as closely matched as possible—but they recognize the limitations imposed by their own natural and moral qualities. It would call for a great deal of fieldwork of a very delicate kind to assess the differences in the marriages of persons of different castes on all the dimensions of unity Bengalis think important. I have not done such work, and I am probably not capable of it. However, I can comment generally on the achievement of unity in marriage, as indexed in gross terms by the incidence of failure of marriage, among the ranked groups of castes established in the *Bṛaddharma Purāṇa* as I have come to know representatives of these castes through fieldwork.

In my experience, marriages among Brahmans and "Brahman-like" Śūdras very rarely fail to achieve the permanent union of husband and wife.[18] Among the "Vaiśya-like" Śūdras, including the Goldsmiths and Gold-sellers, marriage failures are slightly more frequent but by no means common. The castes in the category that I have called the "Śūdras of the Śūdras," so far as I know them from my fieldwork, face the prospect of a mismatched bride and groom and of unaccomplished marriages with a kind of resigned disapproval. They try so far as possible to carry out everything correctly, but there is no denying that some men do not succeed in selflessly giving their daughters in marriage or are willing (or able) to pay for a ceremony of only short duration, and that too from a Brahman of inferior quality. Discovering information about unsuccessful marriages among these castes is often not easy; they are shamed by their failures, if for no other reason than that these are demonstrations of their natural and moral inferiority at a time when prospects for increased caste honor are better than ever before.

Shame does not so often seem to me to afflict persons who belong to the castes of the lowest category, those who in the myth are said to be outside *varṇāśramadharma*. Divorce is common among them, and the remarriage of divorced and widowed women is usual. Most of the castes in this category—Leather-workers, Scavengers, Bamboo-workers, Palanquin-bearers, and so on—now have Brahman priests who perform rites only for persons of a single caste. These Brahmans have very ambiguous standing in society at large because they combine qualities of the very highest and very lowest castes. Occasionally *saṃskāras* of the lowest castes are performed by non-Brahman–initiated Vaiṣṇavas, who are their preceptors. It does not matter much who performs a particular rite, however, because the castes of this category often expect of themselves what others generally expect of them—that they will not gain very much effect from rituals. Their naturally and morally chaotic characters, evident in the loud quarrels, brawling, and drunkenness so common in their neighborhoods, and in the promiscuity and lack of modesty of their women, prevent them from accomplishing much through ritual action, even though they carry it out with the greatest resolution possible for them.

The "facts" about rates of divorce or marital discord do not bear on the cultural explanation of failures of solidarity except as they are "cultural facts," that is, symbols whose meanings are shared by a people. I suspect that if the truth were known about such things, the incidence of unhappy marriages in Bengal would turn out to be pretty much the same in all castes. However, the outcomes of such marriages are different for people of different castes: unhappy or unwanted wives of the higher castes more often return to their fathers' houses to live out the rest of their lives in quiet misery or, failing that possibility, end their despair through suicide; badly made unions among lower-caste people are more often publicly acknowledged in divorce and remarriage. In many villages scandalous affairs between higher-caste men and lower-caste women are talked about in whispers, while those of lower-caste men and women are made the subjects of noisy village adjudication. An advantage of the polythetic approach to the classification of the castes used by Bengalis is that the same item of conduct can be used to characterize one caste, even though it is not universal among persons of that caste, and ignored when it is displayed by persons of another caste. Thus, statistical rates need never impinge very heavily on meaning.

Divorce is not a cultural fact for Bengali Hindus, even though a great many of them recognize that it takes place among Bengali Muslims, among Americans, and sometimes even among themselves. Divorce for a Hindu couple is not a statement about the dissolution of marriage but rather about the failure of the achievement of the goals of the marriage *saṃskāra*. There are several reasons why a *saṃskāra* rite might not accomplish its purpose: in the weakened *dharma* of the Kali age any rite might fail, and the abbreviated rites most people perform may be insufficient to achieve the large transformations they seek. But the principal reason for the failure of marriage rites lies in the bodily qualities of the persons these rites attempt to unite. These qualities are seen by Bengalis as, at the same time, both natural and moral. The natural disorderliness brought about by the mixing of different castes is a "biological" expression of the moral chaos from which they were born. Human bodies born from persons of more mixed caste ancestry are more entropic—have lower potential capacity for the marital transformation—than bodies of persons born of less mixed ancestry. The Bengali expressions *biye-kāṭā* and *vivāha-viccheda*, "cutting a marriage" or "putting asunder a marriage," sound as though they mean more or less the same thing as the English term "divorce." But in Bengali Hindu culture, two persons who have been successfully joined together by the *saṃskāra* of marriage cannot be put asunder by human agency, for their relationship is not only a legal or moral one—a relationship only in culture—but also a permanent, natural relationship.

NOTES

1. This essay was written in 1978 for presentation at the Tenth International Congress of Anthropological and Ethnological Sciences held in New

Delhi. It was conceived as an appendix to *Kinship in Bengali Culture*, which had then been recently published and which was criticized for ignoring the realities of kinship and marriage in favor of idealized representations. I have conducted many household censuses in Bengali villages and have a lot of data on "divorce rates" and the like. The purpose of the present exercise, obviously, is not to talk about why and how often marriages fail but rather to explore the way people explain such failures at the highest level of generality. Focusing on caste differences, as I have done here, may make some readers want more information about class conflict and low-caste perspectives. I will try to discuss these matters further, but I know enough not to make rash statements about essays that I hope to write. I apologize for making no mention of the important work on kinship and marriage in India published since 1978.

2. Ronald Inden and Ralph Nicholas, *Kinship in Bengali Culture* (Chicago: University of Chicago Press, 1977), p. 36.

3. Ibid., p. 37.

4. Rajendra Chandra Hazra, *Studies in the Puranic Records on Hindu Rites and Customs*, University of Dacca Bulletin no. 20 (Dacca: University of Dacca, 1940), p. 176.

5. Ibid., p. 235.

6. There are two printed editions of this Purana, according to Hazra (*Studies in the Upapurāṇas*. Vol. 2: *Śākta and Non-Sectarian Upapurāṇas* [Calcutta: Sanskrit College, 1963], pp. 396–97), one in Bengali characters published by the Vaṇgavāsī Press and a Devanāgari edition published by the Asiatic Society of Bengal. Unfortunately, I have not been able to obtain either of these and have relied on Hazra's detailed summary and the "popularized," abridged, and expurgated translation by Syama Charan Banerji, *The Bṛhad-dharma Purāṇa* (Lucknow: The Indian Commercial Press, 1915).

7. Hazra, *Studies in the Upapurāṇas*, pp. 448–61.

8. The myth of wicked King Veṇa and his son, the good Pṛthu, is very ancient. O'Flaherty (*The Origins of Evil in Hindu Mythology* [Berkeley: University of California Press, 1976], pp. 321–69) summarizes many versions of it and analyses a number of the recurrent symbolic elements in them. The particularly Bengali version constitutes chapters 13 and 14 of the Uttara-khaṇḍa of the *Bṛhaddharma Purāṇa*. This version is briefly summarized by Inden (*Marriage and Rank in Bengali Culture: A History of Caste and Clan in Middle Period Bengal* [Berkeley: University of California Press, 1976], pp. 49–51), who provides an illuminating discussion of some of its implications. The Dacca *History of Bengal* contains further details about the "thirty-six castes" (see R. C. Majumdar, *The History of Bengal*. Vol. 1: *The Hindu Period* [Dacca: University of Dacca, 1943], pp. 567–70), as does the work of Nihararanjana Raya (*Bāṃālī hindur varṇa-bheda* [Calcutta: Visvabharati University, 1945], pp. 89–94). Another Sanskrit text that underwent a post-Islamic rescension in Bengal, the *Brahmavaivartta Purāṇa*, provides a different narrative of the mixing of castes (Brahmā-khaṇḍa, chapter 10.13–21, pp. 89–137). This is a very popular purāṇa and qualities of the castes mentioned in it are often cited by people today. I have not yet undertaken an analysis of this text.

9. Although mixed, these unions are in the proper direction (*anuloma*, "with the hair"), that is, the man belongs to a higher-ranking group than the woman.

10. These unions are in the improper direction (*pratiloma*, "against the hair"), that is, the woman belongs to a higher-ranking group than the man. Curiously, it is not said that Veṇa compelled a Śūdra man to cohabit with a Vaiśya woman.

11. The list of inferior mixed castes given here is by way of example and is not intended to be exhaustive; it concludes with *ityādi* ("and so forth").

12. The Cāṇḍala is an anomaly in a class defined in this way. A great deal of *smṛti* literature, going back to the *Mānavadharmaśāstra* 10.12.26 (see Georg Bühler, trans., *The Laws of Manu*, Sacred Books of the East, vol. 25 [Delhi: Motilal Banarsidass, 1964]), declares the Cāṇḍala to be the product of a Śūdra father and a Brahman mother, and to be "that lowest of mortals." I surmise that the author of the *Bṛhaddharma Purāṇa* could not avoid the weight of this tradition even though it created an inconsistency in his system of classification.

13. Whether the etymology is historically accurate or not, the *dharmaśāstra* interpretation seems obscure. For an ordinary man, union with a woman of the mother's caste (which would, of course, be the same as the father's caste) is usual. Why it should acquire this special incestlike onus in the case of the mixing of castes is unclear. There are four further instances of such unions among the "examples" of inferior mixed castes, and these are all identifiable with contemporary Bengali castes of very low rank.

14. Stanley Tambiah, "From *Varṇa* to Caste Through Mixed Unions," in *The Character of Kinship*, ed. Jack Goody (Cambridge, Mass.: Harvard University Press, 1982), p. 191.

15. Ibid., pp. 195, 204.

16. Rājputra or Rajputs are today considered by Bengalis not to be indigenous to their country. Whether there was a Bengali caste with such a name six centuries ago is difficult to say, but I know of no textual sources that would support such a supposition. Vārjīvīs are identified with the contemporary Bārui caste of betel-leaf cultivators (those who get their livelihood [*jīvikā*] under a cover [*vāra*], namely, the covered garden [*baroj*] that protects the delicate betel vines from the sun). Bāruis are considered high-ranking Śūdras in Bengal today. There is no apparent reason for excluding them from the discussion of occupations in the myth except as an arbitrary means of creating a "slot" for another caste without going beyond the established number of twenty high mixed castes.

17. Rodney Needham, "Polythetic Classification: Convergence and Consequences," *Man*, n.s., 10 (1975): 249–69.

18. My own fieldwork had not brought me into contact with Vaidyas, although I have a good many acquaintances among persons of this caste in Calcutta and elsewhere. The Āguri caste, who consider themselves the modern representatives of the Ugras and refer to themselves as Ugra Kṣatriyas, are heavily concentrated in Burdwan district and the immediately surrounding areas. There is no caste in contemporary Bengal identifiable with the Māgadha, and the occupation of bard, common in regions of India where a Kṣatriya warrior cultural style is dominant, is not represented among the Bengali Hindu castes.

7

Begetting on Margin: Adultery and Surrogate Pseudomarriage in Hinduism

WENDY DONIGER

The bottom line on sex and marriage in the *dharmaśāstras* (the Hindu texts of religious law) is that neither the husband nor the wife should ever have sex with anyone else. But this rule was, in some cases, more honored in the breach than in the observance. The husband was tacitly allowed to have sex with other women in various circumstances, and the wife was allowed to have sex with another man in one particular circumstance: the levirate or *niyoga* (literally the "appointment" of the woman to be impregnated by a man who is not her legal husband). Each of these forms of nonmarriage serves to define, as well as to challenge, the boundaries of "normal" marriage. Let me begin with adultery.

Adultery

In India it is always assumed that the eternal adulterous triangle consists of the woman, her husband, and her lover—not the woman, her husband, and his mistress (the basic configuration of French comedies). Of course, both configurations occur in India, as in the rest of the world (and, probably, on other planets in galaxies that have the institution of marriage); but only one (in which the wife has a lover) is construed in India as adultery, a crime, *adharma* (the violation of religious law), the pollution of a woman. The other (the French connection, where the husband has a mistress) is simply the way of the world—the man's world, easily overlooked in the polygamous world of *The Laws of Manu* (the most cited of the *dharmśāstras*) and in the two great epics, the *Mahābhārata* and the *Rāmāyaṇa*. As Macdonell and Keith dryly remark, speaking of the Vedic period:

> Adultery was generally regarded among Aryan peoples as a serious offence against the husband of the woman affected. . . . Despite polygamy . . . there is ample evidence that the marriage tie was not . . . lightly regarded as far as the fidelity of the wife was concerned. There is, however, little trace of the husband's being expected to be faithful as a matter of mortality.[1]

Within this basic triangle we may trace each of the points of view in a different genre of Indian literature. The husband's point of view is developed in the *dharmaśāstras*, while the point of view of the woman and her lover is expressed in folklore, in the Sanskrit romances (such as the *Kathāsaritsāgara*), and in the *Kāmasūtra*, the textbook of erotic love. These stories depict not merely different realities but different fantasies: from the lover's point of view, adultery is fun; from the husband's, it is terrifying. From the woman's point of view, it is, our texts presume, both.

Adultery in Vedic Texts

The earliest Indian texts, Vedic texts—the *Ṛg Veda*, the Brāhmaṇas, the *Atharva Veda*, and the Upaniṣads—refer to lovers, both male and female, as a fact of human life. The image of a man between two women begins, like all things Indian, in the *Ṛg Veda* (c. 1000 B.C.E.), which cryptically likens a draft animal between two shafts to a man in bed with two women.[2] Several Brāhmaṇa texts suggest that, on certain ritual occasions, the man should refrain from sex with the wife (*strī*) of another man,[3] and presumably remain faithful to his own wife.

But the contrasting image of a woman with a lover also appears in the *Rg Veda*, in a number of similes that liken various sorts of enthusiasms to a woman's eagerness to meet her lover.[4] It seems to be the emotional intensity of the act that is the point of the simile. The *Rg Veda* assumes that a wife might sleep not only with her husband but with her lover or even her brother, both of whom are casually mentioned in a prayer to protect the embryo:

> The one who spreads apart your two thighs, who lies between the married pair, who licks the inside of your womb—we will drive him away from here. The one who by changing into your brother, or your husband, or your lover lies with you, who wishes to kill your offspring—we will drive him away from here.[5]

There is danger here, but not from the lover; only from the (harmful) demon who assumes the form of the (presumably harmless) lover.

The assumption that the wife of the sacrificer does in fact have lovers is reflected in a Brāhmaṇa text in which the wife is asked not *if* she is having an affair, but with whom (the male chauvinist parallel to the feminist question "Have you stopped beating your wife?"): "He asks her, 'Who are you carrying on with [*kena carasi*]?' For a woman offends Varuṇa if, when she belongs to one man, she carries on with another. And he asks her to keep her from sacrificing while she has an inner guilt; when the sin [*enas*] is spoken [*nirukta*] it becomes smaller, for it becomes a truth."[6]

But to assume that a man's wife has a lover is not necessarily to assume that the husband finds this situation tolerable. The *Atharva Veda* has spells not merely to drive away the potential lover but to make him impotent.[7] The Upaniṣads go one step further and give practical, ritual instructions for taking back the seed from a lover whom the husband hates (implying, perhaps, that there is another category not discussed here, namely, a lover whom he does not hate):

> If a man's wife has a lover whom he hates, he should spread out a row of reed arrows, their heads smeared with ghee, and sacrifice them, in inverse order, into a vessel of fire, saying, "You have made a libation in my fire! I take away your breath, your sons, your cattle, your sacrifices and good deeds, your hope and your expectations. You have made a libation in my fire, you [Mr. X]." If a Brahmin who knows this curses a man, that man dies impotent and without merit. Therefore one should not try to get on "joking terms" with the wife of a learned Brahmin.[8]

This idea of drawing back the seed from a lover is reiterated in several Brāhmaṇas, which provide a verse to be recited by an illegitimate son[9] or by any sacrificer:[10] "If my mother has given in to her desire, going astray and violating her vow to her husband, let my father keep that semen away from me." Presumably what is meant is that the seed will not achieve its ultimate goal, that the mother will not be impregnated by her lover. In *The Laws of Manu*, the (presumably legitimate) son is supposed to say this Vedic verse when he has reason to fear that his mother has strayed from the path of virtue.[11] The Upaniṣadic text presents a basic Indian trope: the metaphor of the vagina as the sacrificial fire and the sexual act as a sacrifice, conflating the image of the legitimate sexual act, whose fruit is a child, with the sacrificial act of pouring melted butter into the consecrated fire, an act whose fruit is, inter alia, immortality.

Adultery in Manu

The idea that one could claim back the seed of another man rests upon another implicit metaphor: the wife viewed not as a sacrifice but as a field. In *The Laws of Manu* there are two different, conflicting models of paternity, expressed through a single agricultural metaphor: the sower of the seed is the biological father, who may or may not be the legal husband; the woman is the field, and the owner of the field is the legal husband. The son born in the field (the wife) by a man other than her legal husband is known as the *kṣetraja* (literally "born in the [husband's] field," the wife's natural son).[12] But there are two ways of looking at this metaphor.

The first assumes that the man who owns the field (i.e., the wife) owns whatever crop is sown in the field. Manu assumes that the field is entirely neutral, and that the crop (son) sown in it will always resemble the seed (the father). Therefore, you should never waste your seed by shedding it in another man's "field" or wife, but you are not harmed if another man sheds his seed in your wife (in that you own the son resulting from that act). Manu thus forbids a man to commit adultery in another man's wife but encourages him to let a brother produce a levirate heir in his own wife, through the Indian practice of *niyoga*, in which the widow of a man who has produced no male heirs is appointed to have a son by that man's younger brother. This argument—that the man owns the woman—prevails in India.

On the other hand, it might also be argued that the man who owns the seed, and who in any case determines the characteristics of the crop, owns the crop. This supplies a reason why a man might want to shed his seed in someone else's field, but it now also argues that a man should make sure that only his own seed is sown in his own field. This argument—that the man owns his own seed—takes a secondary place, as it would both encourage adultery (you would produce legitimate sons in all sorts of women) and make the *niyoga* meaningless (since the son that your brother produced in your wife would be his son, not yours).

Violating the Guru's Bed in Manu

The "learned Brahman" whose wife is sexually taboo is, of course, the author of the Upaniṣadic text that made the taboo; such Brahmans were also responsible for the orthodox view of adultery, as expressed primarily in the *dharmaśāstras*. Hence, it is hardly surprising that the wife of the "learned Brahman" is the object of the most vicious form of adultery in Indian literature, the crime of violating the bed of the spiritual teacher or guru (*gurutalpaga*).

Manu regards this violation as one of the four greatest crimes: "Killing a priest, drinking liquor, stealing, violating the guru's marriage-bed, and associating with those (who commit these acts) are called the major crimes."[13] It is the first sexual crime that Manu mentions, and it catapults him into the first of his many violent denunciations of women (and, incidentally, into a rare explicit reference to incest):

> [The student] should not rub oil on his guru's wife, or bathe her, or massage her limbs, or do her hair. When he is fully twenty years old and understands virtues and vices here on earth, he should not greet his guru's young wife by [touching] her feet. It is the very nature of women to corrupt men here on earth; for that reason, circumspect men do not get careless and wanton among wanton women. It is not just an ignorant man, but even a learned man of the world, too, that a wanton woman can lead astray when he is in the control of lust and anger. No one should sit in a deserted place with his mother, sister, or daughter; for the strong cluster of the sensory powers drags away even a learned man.[14]

And the punishments for violating the guru's bed are horrendous:

> A man who has violated his guru's marriage-bed should declare his error and sleep on a heated iron bed or embrace a red-hot metal cylinder, and by his death he is cleaned. Or he himself may cut off his penis and testicles, hold them in his two cupped hands, and set out toward the southwest region of Ruin, walking straight ahead until he dies. Or he may carry a club shaped like a bedpost, wear rags, grow a beard, concentrate his mind, and carry out the "Painful" vow of the Lord of Creatures for a year in a deserted forest. Or, to dispel [the crime of violating] his guru's marriage-bed, he should restrain his sensory powers and carry out the "Moon-course" vow for three months, eating food fit for an oblation or barley-broth.[15]

The commentators say that the "Painful" vow[16] expiates incest with one's father's wife or a stepmother (who is, according to some commentators, not among the women to whom the verse about the guru's bed applies). Some commentators say that it applies only when one has mistaken her for one's own wife, others that it applies when one does it knowingly, out of lust.

But when we turn to the myths, we find very few instances of the crime of violating the guru's bed, in dramatic contrast with the frequent occurrence of other forms of adultery, particularly incest. The argument that the violation of the guru's bed is overemphasized in Manu because it masks a deeper fear of incest with one's biological father[17] is thus belied by the mythological texts, which have no problem at all in talking about incest with a parent (particularly a divine parent), but don't seem to want to talk about the violation of the (human) guru's wife. One famous exception provides a counterexample. A young Brahman named Uttanka was propositioned by his teacher's wife but resisted her advances. His teacher was pleased, but the wife sent him to get some special earrings which involved him in dangerous adventures in the underworld.[18] Thus the student who does *not* violate his guru's marriage bed risks the wrath of the woman scorned.

An inversion of the theme of the violation of the guru's bed is the story of Sudarśana:

> Sudarśana was a householder who vowed never to disregard a guest. One day Dharma [religious law incarnate in a god] came in the form of a Brahmin and asked Sudarśana's wife to give herself to him. Remembering the command of her husband, she complied. When Sudarśana returned and called for his wife, the Brahman called back, "Your wife is pleasing me with the various guest-rites. Her mind is firm and honest." Sudarśana smiled and said, "May you enjoy your love-making. The pleasure is mine." Then the Brahman revealed himself to be Dharma and he said, "I came to test the truth of your vow. Your wife is chaste and cannot be defiled, and you have conquered death by adhering to the duties of a householder and by conquering your passions, desires, and angers."[19]

Dharma appears in disguise here, as in many other myths, in order to test and prove the virtue of a good man; in this he is to be contrasted with Indra, who often appears in disguise in order to challenge and destroy the virtue of a good man (or, more often, a good woman). It is right to give your wife to Dharma, the paradigmatic Brahman; it is wrong to give your wife to Indra, the paradigmatic warrior king. The myth of Dharma and Sudarśana's wife seems to be saying that the guru can do it, but you mustn't do it to the guru. It also seems to reflect a belief, widely expressed in myths though not sanctioned by law, that a barren woman might be legitimately impregnated by a holy man (a man of the Brahman class who was noted for his spiritual powers) in a kind of pseudo-*niyoga*. Since, as we shall see, the *niyoga* itself was a kind of pseudomarriage, impregnation by a holy man is in a sense twice removed from legitimacy. And the tale of Dharma and Sudarśana demonstrates the extreme case that could be made both for generosity toward Brahmans (always a favorite theme in our Brahman-authored texts) and for the sexual freedom of the guru, in complete contrast to the total lack of sexual freedom of the guru's wife.

Bṛhaspati the Cuckold and the Cuckolder

The paradigmatic case of the violation of the guru's bed is the tale of Tārā, the wife of Bṛhaspati, the guru of the gods. Tārā was abducted by the moon (Soma or Candra), Bṛhaspati's pupil, and gave birth to a child, Budha, the founder of the great lunar dynasty. This episode is told in most of the Puranas, as it is the source not only of a great dynasty but (like the *niyoga* births in the *Mahābhārata*) of a great war ("The War over Tārā"). An early prose version of the tale occurs in the *Viṣṇu Purāṇa:*

> Soma, the moon, was the grandson of Brahmā. Intoxicated with pride, Soma carried off Tārā, the wife of Bṛhaspati, the guru of all the gods. A battle ensued, in which Indra and all the gods sided with Bṛhaspati, while the guru of the demons (Uśanas) and all the demons sided with Soma. Finally Brahmā restrained them and gave Tārā back to Bṛhaspati. But when he saw that she was pregnant, Bṛhaspati said to Tārā, "This child of someone else should not be kept in my field. Get rid of it. Enough of this raping." She being a faithful wife [the commentary says she was still a faithful wife because Soma had taken her by force] did as her husband said and got rid of the embryo in a clump of grasses.
>
> He was a beautiful child, and both Bṛhaspati and Soma wanted him. The gods, in doubt, asked Tārā, "Tell the truth. Whose son is he? Soma's or Bṛhaspati's?" But she was ashamed and did not answer. Then the child began to curse her, saying, "You filthy woman! Mother, why don't you tell about my father? I am going to give you a punishment for your false modesty, right now, so that no other woman will lie about being raped like that." But then Brahmā, his great-grandfather, restrained the child and himself asked Tārā, "Tell me, my little calf. Whose son is he? Soma's or Bṛhaspati's?" Paralyzed with shame, she said, "Soma's." Then the moon beamed and embraced the child and said, "Well done, my little calf. Since you are so wise, your name will be Budha [from the verb *budh,* to be enlightened]."[20]

The concern for the "field" (i.e., the legitimate wife) and the paternity of the child are echoes of the paradigm that we have seen in Manu.

The *Bhāgavata Purāṇa* retells the story in verse and adds some new details: Bṛhaspati tells Tārā to abandon what had been placed in his field by others (in the plural!); the child is said to be infuriated by his mother's false modesty but does not mention it, or any threat, when he begs her to tell him the "unspeakable" thing that she has done; and Brahmā takes Tārā aside in private when he persuades her to name the culprit.[21] The translator of this text, however, adds some very fine flourishes:

> Both Bṛhaspati and Soma desired to have the son as his own (as a *kṣetraja* son—born of his field, viz. wife in the case of the former, and as a *vīryaja* son—born of his own semen—in the case of the latter). While they [Bṛhaspati and Soma] were wrangling vociferously, "This [son] is mine and not yours," sages and gods enquired [of Tārā], but through sense of shame, she kept mum.[22]

The Bṛhaspati/Tārā story may also be read as an astronomical allegory, for Soma is the moon and Tārā means "star," while Bṛhaspati, Budha, and Uśanas are all planets. But as a narrative this story is a class for which there is one famous paradigm (this myth) but no members: what other stories are there about the violation of the guru's bed?

Perhaps because of that very dearth, this particular story is told over and over again. There is an especially wonderful Telugu version of it, which refers to the moon by his epithet of Candra rather than Soma:

> Brahmā created Candra, the moon, so handsome that all women loved him. His father, Atri, sent him to be educated by Brihaspati, and as he grew older, Tārā, too, felt desire waken in her; she began to imagine what it would be like to make love to him. She would seek him out in narrow passageways, where there was no way to step aside, and, her sari slipping from her shoulder, would press against him with her breasts. After a while, he began to melt within with desire for Tārā. He strove valiantly to defend himself against this feeling, but one day when Brihaspati was absent she rushed to Candra. He protested, "Your father-in-law will crush you in the betel-nut press; your husband, if you talk about it, will try to kill you." But she replied, "You've got it all wrong; you say a woman should not sin against her husband, and I agree. The man a woman loves, that man who is pleasing to her eyes—*he* is her husband; if she denies this and makes love to another, that is truly not right. Even your guru [Brihaspati] forgot about kinship when he slept with his elder brother's wife [Mamatā, wife of Utathya]! Your fellow-student, Indra, grabbed Ahalyā, though she was a sage's wife." She fell on Candra, and they embraced; he wanted to kiss her, but still he hesitated. She mocked him: "Already on the bed, and you're thinking about kinship rules!" She kissed him quickly, and he responded at last.
>
> When Brihaspati returned, he discovered at once that his wife and Candra were lovers. She told him the truth, and he wanted to curse her, but she said to him: "Don't use your *brahmāstra* weapon against a sparrow. Is there anyone in the world

> who doesn't make mistakes? Even Ahalyā, Brahmā's own daughter, erred like this. Husbands should be patient; otherwise, you'll be laughed at for nothing." She cried, and he lifted her up and forgave her. But when the adultery persisted, the gods intervened, and Tārā returned—pregnant—to Brihaspati's house. Upon the birth of her child, Budha, Candra appeared to claim him. Tārā confirmed that Candra was the father, and Brahmā forced Brihaspati to give Candra the boy.[23]

This text, created in the context of Nāyaka eroticism, is far more interested in the arguments in favor of adultery (which I have had to abbreviate greatly in this summary of a much longer text) than in the arguments about parentage. But, just as other texts cite myths about parentage, so this text cites myths about adultery. As David Shulman remarks, "There is a nice touch of poetic justice in recalling Brihaspati's own violation of Utathya's wife, in the context of Tārā's eagerness to betray *him*."[24] Indeed, there is even greater irony (or is it just female tact?) that, though Tārā cites as role models both Ahalyā and Bṛhaspati when she is seducing Candra, she cites only Ahalyā, omitting Bṛhaspati, when she argues with Bṛhaspati himself.

But Bṛhaspati is indeed better known as the villain, rather than the victim, in adultery. His seduction of Mamatā is told in the *Bhāgavata Purāṇa* only a few chapters after the tale of Tārā and Soma, but it is also told much earlier, in the *Mahābhārata*[25] and in this version from the still earlier *Bṛhaddevatā:*

> The sage Bṛhaspati tried to rape Mamatā, the wife of his brother Utathya, when Mamatā was pregnant. But the unborn embryo [the future Dīrghatamas] protected his mother by kicking out the intruding penis, shouting, "Get out, uncle! There's only room for one in here, and I was here first!" The infuriated rapist cursed the embryo to be blind; the child was born as Dīrghatamas ["Long Darkness"].[26]

Here, as in the birth of Budha, the child who is the victim of sexual violence speaks out precociously to utter a curse. The fact that Bṛhaspati is Utathya's *brother* further assimilates this story to the problematic *niyoga*. The brothers literally share Mamatā in one retelling of the story of the rape, in which it is said that Mamatā became impregnated by Bṛhaspati, too, and bore two sons; in addition to Dīrghatamas (the son of her husband, Utathya), she gave birth to Bharadvāja (the son of Bṛhaspati). This takes place under complicated circumstances that are merely alluded to by the text but are spelled out by the commentary:

> King Bharata had three highly esteemed wives, but he killed all his sons out of fear of being abandoned [by them], for, he

> said, "They don't look like [me]." [Śrīdhara, the commentator, suggests that he feared some sexual misconduct and, lest the sons, hearing him say this, would say, "He is going to abandon us," he abandoned them.] But when his dynasty was in danger of extinction, the gods gave him a son, Bharadhvāja.
>
> Now, Bṛhaspati had tried to have sex with Mamatā, his brother's wife, when she was pregnant, but when the embryo had prevented him he cursed it and spilt his semen. [The commentator says that the semen, struck by the heel of the child in the womb who was to become Dīrghatamas, fell out of the womb onto the ground and immediately became a child.] Mamatā wanted to abandon the child because she was afraid that her husband would abandon her, but the gods sang this verse which makes the child's name, Bharadvāja: "[Bṛhaspati said,] 'You foolish woman, raise [*bhara*] this child who was born of two [*dva-ja*].' '[Mamatā said,] Bṛhaspati, you raise this child who was born of two.' " But despite the urging of the gods, the two of them regarded the child as born in vain and abandoned him, and the gods gave him [to Bharata] when his own lineage was in vain.[27]

It is certainly appropriate that the child, abandoned by his mother in paranoid fear that she herself will be abandoned, is given to Bharata, who has abandoned his own sons with precisely the same irrational projection of his own fear—a fear based upon the important realization that they do not look like him.

Śrīdhara reads between the lines of the brief divine verse that contains the argument between Mamatā and Bṛhaspati about the name of the child:

> Bṛhaspati says to Mamatā as she is going away, abandoning the son, "Hey, you foolish woman. Raise this son." If she should say, "But I am afraid of my husband," he says, "He is born of the two of us [him and me]: in the field of one, and out of the seed of the other. So he's really his son, too. And so there's no reason to worry." When he has said this to her, she replies, "Hey, Bṛhaspati. *You* raise him. Because he was born of the two of us—you and me. So I won't raise him all by myself."

This remarkable conversation assimilates the question of dual fatherhood occasioned by an adultery (the owner of the field versus the owner of the seed) to the duality of *all* births, legitimate or illegitimate (the father versus the mother), and argues, long before feminism, that the father should share in the child care.

Sanctioned Adultery?

Of course, these are myths, not social laws, and it is often the case that the text of a myth is in blatant conflict with the "text" of social practice.[28] Certainly the myth in which the wives of the cowherds commit adultery with Kṛṣṇa was never used as a charter for adultery.[29] The tale of Dharma and Sudarśana, similarly, can hardly stand as proof that people in ancient India routinely offered their wives to their Brahman guests. Indeed, the texts themselves take up this challenge, imagining a situation in which religion seems to sanction adultery and then deconstructing that situation to show that this is not, in fact, the case.

Such a text appears in a medieval Purana in the form of a wonderful long story that I can only summarize here:

> There was a Brahman woman of loose morals who used to go with her lover, Devadatta, to the Temple of the Four-Headed God, Brahmā, and make love with him. When someone caught them in flagrante and told her husband, he beat her, but the shameless woman swore that she was free from blame, and offered to enter fire to prove the truth of what she said. But the ordeal by fire demonstrated that she was pure and sinless, whereupon the furious husband cursed Agni, the God of Fire, for giving false witness. The God of Fire appeared to the Brahman and said, "It is true that your wife has had a lover for a long time, and that today you caught her in the act. But I could not burn her to ashes because she has become purified of her sin. There is an image of Brahmā with Śiva on his head in that temple where she made love to her lover. She had her fun with her lover, and then she looked up at that image and washed her body in the water of the tank in front of the image and was purified. In that same temple long ago, Brahmā himself was purified after he had sinned by looking with lust on the face of Satī, Śiva's wife."
>
> The Brahman said, "I shall not take my wife home with me even if she has been purified, for I have seen her making love to her lover with my very own eyes." And he left his wife there and went home. The wife was delighted, even though she had been abandoned, for she had learned the miraculous powers of that temple by listening to the God of Fire. She indulged herself totally in sexual delights with her lover right in that temple, and always remembered to bathe afterward in the water of that tank. In time, other women who had been chaste, moral, and faithful to their husbands only out of fear of some terrible retribution in the next life

> began to come from far and wide to that temple in which there was that image of Brahmā with Śiva on his head. There they held a veritable orgy, after which they all bathed in the tank that destroyed their sin, and were also freed from sin by gazing on the image of Brahmā with Śiva on his head. So it came to be that the very idea of a woman's being faithful to her husband vanished, and men were no longer faithful to their wives. Whenever a man saw a beautiful woman, even if she was of good family, he would take her to that temple and enjoy her there. And whenever a woman saw a man that caught her fancy, she would take him to that temple and have a veritable orgy with him there. Neither man nor woman would be stained by any sin for what they had done, because of the miraculous powers of that place.
>
> In time the king of that region became old, and his young wife, who did not love the old and feeble king, would go to that temple and make love to any man she desired. The king found out and became furious; he filled the tank of water with mounds of dust and razed the temple. He then swore, "Whoever shall dig out this tank that I have filled with dust or rebuild this temple will take upon himself all the sins of adultery committed here by men and women, blinded by their lust." One day the king's young wife went to his bed to kill him. She made love to him until he fell into an exhausted sleep, and then she took out a knife that she had hidden in her hair and took his life. Thus the king paid for destroying that wonderful holy site, a terrible, terrible act that everyone had condemned.[30]

This text begins with the premise (shared, after all, by Manu and most other Sanskrit texts) that everyone wants to commit adultery: "Women . . . had been chaste, moral, and faithful to their husbands only out of fear of some terrible retribution in the next life." It then removes that obstacle, and everyone does commit adultery, since the idea of faithfulness, which had previously overpowered the desire to be unfaithful, vanished: "The very idea of a woman's being faithful to her husband vanished, and men were no longer faithful to their wives." It argues, further, that there is a divine precedent for the removal of such an obstacle: "In that same temple long ago, Brahmā himself was purified after he had sinned by looking with lust on the face of Satī, Śiva's wife." This is a clever inversion of another well-known theme, the story that tells how, after Brahmā gazed lustfully upon Satī, Śiva beheaded Brahmā, and Brahmā's head stuck to Śiva's hand until he was released from *his* sin at the temple of "The Release from the Skull" (Kapālamocana) in Benares.[31] In this text, instead of Brahmā's head on Śiva's hand, Śiva himself is on Brahmā's head, and instead of freedom from the sin of murdering a Brahman (an adulterous Brahman), one here gains freedom from the sin of being oneself an adulterous Brahman (or an adulterous anything else). So, too, the theme of destroying a temple, which Phyllis Granoff wisely relates to the problem of the destruction of Hindu temples by Muslims during this period, is also a variant on a more general theme of the destruction of shrines that allow people of all castes to go to heaven.[32] And the king's curse, that anyone who revives the shrine "will take upon himself all the sins of adultery committed here by men and women, blinded by their lust," is a variant of the more ancient theme of the transfer of the sin of adultery from the god Indra to any human adulterer.[33]

But which side is the text on? At first, it presents what may be seen as an antireligious, commonsense view: adultery is adultery, no matter what the gods say. Thus the Brahman grumpily remarks, "I shall not take my wife home with me even if she has been purified, for I have seen her making love to her lover with my very own eyes." And, of course, the condition of sinlessness is not allowed to endure: now that the temple is gone, adulterers will be punished. Yet the author betrays his wistful appreciation of the brief divine escape clause through his evident satisfaction about the murder of the king who destroyed the temple, and in his final statement: "Thus the king paid for destroying that wonderful holy site, a terrible, terrible act that everyone had condemned." To this extent, at least, the dharmic view of adultery is ultimately condemned, even while it is conceded as the way things have to be.

A hilarious, but ideologically similar, series of arguments in favor of adultery appears in Tārā's education of Candra: "Making love with one's wife is for having children. It's no fun. Courtesans cost money. Hunting women in the alleyways is hard work, and not too comfortable. If you think about it, only sex with other men's wives is any good. The whole world sings its praises.[34] Impotent men, unable to satisfy their wives, very cleverly wrote down on palm leaves that it's a sin to make love to someone else's wife. They just wanted their own wives untouched. There is no reason to be disturbed by such dried-up, fallen leaves."[35] Candra, at least, found this argument entirely convincing. One wonders who else it was meant to convince.

The Niyoga

If violation of the guru's wife is the paramount sin, it follows from the logic of misogyny that, at least in myths, the guru himself is allowed to have sex with otherwise proscribed women in general (as in the tale of Dharma and Sudarśana's wife) and with one sort of woman in particular: a woman whose husband fails to give her children. This tradition intersects with the real-life tradition of the *niyoga*, the only other instance in which a woman is legally permitted to have sex with a man other than her husband.

The levirate union, derived from the late Latin *leviratus* (son-in-law), is sometimes (apparently wrongly) said to be so called because of its occurrence in the Hebrew Bible, where Levi's brother begets a son on his behalf (and where a descendant of Levi, Onan, invents the sin of onanism in order *not* to function as a levirate father). Levirate union is a form of nonmarriage invented in order to accomplish the most important goal of marriage (in Hindu or, for that matter, Jewish law): the birth of a son.

The *Rg Veda* speaks of the wife of a dead man sleeping with his brother: "Who invites you, as a widow takes her husband's brother to her bed, as a young woman takes a young man to a room?"[36] The commentators, though not the text itself, also identify as the brother-in-law the man who extends his hand to the widow as she lies down on her husband's grave.[37] But this describes what seems to happen, not what is prescribed by law; after all, the verse goes on to talk about premarital sex (the young woman taking the young man to her room), which has no legal status here (though it is not condemned, as it will be in later Hinduism). Moreover, the *Rg Veda* says nothing about legal progeny resulting from this union with the husband's brother.

The substitute father, the levirate father, must produce a son on the husband's behalf. The surrogate is always said to act in accordance with the man's will, and usually with the woman's, but sometimes she is unwilling. For the myths of levirate union are, like so many myths (as Lévi-Strauss teaches us), about an insoluble contradiction: on the one hand, a man must never have sex with his brother's wife; on the other hand, he must have sex with his brother's wife if the brother is dead. The tension gives rise to the myth. Whether or not the brother is doing his dead brother a favor or an injury is a much debated question, the source of considerable tension within the mythology. Legally and biologically, the person you most want to have sex with your wife, when you are dead, is your brother, because he has your genes. But psychologically, the last person you want to have sex with your wife, even when you are dead, is your brother, because of sibling rivalry (remember Jacob and Esau). For this reason the *niyoga* is the most liminal form of Hindu pseudomarriage, poised on the volatile fault line that distinguishes and connects marriage and adultery: *niyoga* is paradigmatic in myth but stigmatized in *dharmaśāstra*, secretly longed for but publicly disavowed.

Moreover, there are two different duties at stake here: the brother has a duty to give an heir to his dead brother, but he also has a duty to allow the woman, his brother's wife, to fulfil her own duty to produce a child. This is less important than the first, but it, too, counts.

Thus Hindus speak of the *ṛtugamana,* the law that a man must have sex with his wife during her fertile season. In the myth of Uttaṅka, for instance, a married woman attempts to seduce a man who is not her husband by arguing that otherwise her fertile period will be in vain.[38]

Usually the need for the substitute arises when the intended father of a child has died or become impotent before begetting a child; one rather extreme solution to this problem is to invoke the dead man himself, whose corpse miraculously returns to impregnate his widow.[39] But the usual male sexual substitute was, in the Vedic period, the dead man's brother, whose right (indeed whose duty) to beget a child upon his brother's widow was legitimized and institutionalized in the custom of the *niyoga.* Later, the epics speak of the practice of inviting a learned Brahman to beget a son on behalf of a dead man.

Let me now consider the paradigmatic mythic cycle that illuminates the paradox of the *niyoga,* the cycle of Vyāsa and Dīrghatamas, first as it appears in the epics and Puranas and then as it appears in *The Laws of Manu.*

Vyāsa and Dīrghatamas in the Epics and Puranas

Vyāsa, a man of the Brahman class who is a sage and the author of the great epic, the *Mahābhārata,* is implicated in a cycle of stories about *niyoga* impregnations. His situation is made further ambiguous by the fact that he is both the brother of the dead man and a Brahman sage, the two acceptable *niyoga* surrogates. He is, moreover, both an actor in the story and its narrator, who partially redeems, through telling the story of the five Pāṇḍava brothers, the guilt that he incurred in his flawed begetting of those very Pāṇḍavas.[40] This cycle begins in the *Bṛhaddevatā,* roughly contemporaneous with the early Puranas, which tells the tale of Dīrghatamas, involving both male and female sexual surrogates:

> A childless king asked the blind and aged sage Dīrghatamas to beget a son on behalf of him in the chief queen; the sage agreed, but the queen, who considered the sage too old and disgusting for her bed, sent her maid in her place, and the maid gave birth to the great king Kakṣīvat.[41]

Since Dīrghatamas is not the brother of the king, this is an example of the pseudo-*niyoga* practice of inviting a Brahman to act on behalf of the childless father.

The story of Dīrghatamas's begetting of Kakṣīvat is retold a few centuries later in the great epic, the *Mahābhārata,* on an apt occasion; the fathers of the heroes of the *Mahābhārata* are born when the aged sage Vyāsa is called in to beget children upon the childless wives of the dead king, Vicitravīrya, his half brother by a different father. For Satyavatī first bore Vyāsa to the sage Parāśara, who afterward restored her virginity and went away forever; later she married a king and gave birth to Vicitravīrya. Satyavatī is unwilling to allow her daughters-in-law to be impregnated by anyone other than her dead son, until she is told the paradigmatic story of Dīrghatamas's begetting of Kakṣīvat. It is then suggested that they call in "some Brahman who has good qualities, and pay him, and let him beget progeny in the fields of Vicitravīrya." But Satyavatī suggests, instead, that they call in her illegitimate son, Vyāsa, who is both the brother, as in the older *niyoga*, and a Brahman, as in the later, the pseudo-*niyoga* represented by Dīrghatamas.

Vyāsa agrees to impregnate the women, but the first wife, Ambikā, closes her eyes in revulsion (in addition to being old and ugly, Vyāsa, whose grandmother was a fish, smells fishy), and so her son, Dhṛtarāṣṭra, is born blind (like Dīrghatamas, the paradigmatic pseudo-*niyoga* begetter); when the second wife, Ambalikā, turns pale, her son, Pāṇḍu, is born pale. And when the first wife, Ambikā, is subjected to Vyāsa for a second time, the folk theme of the maid sent in disguise is attracted to the myth: Ambikā sends a servant girl in her place, and the resulting son, Vidura, is a servant instead of a king.[42]

Thus the *niyoga* of Vyāsa (who appears in the epic as a kind of walking semen bank) is highly problematic. The widows of Vicitravīrya reject him. Moreover, since Vyāsa's relationship to Vicitravīrya is clouded, being primarily maternal rather than paternal (he and Vicitravīrya have the same mother but different fathers), he is far from the perfect *niyoga* surrogate. The tension for and against the *niyoga* persists in the myths, both in the form of two different sets of myths and in the form of unresolved paradoxes within each myth. Thus the wives of Vicitravīrya both do and do not want to sleep with Vyāsa, and their ambivalence is the direct source of the tragedy of the *Mahābhārata*, a tragedy that stems from a problem in the paternity and birth of Pāṇḍu and Dhṛtarāṣṭra, the fathers of the warring cousins in the great epic, who are the *niyoga* offspring of Vicitravīrya.

The next episode in this series involves deities and is generally regarded as part of the mythical level of the epic:

> When the pale son [Pāṇḍu] reached maturity, he was cursed to die if he ever made love to his beloved queen, and so he, like his father, invoked substitute fathers for his sons; but this time his wife, Kuntī, had been given the boon of invoking gods for this purpose, and so Pāṇḍu's sons were fathered by gods.[43]

Pāṇḍu's progeny problems do not end here, however. Kuntī invokes not one god but five (or, in fact, six, one illicitly): before she married Pāṇḍu, she tried out her boon on the Sun God, resulting in the illegitimate birth of Karṇa (who remains a tragic problem throughout the epic); then, after Pāṇḍu's curse, she invokes the gods Indra (king of the gods), Dharma (religious law incarnate), Vāyu (the wind), and the two Aśvins (twin equine heroes like the Gemini or the Dioscuri) to produce the Pāṇḍavas. This is not true polyandry, since her husbands are gods. Nor is it a true *niyoga*, since the gods are not her brothers. But it functions in the pattern of the *niyoga* rather than of polyandry: the surrogates are invoked because her husband has failed to give her sons. The final solution in this steadily escalating hierarchy of male surrogates is the invocation of the gods—traditional fathers of so many special sons of virgin mothers. Only on this highest, mythical level is the substitute satisfactory to the woman, freeing her at last from having to supply her own female surrogates to accommodate the unsatisfactory male surrogates provided for her bed.

But is it the final solution? The felony is compounded in the next generation, when the Pāṇḍavas themselves, mortals, not gods, together marry a single wife, Draupadī, while any one of them is capable of giving her a son, and several do.

The epic thus offers us, in three successive generations, positive images of women who have several husbands, the first generation through a *niyoga*, the second through a pseudo-*niyoga*, and the third through simple polyandry. First, the three wives of Vicitravīrya have two husbands: Vicitravīrya and Vyāsa. Then Kuntī has six husbands (the six gods listed previously). Finally, Draupadī has five husbands, the five Pāṇḍava brothers.

The *Mahābhārata* is as troubled by this last situation as it is by the others, and gives too many excuses. This sort of polyandry is rare, if not unique, in Hindu mythology, and the epic goes to various awkward lengths to rationalize it. First, it is said that Kuntī (herself polyandrous), without looking up when her sons said of Draupadī, "Look what we found," replied, like every good mother, "Share it with your brothers," but when she saw Draupadī she cried out, "Alas, what have I said?"[44] Draupadī's father protests bitterly, but someone else counters with the example of a kind of inverted *niyoga* ("An elder brother can unite with the wife of a younger brother and still remain virtuous"),[45] inverted because in the normal *niyoga* it is the younger brother who replaces the elder brother.

In the midst of this complex discussion, Vyāsa (the *niyoga* partner of polyandrous women) is called in to arbitrate, and he tells an elaborate myth establishing that the Pāṇḍvas are five forms of the god Indra, five Indras cursed to become incarnate, and Draupadī is Lakṣmī, the goddess of royal prosperity. To cap it, he tells yet another story of a previous incarnation of Draupadī in which she was so eager to get a husband that she kept asking—five times, in fact—and yet another god, Śiva, granted her boon.[46] And then it is said that each time one of the men "took her hand" she became a virgin again.[47]

Even the relatively permissive *Kāmasūtra* commentator is troubled by the sexual mores of the epic. When the text asserts that a woman who has slept with five men can be had by anyone,[48] the commentator remarks, "Now, Draupadī [the wife of the five Pāṇḍava brothers] is unapproachable by other men because she had Yudhiṣṭhira and the others *as her husbands*. But one might ask of the people who made the ancient stories, 'How can one woman who is good have more than one husband?' (to which the text replies), 'The wives of relatives, (male) friends, learned Brahmans, and kings cannot [be regarded as promiscuous even if they have five husbands].' "[49]

Vyāsa and Ṛṣyaśṛṅga in Manu

Vyāsa's dilemmas are glossed in *The Laws of Manu*. Indeed, the commentaries on Manu adduce mythological instances from the epics in support of both points of view, for and against the *niyoga*, and it is interesting to note that Vyāsa plays a pivotal role in the two opposed views of fatherhood. In glossing Manu 9.34 ("Sometimes the seed prevails, and sometimes the woman's womb"), the commentaries cite two different sets of myth. In neither case does the womb actually prevail in the sense of producing children that resemble the mother; this would contradict the basic interpretation of the agricultural model to which Manu is committed. Rather, in the first case the seed claims the child (following the model which Manu generally rejects), and in the second the womb (that is, the owner of the womb) claims the child (following the model which Manu endorses).

Thus Vyāsa and Ṛṣyaśṛṅga, great sages whose fathers were priests and whose grandmother and mother were a female fish and a female antelope, respectively, but who were regarded as the sons of the men who begot them, are cited by the commentators as examples of the prevalence of the seed.[50] (Elsewhere, however, Manu explicitly prohibits sex with a female animal.)[51] This is the agricultural model: children resemble their fathers, and no matter what female they are born in, they belong to their fathers. This model, purely mythical, supernatural, and relegated to more ancient times, is superseded, however, by the second example, more realistic and modern: the commentators go on to cite, as an example of the prevalence of the womb, the case of Dhṛtarāṣṭra, the blind child whom, as we have seen earlier, Vyāsa begot in the "field" of Vicitravīrya but who was regarded as Vicitravīrya's son. This is the predominant model for the *niyoga*.[52] And it should be noted that there are genuine problems acknowledged in both sets of myths: the father may prevail in the supernatural examples because the mother was not just of the wrong caste but of the wrong species entirely; and the children are born with severe physical or social handicaps (such as Vyāsa's fishy smell or Dhṛtarāṣṭra's blindness), maternal inheritances, and, moreover, inherited acquired characteristics, in keeping with the theories of Lamarck and of most mythologies.

Manu's basic ideas about the seed and the field provide the trope for his consideration of adultery and the *niyoga:*

> Men who have no field but sow their seed in other men's fields are acting for the benefit of the men who own the fields, and the man whose seed it is does not get the fruit.[53] If no agreement about the fruit is made between the owners of the fields and the owners of the seed, it is obvious that the profit belongs to the owners of the fields; the womb is more important than the seed. But if this [field] is given over for seeding by means of an agreed contract, then in this case both the owner of the seed and the owner of the field are regarded as [equal] sharers of that [crop].[54]

The "contract" for seeding would presumably be the *niyoga,* in which the "equal" claims to the child produce problems in the mythology.

It is in the light of his complex attitude to procreation that one must consider Manu's treatment of the more specific problem of the *niyoga.* He both justifies the practice of *niyoga* and expresses, in no uncertain terms, his revulsion toward it and his complex reasons for disapproving of it:

> A man is known as a man who marries his older brother's widow if, out of lust, he conceives a passion for the wife of his deceased brother—even if she has been appointed [to have a child by him] in accordance with law.
>
> If, when he is not in extremity, an elder brother has sex with the wife of a younger brother, or a younger brother with the wife of an elder brother, both of them fall, even if they have been appointed [to have a child]. When the line of descendants dies out, a woman who has been properly appointed should get the desired children from a brother-in-law or a close relative. The appointed man, silent and smeared with clarified butter, should beget one son upon the widow in the night, but never a second. Some people who know about this approve of a second begetting on [such] women, for they consider the purpose of the appointment of the couple incomplete in terms of duty. But when the purpose of the appointment with the widow has been completed in accordance with the rules, the two of them should behave toward one another like a guru and a daughter-in-law. If the appointed couple dispense with the rule and behave lustfully, then they both fall as violators of the bed of a daughter-in-law and a guru.
>
> Twice-born men should not appoint a widow woman to [have a child with] another man, for when they appoint her to another man they destroy the eternal religion. The appointment of widows is never sanctioned in the Vedic verses about marriage, nor is the remarriage of widows mentioned in the marriage rules. For learned twice-born men despise this as the way of animals, which was prescribed for humans as well when Veṇa was ruling the kingdom. Formerly, he was a preeminent royal sage who enjoyed the whole earth, but his thinking was ruined by lust and he brought about a confusion of the classes. Since that time, virtuous men despise any man who is so

deluded as to appoint a woman to have children when her husband has died.[55]

But even here Manu tacitly acknowledges that this will be done, and finally he takes it for granted: "If a younger [brother] begets a son on the wife of the elder [brother], there should be an equal division between them. This is the established law."[56]

The myth of Veṇa expresses the tension in Manu (a king did establish the practice, but he was an evil king), but it is not merely part of the solution; it is also part of the problem, a myth that is the starting point for one of the great theodicies in Indian mythical history.[57] It is as if a Jew or Christian spoke of the sanctions for murder by citing the story of Cain from the Bible.

The Later History of the Levirate in India

The *niyoga* fell into desuetude and disrepute in later Hinduism—perhaps due to the sort of abuse depicted in the story of Bṛhaspati and Mamatā, his brother's wife—and was replaced, in the mythology at least, by the widespread custom of inviting a Brahman to impregnate a woman whose husband was, for one reason or another, unable to do this. The idea of the *niyoga* has been further problematized in contemporary India, as Sudhir Kakar has demonstrated in his analysis of a novel in which a brother forced to marry his older brother's wife is deeply troubled. The novel, *A Sheet, Somewhat Soiled,* by the Urdu writer Rajinder Singh Bedi,[58] tells of a young man named Mangla, whose older brother Tiloka, is murdered.

> The village elders' council decides that it would be best for the community and the bereaved family if Mangla, who now drives the *tonga* and has otherwise taken his brother's place, also takes over his wife. He should, in the language of their community, "cover her with a sheet." Rano [the wife], who had brought up Mangla as her own son, giving him her breasts to suck when at the birth of her daughter the little boy too had insisted on being fed, is initially averse to the idea of this marriage. However, she soon overcomes her scruples. . . . Mangla, though, cannot bear the thought of a marriage with such a strongly incestuous coloring.[59]

Mangla refuses to consummate the marriage until one day he beats her, as his older brother had done. Now "her body has ceased to be an object of avoidance. It has been man-handled, touched by Mangla as a husband. The marriage is consummated the same night and the couple begin to live together as husband and wife."[60]

Kakar has interesting things to say about this episode in the novel:

> Mangla's suffering . . . in the face of a long-awaited denouement to the incestuous wish, the embodiment in the flesh of fantasy hitherto entertained in the imagination alone, is much greater than Rano's. . . . Perhaps like many other women, she seems better able to cope with the guilt of incestuous urgings than her "son" who must first beat her for their impending transgression before he can accept his disturbing and dangerous sensual immersion.[61]

It might be argued that not all *niyoga*s bear the burden of the double incest—with the mother as well as with the brother's wife. Yet this reading (which is, in any case, the reading of the Urdu novel) is supported by the general tendency of Hinduism to bracket all potentially explosive sexual situations by defining the forbidden woman as the mother.

Incest aside, Kakar has even more interesting things to say about the persistence of the idea of the *niyoga* in contemporary India:

> For a time in Indian social history, the erotic importance of the brother-in-law—in the sense that he would or could have sexual relations with his elder brother's widow—was officially recognized in the custom of *niyoga*. . . . Though the custom gradually fell into disuse, especially with the prohibition of widow remarriage, the psychological core of *niyoga*, namely the mutual awareness of a married woman and her younger brother-in-law as potential or actual sexual partners, is very much an actuality even today. . . . In clinical practice, I have found that women who are on terms of sexual intimacy with a brother-in-law rarely express any feelings of guilt. Their anxiety is occasioned more by his leaving home or his impending marriage, which the woman perceives as an end to her sensual and emotional life.[62]

This is not a new problem. The *Kāmasūtra* gives a hint of what lies behind Manu's terror of the *niyoga* when it lists, among women who are quite likely to commit adultery, the wife of the oldest of several brothers.[63] (It also demonstrates how easily adultery and the *niyoga* could be conflated in the Hindu mind.) But it is not an old problem in India, either. The ambivalent relationship between a woman and her husband's brother is a paradox that arises in any society that simultaneously equates and opposes the virility of two brothers, but it is particularly acute in a society, such as India, that simultaneously legitimates and forbids the *niyoga* as a liminal form of marriage. Hovering on the borders of legitimate marriage to define it by demonstrating what it is not, adultery and the *niyoga* together demonstrate that Hindu marriage is, in itself, an elusive institution caught between a rock and a hard place.

NOTES

1. Arthur Anthony Macdonell and Arthur Barriedale Keith, *Vedic Index*, 2 vols. (London: John Murray, 1958), 1:396, 479.

2. *Ṛg Veda*, with the commentary of Sāyaṇa, 6 vols. ed. F. Max Müller (London: Oxford University Press, 1890–92), 10.101.11. Translated by Wendy Doniger O'Flaherty, *The Rig Veda: An Anthology of One Hundred and Eight Hymns* (Harmondsworth, Eng.: Penguin, 1980), p. 67.

3. *Taittirīya Saṃhitā* (Calcutta: Bibliotheca Indica, 1860), 5.6.8.3; *Maitrāyaṇī Saṃhitā* (Wiesbaden: Harassowitz, 1970), 3.4.7.

4. See, for example, the Soma hymns in the ninth *maṇḍala* of the *Ṛg Veda*.

5. *Ṛg Veda* 10.162.4–5; O'Flaherty, *The Rig Veda*, p. 292.

6. *Śatapatha Brāhmaṇa* (Benares: Chowkhamba Sanskrit Series, 96, 1964), 2.5.2.20. See also *Maitrāyaṇī Saṃhitā*, 1.10.11; *Taittirīya Brāhmaṇa* (Calcutta: Bibliotheca Indica, 1859), 1.6.5.2. The commentator, Sāyaṇa, helpfully glosses "with whom" as "with what lover" (*jāreṇa*).

7. *Atharva Veda*, with the commentary of Sāyaṇa, 5 vols. (Hoshiarpur: Vishveshvaranand Vedic Research Institute, 1960), 6.138.7, 9. See also Wendy Doniger O'Flaherty, *Women, Androgynes, and Other Mythical Beasts* (Chicago: University of Chicago Press, 1980), p. 30.

8. *Bṛhadarāṇyaka Upaniṣad* (in *One Hundred and Eight Upanishads*, ed. Wasudev Laxman Shastri Pansikar (Bombay: Nirnaya Sagara Press, 1913), 6.4.12; O'Flaherty, *Women, Androgynes, and Other Mythical Beasts*, p. 10.

9. *Śaṅkhāyana Gṛhya Sūtra* (Delhi: Munshi Ram Manoharlal, 1960), 3.13.5.

10. *Āpastamba Śrauta Sūtra*, 3 vols. (Calcutta: Asiatic Society of Bengal, 1882–1902), 1.99.

11. *The Laws of Manu* (*Manusmṛti*), ed. J. H. Dave, 6 vols. (Bombay: Bharatiya Vidya Bhavan, 1972–84); translated by Wendy Doniger with Brian K. Smith (Harmondsworth, Eng.: Penguin, 1991) [henceforth Manu], 9.20.

12. The *kṣetraja* is defined by Manu at 9.167.

13. Manu 11.55.

14. Manu 2.211–15.

15. Manu 11.104–7.

16. The "Painful" vow is explained in Manu 11.212.

17. See A. K. Ramanujan, "The Indian Oedipus," in *Oedipus: A Folklore Casebook*, ed. Lowell Edmunds and Alan Dundes (New York: Garland, 1984), pp. 234–61.

18. *Mahābhārata*, critical edition, ed. V. S. Sukthankar et al. (Poona: Bhandarkar Oriental Research Institute, 1933–69), 1.3.85–195.

19. *Mahābhārata* 13.2.36–85; cf. *Śiva Purāṇa* (Benares: Pandita Pustakalaya, 1964), 2.3.35.10, 34. Cited in Wendy Doniger O'Flaherty, *Śiva: The Erotic Ascetic* (London: Oxford University Press, 1973), p. 197.

20. *Viṣṇu Purāṇa*, with the commentary of Śrīdhara (Calcutta: Sanatana Sastra, 1972), 4.6.5–19.

21. *Bhāgavata Purāṇa*, with the commentary of Śrīdhara (Calcutta: Pandita Pustakalaya, 1972), 9.14.9–12.

22. *The Bhāgavata Purāṇa*, 4 vols., translated and annotated by Ganesh Vasudeo Tagare (Delhi: Motilal Banarsidass, 1976), 3: 1198.

23. Velcheru Narayana Rao, David Shulman, and Sanjay Subrahmanyam, *Symbols of Substance: Court and State in Nāyaka Period Tamilnadu* (Delhi: Oxford University Press, 1992), pp. 150–57.

24. Ibid., p. 158.

25. *Mahābhārata* 1.99.

26. *Bṛhaddevatā* of Śaunaka, Harvard Oriental Series, 5 (Cambridge, Mass.: Harvard University Press, 1904), 4.11–15.

27. *Bhāgavata Purāṇa* 9.20.34–38.

28. I am grateful to Paul Courtright for pointing out the relevance of this distinction in the present context.

29. See Wendy Doniger, "When God Has Lipstick on His Collar," Mackay Lecture, St. Lawrence University, 1991.

30. The *Tāpī Khaṇḍa* of the *Skanda Purāṇa*, chapter 78, verses 3–53, cited and discussed by Phyllis Granoff on these occasions: in "When Miracles Become Too Many: Stories of the Destruction of Holy Sites in the *Tāpī Khaṇḍa* of the *Skanda Purāṇa*," *Annals of the Bhandarkar Oriental Research Institute*, vol. 72, 1991; and an essay, "Halāyudha's Prism: The Experience of Religion in Medieval Hymns and Stories," in *Gods, Guardians, and Lovers: Temple Sculptures from North India, A.D. 700–1200*, ed. Vishakha N. Desai and Darielle Mason (New York: Asia Society Galleries, 1993), pp. 66–93. I have abbreviated and occasionally reworded the translation offered in this latter source.

31. See Wendy Doniger O'Flaherty, *The Origins of Evil in Hindu Mythology* (Berkeley: University of California Press, 1976), pp. 272–320.

32. Ibid., pp. 248–71.

33. *Rāmāyaṇa of Vālmiki*, ed. G. H. Bhatt et al. (Baroda: Oriental Institute, 1960–75), 7.30.20–45); O'Flaherty, *The Origins of Evil*, p. 165.

34. Narayana Rao, Shulman, and Subramanyam, *Symbols of Substance*, p. 156.

35. Ibid., p. 155.

36. *Ṛg Veda* 10.40.2.

37. Ibid., 10.18.6.

38. *Mahābhārata* 1.112.30.

39. Ibid., 10.18.6

40. See Bruce M. Sullivan, *Kṛṣṇa Dvaipāyana Vyāsa and the Mahābhārata: A New Interpretation* (Leiden: E. J. Brill, 1990).

41. *Bṛhaddevatā* 4.21–25; cf. also Sāyaṇa's commentary on *Ṛg Veda* 1.51.13.

42. *Mahābhārata* 1.99–100.

43. Ibid., 1.90, 1.109.

44. Ibid., 182.1–3.

45. Ibid., 1.188.10.

46. Ibid., 1.189.41–48.

47. Ibid., 1.190.14.

48. *Kāmasūtra of Vātsyāyana*, with the commentary of Śrī Yaśodhara (Bombay: Laksmivenkatesvara Press, 1856), 1.5.30.

49. Ibid., 1.5.31.

50. *Mahābhārata* 1.57, 3.110.

51. Manu 11.174.

52. *Mahābhārata* 1.57, 3.110, 1.96–100.

53. Manu 9.51.
54. Ibid., 9.52–53.
55. Ibid., 3.173, 9.58–68.
56. Ibid., 9.120.
57. See Doniger O'Flaherty, *The Origins of Evil,* esp. chapter 11: "The Split Child: Good and Evil Within Man."
58. Retold and analyzed by Sudhir Kakar in *Intimate Relations: Exploring Indian Sexuality* (Chicago: University of Chicago Press, 1990), pp. 9–14.
59. Ibid., p. 10.
60. Ibid.
61. Ibid., p. 14.
62. Ibid., pp. 13–14.
63. *Kāmasūtra of Vātsyāyana* 5.1.52–54.

8

Satī, Sacrifice, and Marriage: The Modernity of Tradition

PAUL B. COURTRIGHT

> *Satī is the* nicoṛ *[essence] of* pativratādharma *[moral action appropriate for married women].*
>
> Agehananda Bharati

Satī *and the Problem of Interpretation*

Of the many images of India that Westerners have implanted in their imaginations over the centuries of contact, the spectacle of the dutiful wife calmly taking her place on the pyre of her deceased husband has provoked both moral revulsion and voyeuristic curiosity. Westerners called such ritual immolations "suttee" (*satī* according to current transliteration practices), taking the Sanskrit term meaning a wife who possesses great virtue. The specter of a married woman walking toward the funeral pyre and joining her husband in cremation presses the interpretive process to its margins. Both traditional Hindu and modern Western or Indian interpreters might well agree that such an action cuts against the grain of a universal and innate human reflex for self-preservation. At the same time it raises the question of the *satī*'s agency: did she choose this act of self-annihilation freely, and if so, what is the context for such a "free" choice?

Two conclusions might be drawn from the spectacle of the *satī* immolation. Either she is not human, or she is not acting out of her own free will.[1] Traditional Hinduism has tended to take the former interpretation, stressing the ways in which the *satī*, particularly during her final moments prior to immolation, behaves in ways that make her indistinguishable from a goddess. She distributes gifts, confers blessings, inflicts curses, and acts as if the pain of her immanent fiery death and the social and physical world of *saṃsāra* were an illusion. Within the fire itself she does not exhibit the involuntary reflexes of pain that one would expect of a human being. Western and modern Indian interpretations, beginning with the late eighteenth century, have often argued that the *satī* was coerced into her actions either directly through the use of opium or other drugs that left her stupefied or, more subtly, by the patriarchal ideology that convinced her that her self-annihilation was her duty or opportunity. With either of these broad interpretations the agency of the *satī* as a woman becomes erased, toward divinity in one case and toward coercion in the other. Consequently the issue of *satī* as an interpretive issue in cross-cultural studies has far outweighed the relative importance that *satī* as an actual event has played in the long history of Hindu culture. The increased attention being paid in recent years to issues of gender and power has added new emphasis to the fact that it is only women who become *satīs*, and the sacrifice of women in a religious or pseudoreligious context connects issues of gender, power, religion, and violence in compelling ways.

Historical evidence suggests that before the British colonial period incidents of such immolations were rare, confined largely to politically elite and martial classes, especially Rajputs, along India's border regions with the largely Islamic cultures of western Asia.[2] Since the sixteenth century Western travelers to India have frequently included purported eyewitness accounts of such events, frequently with lengthy descriptions of ritual details and comments about their own moral horror at Hindus' apparent callous disregard for the woman undergoing such a death along with deep admiration for her (misguided) devotion to her late husband. In the imagined India of Western experience and interpretation, *satī* came to stand for the whole of Hinduism as an irrational, perverse, and heroic religious orientation to life.

By the turn of the nineteenth century, as Britain was establishing its sovereignty over much of India, incidents of *satī* became more common in Bengal in districts under its jurisdiction. A lengthy debate took place over how *satī* was to be understood. Consensus emerged among colonial authorities and some Hindu reformists that *satī* was not an integral part of Hinduism but a medieval perversion of its core values. The principal beneficiaries of these religiously glossed murders of women were Brahman priests who collected fees for performing the rituals and family members who stood to benefit from inheritances that otherwise might have come to the surviving widow. Consequently the British authorities and their client Hindu states banned the practice.[3] A similar policy has been followed by the government of India since 1947.

In recent years accounts of immolations of women that took place in largely isolated areas continued to be reported.[4] The issue of *satī* has emerged now as an important part of the discourse of feminist criticism of Hindu culture's patriarchal structure. From this perspective *satī* is the most egregious example of an attempt to simultaneously repress women and celebrate to the point of deification their self-annihilation in the name of religion. In both the early colonial period and the contemporary moment Hindu traditionalists have argued that *satī*, when properly understood and undertaken, is a sacred religious act that only the most extraordinary women who have a highly evolved moral vision and discipline are capable of performing. In those rare cases, it is argued, such women should not be impeded by the state from carrying out their religious destinies. For both critics and admirers of *satī* there is a shared sense that it fits into the total system of Hinduism as an emblem of its moral bankruptcy or its noble heritage. In the contemporary debate between religious and secular visions of Indian society, *satī* has taken on renewed meaning as a contested symbol that contains contradictory interpretations.

Agehananda Bharati, the late Austrian-born anthropologist and Hindu monk, once commented that *satī* was the *nicoṛ* of *pativratādharma*.[5] His comment warrants some interpretive analysis and investigation of terms. The term *pativratādharma* was discussed in the introduction to this volume.[6] My intention here is to stress some features of this notion that are particularly germane to the issue of *satī*. *Pativratādharma* may be interpretively translated as those morally significant actions, duties, and attitudes that are appropriate to the status of a married woman, the central focus of which is the welfare of her husband and all that adheres to him: household, reputation, kin, ancestors, descendants, deities, and life circumstances. Etymologically, the term means moral action (*dharma*) that is rooted in vows (*vrata*, from the Sanskrit root *vṛ*, 'turn') undertaken for the protection and well-being of the husband or lord (*pati*). These duties, and the orientations that frame them, are presented formally in classical treatises on morality (*dharmaśāstras*) and informally through patterns of behavior and expectations regarding married life passed through generations, encoded in rituals, and celebrated in mythology and folklore.

Pativratādharma may be seen as a subset of the more generic category *dharma* (morally significant action). There are many *dharmas* according to the various classes and stages of life. Kings, priests, ascetics, students, servants, warriors, and so forth all have their particular normative codes of action appropriate to their life situations. At the center of this moral universe is the notion of service or self-subordination: priests serve gods, kings serve the well-being of the populace by maintaining order and patronizing the worship of the gods, warriors serve kings, students serve teachers, children serve parents, servants serve masters, ascetics serve the goal of renunciatory liberation (*mokṣa*), and married women serve their husbands. Within this life context of service is the notion that orientation to a single set of commitments provides the environment and discipline that enable one to be effective in the world while keeping one's sights on ultimate liberation amid the interminable repetition of life. Ideally, if everyone did their service properly, harmonious order would prevail. As with any normative moral system, the ideal of an overarching, coherent *dharma* was and continues to be subverted in various ways: warriors have rebelled against kings, priests have protested against gods, students have disobeyed their teachers, and wives have rebelled in various ways against the authority of their husbands, as several essays in this volume demonstrate. As constructions largely of male Brahman elites over a period of centuries, formulations of *dharma* tend to privilege Brahmans over other orders of society, and men over women. The extent to which women historically or in contemporary Hindu society subscribe to this formulation of their natures and destinies, or how they receive and reformulate it, as the essays by Raheja, Hancock, Gold, and Harlan (see chapters 2, 3, 5, and 9, this volume) especially explore, is a complex and contentious question.

The other term Bharati used in his comment, *nicoṛ*, also requires an etymological detour, for it contains important insights into the relationship between *satī* and the ethos of marriage. The Hindi word *nicoṛ*[7] literally means the summary, gist, essence, or sum and substance of something. It is synonymous with *tattva*, a Sanskrit word meaning the essence of something. The etymological root, however, reveals a deeper resonance. The noun *nicoṛ* is derived from the verb *nicoṛnā*, meaning to wring or squeeze dry. It usually applies to squeezing juice out of fruit, water out of clothes, the essential meaning out of a conversation; extracting money from someone; or reducing a person to nothing. *Nicoṛ* refers to the process by which the juice or essence is extracted through hard pressing or squeezing. It also refers to the product, what is left over after the wringing out has taken place: the juice, essence, money, that which is of value that is left after all the contexts that located it have been stripped away. This double significance of the act and the product of hard effort gives the word a rich semantic range.

That *satī* would occupy the place of *nicoṛ*, the process and result of the wringing out of the ethos of the wife living her life in service and devotion to her husband, requires some further comment. The ethos of *pativratādharma* places much of the power and responsibility for the husband and his social context in the hands of his wife. Through ritual acts of devotion such as prayer, fasting, and service, the wife gathers together her inherent generative power (*śakti*) and focuses it toward the well-being of her husband. In north India, when this *śakti* is focused on the goals of *pativratādharma*, it transforms itself into *sat*, the capacities of dharmic perfection.[8] In the wife's ideal moral universe, the husband functions as the point of orientation for her actions, as the king does for the warrior, the teacher for the student, the deity for the priest, and so forth. Her devotion, therefore, is not necessarily borne out of romantic affection or even friendship with her husband. Indeed, in terms of the logic of *pativratādharma*, his behavior toward her is irrelevant to her commitments to her own moral orientation; her actions have a kind of radical independence that are not derivative of his. Indeed, a neglectful or even abusive husband may be construed as a more demanding challenge for a wife's devotion, just as Kṛṣṇa's neglect of his *gopī* lovers only intensifies their devotion to him.

In the normative configuration of traditional Hinduism, in addition to being empowered and responsible for the husband's well-being, the wife is also understood to be his "half body," merged ontologically through the ritual of marriage. In the process of moving from her natal to her conjugal home, she is expected to abandon her identification with her natal kin and assimilate herself into the identities of her husband's family, ancestors, deities, moral codes, and behavioral practices. Nicholas's essay (see chapter 6, this volume) explores aspects of the textual warrants for this process, and Raheja's essay (see chapter 2, this volume) uncovers a countertradition among women who find themselves defined by and resisting this formulation of their roles as wives.

Satī: *The Double Bind*

In the ideal construction of *pativratādharma* the wife empties herself in service to her husband's well-being. This emptying in turn generates *sat*, which regenerates her capacity for service. The expected consequence of this pattern is that she and her husband will have a long life together. When death comes, it will come to her first, as many Hindu women pray will happen as part of their ritual practices for the protection of their husbands. In the perfect Hindu moral universe, there would be no widows. However, such a perfect moral universe does not exist within the realm of *saṃsāra*. It is the widow, more than any other person, who exemplifies the tension between the ideal version of reality and its manifestation in ordinary life. The widow is the most ideologically and ritually marginalized. She is the emblem of the culture's failure to perfect the ordinary world of experience. When the husband dies first, the wife is faced with a dilemma. As his "half body" she is, in principle, inseparable from him; but as a person in a social world she is alive and he is dead. Traditional Hindu culture regards the widow as one who is dead in life, and many of the avoidances and perceived contaminations associated with death are transferred to the widow, as Wadley's essay (see chapter 4, this volume) explores.

The predicament of the deceased husband is one of the places in the Hindu world where the ideal construction and the existential situation facing the woman takes the form of a double bind. Her own powers of protection and generative moral force (*sat*) are insufficient to overcome the vagaries of her or her husband's *karma*, and the ripening of misdeeds of previous lives has now come to take its toll. She is confronted with the limits of the protective powers her culture presumes her to have. Because the husband's and wife's lives are religiously construed to be indivisible, she faces a crisis of interpretation of the meaning of her own life. If the moral force of *pativratādharma* is "real," and the world of *saṃsāra* is "illusion," as Hindu philosophy teaches, and if the wife has generated the moral capacities (*sat*) from years of service and devotion to the well-being of her husband, then she may wish to go with him in death as she did in life. While she has not been successful in keeping him alive, she retains the capacity to decide whether she should remain alive as a survivor and keep her connections with him in place through continued ritual veneration, or whether she should go with him in a single and spectacular display of violent self-annihilating devotion. The Sanskrit term for the rite of immolation with the deceased husband, *sahagamana* (going with), carries this sense of what is taking place. Such a "going with" confirms the priority of the religious construction of reality over the existential situation of the "natural" fear of death, let alone burning alive. From the religious perspective, the death of the body does not take place until the indissoluble spirit (*ātman*) is released through the purification of the cremation fire. The wife does not become a widow until her husband is cremated. By joining him on the pyre she dies together with him as his "half body," bypassing the status of widowhood and avoiding the ritual contamination and social marginality it would bring on her and those around her. This display of devotion releases a surplus of religious merit, which the *satī* distributes to her kin and community at the time of her death and afterward in the form of her continuing presence as a beneficent ancestress to her lineage. Subsequent generations of her lineage appeal to her for protection, as she had protected her husband in the transition from one cosmological plane to another. This, I think, is what Bharati had in mind when he called *satī* the *nicoṛ* of *pativratādharma*. It is the place where the double bind of the Hindu construction of marriage, body, and *dharma* wrings itself out. And it is the wife, the *satī*, who becomes the vehicle for it. She is the field of battle for this internal conflict of the tradition. She is the *nicoṛ:* the substance and the wringing. From the perspective of the logic of Hinduism as a system, the perfection of *pativratādharma*, the *satī* is its embodied substance. She is the context or form in which the normative religious world and the existential moment converge in an act that is at one and the same time one of annihilation and deification. Hence, she takes on a supernatural persona. She walks calmly to the pyre, whereas ordinary people would shrink in terror. She dispenses blessing on those who venerate her and invokes curses on those who resist her. From the perspective of her as a person, she is the victim, the one wrung out of the system, the one who is backed into the corner of choosing between a death of life in the fire or a life of social and ritual death as a widow. This double bind, or *nicoṛ*, is what gives *satī* its religious character, its emotive power, and its moral dissonance. As a sacrificial act it carries within it the burden of the validity of the religious world from which it takes its definition. A religious interpretation, which foregrounds the normative world of *pativratādharma* and existence as *saṃsāra*, could account for what might be going through the mind of a wife when facing the choice of going with her husband in the fire or staying behind as a widow. Once the religious frame of reference is removed, as the colonial and secular state ideologies and practices have done, then what is left or wrung out is some form of suicide or murder, both of which are criminal actions under the law. Religion moves to the margin as the "mystification" appealed to in hiding the actual criminal act of the murder of a woman. The *satī* becomes a victim, and the devotees become accomplices in her destruction.

Satī *and the Modernity of Tradition: The Story of Bāḷāsatīmātā*

Nearly two centuries of colonial and secular governance have undermined *satī* as an uncomplicated act of religious heroism, removed it from its religious context altogether as far as the legal system is concerned, and relegated it to the category of the criminal. Anyone attempting to become a *satī*, assisting a *satī*, or displaying one's regard for a *satī* as a deity in rituals of veneration faces the threat of severe criminal penalties. Yet the underlying religious values that *satī* embodied have not disappeared in contemporary India, especially in the rural areas in the northern and northwestern parts of the country. In addition to the occasional cases of actual immolations that frequently receive considerable media attention, there are other, quieter expressions of the continuity of the religious importance of *satī* and its underlying moral and religious values, which have adapted themselves to changing circumstances.

In the state of Rajasthan in the northwestern part of India, there is a tradition of religious devotion to women who are called *jīvit satīmātā* (living *satī*-mothers). These are women who sought to be *satī*s when their husbands died but were prevented from carrying out their objective by their kinsmen, who feared criminal prosecution for assisting them. Consequently, they turned to saintly lives of ascetic surrender, no longer eating, drinking, or sleeping. Because they declared their intention to become *satī*s, they have retained much of the aura associated with wives who completed the sacrifice. I first learned of this tradition from Lindsey Harlan, who had been conducting research on high-caste women's religious traditions. According to Harlan, the living *satīmātā* tradition appears to be quite recent, probably emerging only after the criminalization of the actual ritual immolations of wives in Rajasthan in the mid–nineteenth century.[9] While there are not many of these women, as indeed there were not many *satīs*, their personal charisma attracts followers, predominantly women, and stories of their miraculous powers circulate through the regions in which they live. So far as I know, this *satīmātā* tradition is not found outside of Rajasthan and parts of Gujarat that border on it.

On the walls of homes I visited of people in the Rajput community in Jaipur, I noticed a number of portraits of a kindly looking, saintly woman (see Fig. 8.1). There was a clarity and simplicity about her face and eyes that struck me the first time I saw her portrait. When I asked who she was I was told that she was Bāḷāsatīmātā, a Rajput woman who had "left her body" the previous year. She had lived in the village of Bala, near Jodhpur, and many regarded her as a divine being. This was the same person that Harlan had told me about, and later wrote about in her book on the religious traditions of Rajput women.[10] People told me that when she was a young wife her husband died quite suddenly, and she announced she would become a *satī*. But, because it was against the law, her family prevented her. In the years that followed she became more and more saintly and began to gather devotees around her, performed miracles, cured diseases, and shed the radiance of her divine being to all who came into her presence. Harlan comments on the symbolism surrounding the *satīmātā:*

> The living satīmātā remains in this world but is no longer of it. She is no longer a *pativratā* in the standard sense of the term, nor is she technically dead. She breathes yet requires no food, drinks no water, and needs no sleep. The fuel that keeps her alive is *sat*, the internal heat that she has accumulated as a *pativratā*.[11]

Intrigued by this new saint, I visited her shrine in the village of Bala, not far off the main road linking Ajmer and Jodhpur. There I found a small temple in her honor, a few residences, and a modest pilgrimage center. The centerpiece of the complex was a small hut, called the *kuṭiyā*, where she had spent much of her life in meditation and which came to be associated with her as the locale of her extraordinary powers and presence.[12] The peaceful atmosphere of the place and the quiet hospitality of its residents reminded me of other ashrams I had visited whose clientele were regional and were largely unknown to foreign visitors and devotees.

A member of the trust committee of the shrine gave me a copy of a hagiography of Bāḷāsatīmātā entitled *Śrī satī mātā caritāmṛt*, which was

Figure 8.1 Bālāsatīmātā (contemporary lithograph).

published in Hindi in 1986 by Rup Kunwar Mehta, one of her devotees. Like other hagiographies of saints in India and elsewhere, in terms of genre the text stands somewhere between myth and biography. The historical detail of events gives way to the moral point of the story, or the story as an exemplification of the power and grace of the *satī-mātā*. The information for this portion of the essay has been compiled from interviews with Bāḷāsatīmātā's devotees in Jaipur, Jodhpur, and

Figure 8.2 The *kuṭiyā*, or small hut, in which Bālāsatīmātā spent much of her later life. (Photograph by Paul Courtright)

Bala, during a visit to Rajasthan in the summer of 1987, and from Mehta's book.

Although the text of the *Śrī satī mātā caritāmṛt* was published in 1986 and distributed in an inexpensive paperback format, it presents the life and work of Bāḷāsatīmātā within a traditional mode of remembrance and narration that reaches deeply into the religious sensibilities of its Hindu readers. The term *caritāmṛta*, literally translated as "life-giving nectar of the acts (of, in this case, Bāḷāsatīmātā)," draws upon a Sanskrit and vernacular *carita* or *caritra* genre of literature dating back at least a millennium. Texts of this genre praise a particular deity or individual for deeds that have extraordinary religious meaning. They, in turn, were probably modeled on the even older *mahātmyā* and *aṣṭaka* literatures, often embedded within Purana texts, which eulogize a sacred place and celebrate its redemptive powers for pilgrims who come there.

In Bengal the medieval *maṅgal kāvya* literatures extol the auspicious (*maṅgal*) qualities attending to the works and lives of deities. By the seventeenth century, among Bengali Vaiṣṇavas, Kṛṣṇadāsa's *Caitanya Caritāmṛta* celebrates the works and teachings of its most famous saint. The chief characteristic of the *caritāmṛt* as a genre of text is its tendency to combine an anecdotal life "history" with theological reflections on the meaning of particular events that, in turn, display the sacredness of the life being narrated. The *caritāmṛt* text is a sort of narrative epiphany, drawing the reader—or listener, as these texts are more often recited than read—to see the divine character of the life being reviewed. The goal of this kind of religious writing is less to provide a biography, in the modern sense of the term, than to offer a series of episodes in which divine reality emerges through the situations in which the saint finds herself or himself. Hence, the *caritāmṛt* reads as much like myth as it does like history. The text attempts to narratively embody its subject as an exemplar of human perfection as viewed through the lens of Hindu religious values. The particular details of the life being narrated become reorganized in subordination to that overall religious objective. Consequently, such texts cannot simply be read for their biographical or historical content; they must also be read for their *religious* content, the theological vision that animates both the life being narrated and the devotion of the narrator.

The expanded sense of the title of the hagiography is that the hearing or reading of the text is an act of ingesting the nectar (*amṛt*), which has the properties of immortality (*amṛt*) that one derives from knowing about the actions of Bāḷāsatīmātā. These characteristics of the *caritāmṛt* as a religious text bear sufficient resemblance to Western premodern hagiographies, or sacred biographies of saints, as to enable us to consider the *Śrī satī mātā caritāmṛt* a hagiography.

Despite this mixing of biographical and devotional material, I will attempt here to reconstruct a bare outline of Bāḷāsatīmātā's life and significance for her devotees drawn from episodes presented in this text and from the narrative summaries of her life story that I heard during my visit to Bala. There are some discrepancies between what I learned from talking with devotees in Bala and Jaipur and what is contained in the *Śrī satī mātā caritāmṛt,* principally whether her attempted *satī* was in response to her husband's or her nephew's death. From the perspective of the devotees, the religiously significant issue was her determination to surrender her body in response to her sense of her *dharma.* Indeed, when her devotees and hagiography speak of *satī* in relation to Bāḷāsatīmātā, it is the broader, more generic meaning of her as one whose moral perfection has been achieved.

She was born Rup Kumari, the daughter of a Shekhewat Rajput family, in nearby Bilara district, on August 16, 1903. Her birth was surrounded by auspicious signs such as cool breezes that enabled nearby temple bells to ring, announcing her arrival.[13] Her astrological chart closely resembled that of Mīrā Bāī, with whom she identified as a young woman. Her paternal uncle was a religious man and predicted at the time of her birth that she would become a great spiritual being. Although her caste did not prohibit the eating of meat, her own family followed a strictly vegetarian diet.

Even as a child Rup Kumari exhibited religious inclinations. She spent long hours in meditation, enjoyed the company of mendicants who came through her village, and often engaged them in theological conversations about the forms and formlessness of god. Her uncle tutored her in religious matters, and she developed the reputation of one who had remarkable spiritual proclivities. During her childhood, Rup Kumari suffered a series of losses: her mother died when she was twelve, and three years later her father and sister died from a plague epidemic. These experiences may have only served to reinforce her commitment to renunciation and her perception of the world as a transient and unreliable place.

She resisted attempts by her family to arrange a marriage for her, but finally her uncle advised her to proceed with making arrangements. He read her palm and predicted she would become a great *satī;* hence, a marriage would be an essential step. He reassured her that he would protect her celibacy. When she was sixteen she was engaged to one Junkar Singh of Bala village. He had been away for a number of years serving with the Indian army. He had previously been engaged to Rup Kumari's elder sister, but she died before the wedding took place. Her wedding was set for May 10, 1919, despite her uncle's warning that the astrological calculations for the ceremony were incorrectly followed. She joked with her uncle that while her worldly husband was approaching her in full royal dress, she was dreaming about her spiritual husband, Kṛṣṇa, from her previous births. Mīrā Bāī had a similar understanding about her worldly and spiritual relationships, as explored in Harlan's essay (see chapter 9, this volume).

As the bride and groom sat before the sacred fire, the priest joined their hands together. When Junkar Singh's hand touched Rup Kumari's, he felt an intense shock as though from a hot fire or electricity. Immediately the vermilion decoration of her hand *(hīnā)* disappeared from Rupa Kumari's hand. The intense heat in her body that Junkar Singh felt was from her *sat,* the physical manifestation of her spiritual attainments resulting from her meditational practices. He immediately came down with a high fever, and was only half conscious during the remainder of the ceremony.

The bride and groom moved to his family home in Bala, but his fever did not subside, and doctors were unable to help him. His army leave was about to expire, and he managed to get to the town of Bilara nearby to send a telegram to his commanding officer about his ill health. As he lay dying, Rup Kumari took water for him to drink. He told her that as he looked at her he had a vision of Durgā. On May 25, nine days after the wedding, Junkar Singh died, never having recovered from the fever resulting from Rup Kumari's touch.

When Junkar Singh died, Rup Kumari did not exhibit the usual grief reactions. Her hagiographer interprets her response theologically: "She was untouched by happiness and sorrow, accepting whatever god does is for the best. She was not attached to the husband and thought of herself as already given to Lord Kṛṣṇa as Mīrā had done."[14] Nevertheless, after her husband died, she began eating even less, giving her food to animals and guests. In the years that followed, she lived the quiet life of a Rajput widow, doing household work for her in-laws, taking care of the sick animals, constantly reciting the names of Rāma and Kṛṣṇa, and engaging in yogic practices. She frequently remained awake all night, engaged in devotional singing and meditation.

Conversations with devotees in Bala revealed a somewhat different version of her story. According to their account Rup Kumari was married at the age of ten. When Junkar Singh died, Rup Kumari declared that she would join her husband in his cremation, but the king of Jodhpur and other village authorities made an obstacle for her to become a *satī*. From that time she lived alone, sitting under a tree for twelve years in meditation. Then she built the small hut *(kuṭiyā)* and sat inside it all alone. At that time she no longer took any food or water, yet her body did not deteriorate. She lived entirely on the *sat* that she had accumulated. The police came and stayed there for five years to see whether she was eating anything. They verified that she ate nothing. Doctors came from Jodhpur and even from foreign countries to find out how it was possible for her to live without food or water, but they could not understand it.

Her hagiography locates the episode of Rup Kumari's attempt to become a *satī* at a later time in her life. According to this version Rup Kumari lived a life of increasing and intense meditational and devotional practices for over twenty years. During this period Rup Kumari developed a close spiritual relationship with her nephew-in-law, Man Singh. On February 15, 1943, after a week-long session of devotional singing, Man Singh became seriously ill from typhoid and quickly died. When he died his daughter-in-law, Rasal Kumari, who was very devoted to him, dressed up as a bride, announced that she wanted to become a *satī* with Man Singh, and joined him on his funeral pyre. Rup Kumari decided that she too would become a *satī* on the pyre of her adopted son Man Singh. The news about the impending *satī* spread like electricity through Bala village and beyond. Both *satīs* recited the name of Rāma and displayed single-minded determination to follow through on their announced course of action. Rup Kumari's sister-in-law, Bhur Kunwar, resisted her effort, and locked her in the house. Villagers doused Rasal Kumari with water that had leather sandals soaking in it. This polluted her body, her *sat* left her, and she became quiet.

Bhur Kunwar told Rup Kumari that she would make a mistake by attempting to become a *satī*. Rup Kumari resisted by saying that the family would be honored by her devotion. Bhur Kunwar replied that because of her *satī* the government would prosecute the family and asked her why she wanted to inflict such pain on them. Nevertheless,

Rup Kumari bathed and prepared for her cremation. She began to walk toward the temple of Kṛṣṇa, and, as she did not have a veil on her face, many saw a radiance coming from it. She paid homage to the deity and then started out toward the cremation ground. Then family members promised that they would help her become a *satī* if that was her unalterable determination. They told her they would help her with the preparations for the procession they secured a horse for her to ride; and dressed her in her wedding attire. Meanwhile, they took Man Singh's body and cremated it without her knowledge. Seeing that time was passing, Rup Kumari moved toward the cremation ground. Then the village goldsmith, Shankar, covered her with a blanket. At that moment she realized she had been deceived.

After this incident Rup Kumari quit eating altogether. Her family attempted to feed her forcibly. Later she attempted to set herself on fire but was restrained by Bhur Kunwar. People came to visit her more and more frequently. By the late 1940s word had spread about this saintly Rajput woman who had wanted to become a *satī* but was prevented from doing so by her relations. Her reputation spread, and she came to be known as the *satī*-mother from the village of Bala, or Bāḷāsatīmātā. It was about this time that the author of her hagiography became a devotee. By the mid-fifties, regular Vedic ceremonies were performed in front of the temple of Śiva in Bala, and Bāḷāsatīmātā moved out of the house of her in-laws and took up residence in the small hut by the riverbank.

Devotees saw in Bāḷāsatīmātā one who had transcended the limits of worldly attachments and aversions. Stories circulated that she was impervious to cold and heat, and that she did not eat, drink, sleep, or excrete. She appeared to her devotees at times of death or in moments of difficulty. She healed people with various diseases, and she was unaffected by snakebites. Many people who were crippled or who suffered from mental illness came to her for healing. Her allegedly infinite capacity to renounce the connections to this word—food, drink, sleep, bodily functions—and her receptivity to the suffering of others shaped her identity in the imaginations of her devotees as one who had transcended the limitations of worldly life. As one who lived on the margins between the human and the divine, she served as a refuge for those for whom the world was all too present and as an inspiration for those who wanted to travel more lightly within it.

A number of stories about Bāḷāsatīmātā's miraculous powers circulate among her devotees. In 1945 one local saint, Darśanrām, was living in Jodhpur. He had felt his death coming because he knew that a star's location was in a bad position. When he knew his death was immanent he expressed his wish to stay the four rainy months (*caturmās*) in Bala village. Bāḷāsatīmātā told the author of her hagiography in private that no matter what he would die soon in Bala. The saint spent the four-month period there. Bāḷāsatīmātā took care of him, fed him, and gave him great respect. The author asked Bāḷāsatīmātā, since the time had passed during which the saint had predicted his death, how was she to understand his continuing to live on? The next day he was bitten by a snake, and his whole body turned blue. Doctors came from nearby places and many devotees gathered there. The doctors pronounced him dead. Suddenly Bāḷāsatīmātā came out of her meditation. She was very shocked and started crying. She complained to Lord Śaṅkar (Śiva) that if a saint dies like this she would no longer put her trust in him. In the future no one would come to spend *caturmās* at Bala. Bāḷāsatīmātā touched the saint's dead body, and all of a sudden he awoke and sat up as if nothing had happened. This incident was much discussed among her devotees.[15]

Another story that is said to have taken place in 1965 also illustrates Bāḷāsatīmātā's reputation as a healer. A young man named Sadar Sheher was suffering from epilepsy. His family brought him to Bāḷāsatīmātā. When he arrived a wealthy businessman was sponsoring a recital of the *Bhagavadgītā* at Bāḷāsatīmātā's ashram. She asked that the three trays of gold coins, each containing ten thousand rupees, which the young man's father had brought to honor her and two other saints who had attended the recitation, be brought before her. She then asked that one of the coins be heated so that it could be put on the body of the epileptic as a symbol of illusion. The boy recovered, and the money was donated to the local Gandhi school.[16]

As Bāḷāsatīmātā's reputation for spiritual virtuosity spread, she attracted the attention of other important saints and patrons in Rajasthan and Gujarat, including Shanta Maharaj at Mount Abu; Gulba Ma, a much-revered woman saint in Gujarat who had been fasting for the past fifty years; and Kishori Devi of Ayodhya. The president of India, Rajendra Prasad, invited her to Delhi with Sherananand, founder of the charitable Human Service Association. On another occasion she met President Radhakrishnan; and Indira Gandhi met her with Andandamayi Ma, the famous saint from Benaras, when the future prime minister was Minister of Information and Broadcasting.

One component of Bāḷāsatīmātā's religious charisma is the number of stories of her out-of-body manifestations to her devotees. The author of her hagiography relates an incident that took place at the time of her wedding in 1946.

> At the time of my wedding, Satīmā promised to come to our house. It was very small and crowded, so she didn't come visibly. We were very disappointed but we could not do anything. She did come but stayed invisible. Before she left she told Lakhari Bai of Bala to tell my father-in-law, Chanchanmal, that she had kept her promise. All of a sud-

den the sound, "hari oṁ," could be heard in the room where I was sitting. I didn't see anyone, and I became frightened of the sound. Then there was a strange stillness in the room. Later, when I went to Bala, Satīmā asked me if anyone was frightened of the sound of "hari oṁ." She said, "I was the one in that room doing the chanting and praying."[17]

Another story told to illustrate Bāḷāsatīmātā's generosity, her capacity to be the ever-giving mother, is reminiscent of the story of Jesus and the loaves and fishes in the Gospels.[18]

A few years ago on Holi festival, the whole of Bala village gathered and was singing devotional songs. There was a plate full of white sugar candy (*batāśā*), covered by a cloth and placed in front of [Bāḷāsatī] Mā. She started to give everyone the food offering. As soon as the plate became a little empty she shook it, stirring the sweets, and the plate would fill up immediately. Thus she distributed it to all. I was dumbfounded that a small plate could be distributed to the whole village.[19]

The white sugared food, which became sacralized (*prasād*) as the result of having been touched by her, became in the astonished perception of her devotees evidence of her power and her bottomless capacity for self-giving. In a gesture reminiscent of the ancient story of the churning of the ocean of milk to form the cosmos, Bāḷāsatīmātā, as the embodiment of the primal divine energy (*ādiśakti*), stirs the plate of sweets to satiate the hunger of those who came to see her.

Bāḷāsatīmātā died on November 16, 1986, at the age of sixty-seven. Her body was cremated in front of the hut where she had spent so much of her life. The ashes from her cremation are considered a sacred and healing substance, the last residue, the *nicoṛ*, of her material form. Her devotees continue to affirm her presence in their lives even though she has "dropped her body." In her life she exhibited the virtues of nonattachment, generosity, service to god and others; in short, she was a model of *pativratādharma*.

Her hagiography opens with a *vandana* (praise poem) in Sanskrit and Hindi written before her death by one Shri Ramsneha Das that summarizes the religious meaning she has for her devotees:

1. This Mother Satī (Satīmātā) is Satī indeed, but she is not the daughter of Prajāpati, Lord Dakṣa. Having relinquished all mundane nourishment without having yet taken her liberation from this world (*samādhi*), subsisting alone on Rām's name, she tirelessly serves all: guests, cows, devotees, and Brahmans.
2. She whose activating power (*krīya śakti*) can in no way be compre-

hended even by the greatest scientists and doctors, she indeed (the self-blessed one) is our Mother Satī.

3. Unpolluted by all natural activities (hunger/thirst, cold/heat, the expelling of feces and urine, etc.), she is at this time accessible (for *darśan*) to all ordinary people: after she departs her body, in the future, it will be difficult for anyone to believe in these unprecedented acts of hers.

4. By the Lord's grace, having given up food and even without defecation and urination, a living being (*prāṇi*) can live for a very long time performing all actions.

5. I honor that Mother Satī whose manifestation is solely in order to firmly establish faith in the hearts of devotees.

6. If anyone should have any sort of doubt in his heart concerning Mother Satī, by going and testing her let him quickly cross over the mud of skepticism.

7. May she who is endowed with miraculous power, unmatched by anyone at present, or in the past or the future, bestow on everyone, by mere recollection (*smaran*), the gift of devotion to the Lord.[20]

The poem celebrates Bāḷāsatīmātā as an embodiment of perfection that goes beyond the limits of ordinary human life and thereby bears witness to a cosmos that is embraced by a gracious deity. Bāḷāsatīmātā is presented here as a kind of incarnation (*āvatāra*) of the fully giving maternal presence, the perfection of traditional notions of *pativratādharma*; as the poems says, she "tirelessly serves all."

The poem opens by playing on the many meanings of the word *satī*. It distinguishes between Satī as perfect wife and Satī as the goddess and wife of Śiva, and it elevates Bāḷāsatīmātā even above the goddess. It does not make reference to *satī* in its meaning as a woman who immolates herself on the funeral pyre, although that episode in her life story is an important feature in the recollections her devotees have about her. The poem draws upon several themes from yogic, tantric, and generic renunciatory traditions to situate Bāḷāsatīmātā within the realm of those beings who, while in human form, nevertheless live as though they were already liberated from the samsaric world. The poem emphasizes her activating power (*krīya śakti*) manifested in her performance of miracles, her ability to live in the world without any physical dependence upon what goes into the body in the forms of food and drink and what passes out, and her capacity to confound the epistemological criteria of the ordinary world symbolized by the skepticism of scientists and doctors. It invites the hearer to leave behind the standards and expectations of knowledge that would call into question the miraculous dimensions of her story, and to cross over into the realm of devotion from which vantage point, through the practice of remembering her and bringing her presence imaginatively into one's awareness, the miraculous becomes ordinary and devotion to the Lord, who transcends the distinctions among particular deities, is the gift that follows from the surrender of doubt. Through this religious method of devotion to Bāḷāsatīmātā, the devotee is promised a share in the miraculous power that she displays. Bāḷāsatīmātā's presence in the world and her powerful activities on behalf of her devotees is, in turn, situated within a cosmos surrounded and pervaded by divine grace (*bhagavan kī kṛpā*).

There is much about Bāḷāsatīmātā that is highly traditional. She participates in the extended renunciatory tradition of persons who have left the world of the householder life behind and through ascetic practices and attitudes collect around themselves reputations of psychic and physical powers that only come to those at the margins of the conventional world. The stories of her miracles and healings resonate with those of holy men and women who continuously fast and never sleep or excrete. Like them, she has reached a condition of autonomy from the physical exchange relationships of the ordinary world: sleeping/waking; eating/excreting. It goes without saying that she observes strict sexual abstinence.[21]

Unlike the traditional *satīmātā* who is venerated within a particular family lineage, the living *satīmātā*, like the guru, draws veneration from a variety of devotees. In this respect she cuts across caste and filiational boundaries and belongs, in principle, to everyone. However, because she is Rajput by caste, most of her devotees are drawn from that community.

Her geographical base in west central Rajasthan, Bala village, is about halfway between Ajmer and Jodhpur, and her communications in the local Marwari dialect have limited her range of appeal. However, the technology of mass communications has brought her into contact with the larger world of India and the diaspora of Rajputs and Rajasthanis abroad in East Africa, Europe, and North America has brought her presence to the attention of Hindus who would not have heard of her.

Bāḷāsatīmātā spent most of her time in her modest ashram in Bala village, worshiping Śiva, giving *darśan* to her devotees, and visiting sacred places around north India and the Himalayas. Much of Bāḷāsatīmātā's lifestyle was that of a widow. She wore a simple white sari, devoid of ornamentation, and her renunciatory way of life made the average widow's privations look like self-indulgence. Many of the women I saw at her ashram were dressed as widows. Though she was, in some sense, a widow, because her husband had died before her, she did not intend to be a widow by complying with the funeral observances. She intended to be a *satī* but was a victim of her family's restraint on her actions. It was her intention that confirmed her sacred status and gave her the capacities to live outside the world of desires and appetites. Her designation as a *satīmātā* seemed to relieve her of the associations of ritual pollution usually accompanying the status of the widow. There is nothing about her presence, so far as her devotees are concerned, that conveys the inauspicious and contaminating power of the dead that would lead anyone to avoid her.

Satīmātā *on the Margins of Hindu Marriage*

In an earlier generation, before the modern state used its power to constrain the practice of *satī*, Bāḷāsatīmātā might have carried through with her plan to become a *satī* on the funeral pyre of her nephew. While the pressures of modernity prevented Bāḷāsatīmātā from immolating herself, they have not prevented her from transforming her intention to become a *satī* into a life of sainthood. She took on the life of the renouncer. The emerging tradition of the *satīmātā*, as we see in the case of Bāḷāsatīmātā, stakes out a modality for the exceptional woman to occupy in the context of one of the most thoroughgoing patriarchal communities in India. In her life the *satīmātā* has fulfilled the expectations of *pativratādharma* yet resists the abject state of widowhood through her exceptional displays of personal autonomy, symbolized by her detachment from bodily functions and her supernatural powers. Her ability to work miracles and confound foreign doctors displays capacities that place her outside the networks of conceptual and operational control by conventional patriarchal society. Her charismatic presence provides a secure and religiously legitimate zone for women devotees to assemble in order to draw from her the strengths they need to carry out their own efforts at *pativratādharma.*

As Mary Hancock's essay (see chapter 3, this volume) argues, women in circumstances of high levels of role definition have been able to mobilize the Hindu system of devotion and religious practice to establish significant levels of autonomy and authority. From her location on the margin of Hindu marriage, Bāḷāsatīmātā subverts the institution in the context of calling into question the entire system of the samsaric universe, of which marriage and *dharma* are the cornerstones. Bāḷāsatīmātā does not offer an alternative to marriage in this world but marginalizes its totalistic claims on women by providing a model of the strong woman who has transformed what might otherwise have been the oblivion of widowhood into the inspiring visibility of sainthood. As Harlan points out, this transformation and recombination of traditional structures of *satī*, marriage, *pativratādharma*, asceticism, and devotion provide an example of the adaptability of what otherwise might appear to be an inflexibly conservative society.[22] Bāḷāsatīmātā is not a social revolutionary, nor is she likely to become a compelling paradigm for women with secular or feminist orientations. Yet for the many traditional women at the grass roots of Hindu culture, the living *satīmātā* is an icon of strength and steadiness, one who gives all she has and brings strength and healing to many who come to her for help. She was radically independent and traveled widely, albeit within traditional religious patterns of pilgrimage. Her life and continuing presence among her devotees—many of whom are men—speak to the cultural complexity and subtlety of the powers of women. Bāḷāsatīmātā found a place of status and authority for herself as a woman by a paradoxically subversive perfection of the values of *pativratādharma*.

NOTES

This essay is dedicated to the memory of Agehananda Bharati. I have benefited greatly from his ideas, perspectives, and critiques at earlier stages of my research on *satī*. I would also like to thank Lindsey Harlan, Wendy Doniger, Joyce Burkhalter Flueckiger, Bhoju Ram Gujar, Tony Stewart, Dharma Chandra, and Philip Lutgendorf for their help at various stages of my research.

1. I am grateful to Richard Schweder's insights in formulating the issue in this way.

2. Romila Thapar, "Death and the Hero," in *Mortality and Immortality: The Anthropology and Archaeology of Death*, ed. S. C. Humphreys and Helen King (London: Academic Press, 1981), pp. 293–315.

3. Lata Mani, "The Production of Official Discourse on *Sati* in Early Nineteenth-Century India," *Economic and Political Weekly* 21 (1986): 32–40.

4. Kumkum Sangari and Sudesh Vaid, "Satī in Modern India," *Economic and Political Weekly* 25 (1990): 1464–75, 1531–52.

5. Personal communication, November 20, 1988.

6. See especially pp. 11–15.

7. Hardev Bahri, *Learner's Hindi-English Dictionary* (Delhi: Rajpal and Sons, 1989), p. 348; R. C. Pathak, *Bhargava's Standard Illustrated Dictionary of the Hindi Language* (Varanasi: Bhargava Book Depot, 1986), p. 569.

8. For a discussion of *sat*, see Lindsey Harlan, *Religion and Rajput Women: The Ethic of Protection in Contemporary Narratives* (Berkeley: University of California Press, 1992), pp. 124–33.

9. Ibid., p. 179.

10. Ibid., pp. 172–75.

11. Ibid., p. 173.

12. See Fig. 8.2.

13. In north India it is a common practice to ring a bell to announce the birth of a male.

14. Mehta, *Śrī satī mātā caritāmṛt*, p. 59.

15. Ibid., pp. 67–69.

16. Ibid., pp. 78–79.

17. Ibid., p. 83.

18. Matt. 14: 13–21; Mark 6: 30–44; Luke 9: 10–17; John 6: 1–13.

19. Mehta, *Śrī satī mātā caritāmṛt*, p. 93.

20. Ibid., pp. 11–12. I am grateful to Philip Lutgendorf for his help in the translation and interpretation of this text.

21. On the ascetic practices of women, see Lynn Teskey Denton, "Varieties of Female Asceticism," in *Roles and Rituals for Women*, ed. I. Julia Leslie (London: Pinter Press, 1991), pp. 211–32.

22. Harlan, *Religion and Rajput Women*, p. 179.

9

Abandoning Shame: Mīrā and the Margins of Marriage

LINDSEY HARLAN

Mīrā Bāī is undoubtedly the most famous woman saint in the history of north Indian devotionalism (*bhakti*). Mīrā's story—or, rather, some version of it—is known to people of all ages and from all tiers of society. It has been passed down through generations orally and recently in small religious pamphlets, in schoolbooks, and even in the colorful comic books of which children and Indologists are so fond.

My interest in Mīrā has been limited to the narrative tradition familiar to Rajasthani Rajput women, particularly aristocratic women, among whom I have done extensive fieldwork.[1] Many of the women I interviewed mentioned Mīrā as one of the women they most admired. Their admiration made sense to me: Mīrā was a Rajput princess in Mewar, the area in which I based my research. Moreover, she is an illustrious ancestor in a culture that venerates ancestors.

Mīrā, however, has little in common with the other women frequently mentioned as admirable: while the others behaved in a manner consistent with Rajput normative codes, Mīrā did not. Thus while many Rajput women are quick to claim her as a member of their community and to celebrate her character, they also tend to believe she really was on rather bad behavior. Their commentary on Mīrā's story reveals ambivalence about a great woman who acted shamelessly.

Before exploring some of this commentary, I provide a summary of the Mīrā story as it is often told in Rajasthan.[2] What follows is a standard, bare-bones rendition that varies at a number of points from versions known elsewhere in India.[3]

> Mīrā was a princess in the Mertiya branch of the Rathaur Rajputs. As a child, she adored the cowherd god, Kṛṣṇa, an image of whom she treated as a doll. One day, while watching a wedding procession, Mīrā asked her mother, "Who will be my bridegroom?" Caught by surprise and unsure what to say, her mother replied, "Lord Kṛṣṇa."
>
> Having matured into an attractive young woman, Mīrā was married to Mewar's heir apparent. Her love for Kṛṣṇa undiminished, she set off for her new home at the royal fortress at Chitor (then the capital of Mewar). Soon after she arrived, her in-laws began to pressure her to abandon her affection for Kṛṣṇa and to venerate Ekliṅgī (the incarnation of Śiva associated with the royal household) as well as the royal *kuldevī*. Even though as a daughter-in-law Mīrā was supposed to revere the deities of her husband's family, Mīrā cared only for Kṛṣṇa. She spent her days composing love songs for Kṛṣṇa and dancing for him in a temple she had persuaded her husband to build.
>
> Mīrā's impudence enraged the household. Further aggravating its members, Mīrā denigrated her marriage by speaking of Kṛṣṇa as her true husband and refraining from sexual contact with her human husband, whom she regarded as a brother.
>
> Mīrā's husband died young and heirless. Later, when her father-in-law died, her husband's younger brother (*devar*) succeeded to the throne. The *devar* resented Mīrā's attitudes, particularly her unwillingness to act as a widow on the grounds that her true husband, Lord Kṛṣṇa, was alive. Having failed to induce the princess to behave properly, he contrived to have her killed. First, he ordered her nightly drink to be laced with poison. Mīrā drank this down but Kṛṣṇa rendered the poison harmless. [There were other such unsuccessful assassination attempts.][4]
>
> Mīrā thought it prudent to leave Chitor. Taking up the life of a mendicant ascetic, she communed with male ascetics (*sādhus*, yogis) and as she traveled, she danced and sang for Kṛṣṇa along the roadways and in the woods. In time she arrived at Brindavan, the forest home of Kṛṣṇa's youth.
>
> Eventually, she traveled to Dvaraka, Kṛṣṇa's home in his later years. There she spent her days attending Kṛṣṇa at one of his temples. By this point, much to the royal family's dismay, Mīrā had gained widespread fame as a *bhakta*. At the

> same time that her reputation was spreading, Mewar was suffering from various political problems.[5] Many felt that these problems were either due to or aggravated by the shame that the errant princess was bringing the royal family. They viewed her activities as robbing the king and his kingdom of dignity and strength. To rectify the situation, the king dispatched a retrieval party. Yet when the party members arrived in Dvaraka and entered the temple where Mīrā served Kṛṣṇa, they discovered that Mīrā had disappeared into Kṛṣṇa's icon. Her sari, draped upon the icon, was all that remained to testify to the miracle.

Reflecting on this story, some women explained to me that although Mīrā broke many rules, it was fine for her to have acted as she did because she was who she was. For example, one woman remarked, "Mīrā was above the Rajput rules and regulations. That's okay only if you're a saint."[6] Other women seemed to think that Mīrā's actions were inappropriate even for her. Thus, another woman commented, "Mīrā left everything because of her *pūjā* [worship]. I can't comment on that. Well, she shouldn't have left. Rajput ladies are very much tradition-minded. They are expected to mind their homes."

The women whose comments I have quoted both said they admired Mīrā; they differ in their evaluations of whether Mīrā should have done what she did (given the fact that the actions in themselves are wrong). Many women who admired Mīrā said straight-out that it is better to be a *pativratā* (a devoted wife) than a *bhakta* (a devotee of God).[7] A few women recited the adages "A woman's husband is her god" and "A woman should ask her husband to worship other gods." One went a step further and said, "A husband is higher than a god: you can defame a god, but not a husband."

Hence, while Rajput women understand Mīrā as a superb *bhakta,* they find much of her behavior nonexemplary and actually harmful, as is illustrated by the troubles it brings Mewar.[8] In an insightful and passionate essay about Mīrā, Parita Mukta comments rather critically on what she finds a grudging acceptance of Mīrā among aristocratic Rajputs in the area.[9] She says that the veneration of Mīrā among the Mewari Rajputs is recent and reluctant; it is the result of the spread of Mīrā's image as a national symbol of self-sacrifice during Gandhi's *satyagrāha* campaign. While I gathered no evidence that could either confirm or refute this intriguing speculation, I wonder whether perhaps, some of the women critical of Mīrā's behavior would characterize themselves as admirers.[10] Ambivalence along the lines I have described might account for their grudging acceptance.[11]

Trying to understand fully the ambivalence felt by the women I interviewed toward this much-admired but quite unwifely person, I looked back over the commentary I collected. It struck me that the aspect of the narrative that caused the most concern and occasioned the most reflection was her transgression of *pardā*. Mīrā left a "woman's place," or more specifically, a "married woman's place," when she crossed beyond the *pardā* (curtain) that separates female space from male space and private space from public space. Crossing the literal margin of marriage represents a culmination of nonconformist behaviors and an initiation into a life on the periphery of marital experience.[12] Focusing on this literal departure for a moment will pave the way for a subsequent investigation of the various ways in which Mīrā embodies marginal status and experience.

Transgressing Pardā

That so many women focused their evaluation of Mīrā on her abandonment of *pardā* may well reflect their current concern with the erosion of *pardā* in their community today. In Udaipur the last few years have witnessed a rapid expansion of tourism, commerce, and industry, which has brought many outsiders to the area and has expedited the decline of the old order in which Rajputs could easily identify themselves at the top. Gradually abandoning *pardā* or expanding the definition of *pardā* to include free movement throughout all properties owned by one's extended family or even to one's "hometown," many women, with the support or reluctant acceptance of their husbands, have adapted their behavior to suit the times. One reason for this is that *pardā* has become expensive: family resources have dwindled and servants have become too expensive in postindependence India.[13] In some families women have taken to doing the shopping their servants once did. In others women have begun to run portions of their rambling homes as guest houses for tourists. A few young women have even taken up teaching in nursery schools, though the idea of women pursuing a profession outside the home is still one with which the community is particularly uneasy.

While many women have undoubtedly welcomed the greater freedom allowed them by exigency, the vast majority of women are extremely concerned that the exposure of Rajput girls to the outside and outsiders' conventions will tempt them to marry outside the community or contemplate abandoning their marriages if they become unhappy. Many Rajputs in Udaipur proudly describe themselves as "backward" in such matters and view love marriage and divorce in India as the result of corruption and Westernization.[14] This threat from without seems to have reinforced the Rajputs' desire to define clearly the differences between themselves and others. Community members have expressed great concern about maintaining the purity of Rajput blood lines and cultivating Rajput character and integrity. A number of them commented to me that they must now be especially vigilant about checking up on genealogies because they fear some genealogists can be bribed to create fictitious lists, allowing outsiders to pass for insiders.[15]

Moreover, there is among many Rajputs, both men and women, a persistent nostalgia for the past and its presumed simplicity. Roles are seen as having been clearly defined "back then," when Rajput men were rulers and women were dutiful and secluded *pativratās*, wives wholly devoted to their husbands.[16] Many idealize Rajput ancestors as heroes who sacrificed their lives fighting off invaders or perishing as *satīs*.

Mindful of family heritage and of honor (*izzat*), women in Udaipur have trod carefully as they have redefined and loosened *pardā*. The custom remains very much tied to their identities as wives. The place *pardā* occupies in self-perception is evident in the commentary about Mīrā but also in the ways in which Rajput women represent their community to themselves and to others in general conversation.

A woman whose family was still practicing strict *pardā* when I interviewed her in 1985 commented that Mīrā "abandoned everything, whereas a Rajput woman living in a family must perform her duties. A Rajput woman wouldn't dare go out; everyone can't be like Mīrā." Another woman whose family practiced *pardā* expressed her admiration for Mīrā's action but then distanced herself from it by saying Mīrā was not a *pativratā*. She said: "I certainly admire Mīrā. When people were so orthodox that they wouldn't step out at all, she had the guts to step out. Maybe because I can't step out, I admire her so. She was not a *pativratā*, though;[17] she was devoted to Kṛṣṇa. So we don't consider her an ordinary Rajput woman."

These women, who are so "unsure of their footing" and so anxious about whether their activities today overstep the shifting boundary delineating wifely duty, regard Mīrā's time as one in which the boundary was relatively fixed, visible, and easy to heed. Although many women, like the one who said Mīrā "had the guts to step out," expressed admiration for Mīrā's courage in leaving *pardā*, they did not approve of her leaving *pardā*, particularly as it ruins her family's reputation and brings about unfortunate consequences in the kingdom.[18]

Today relaxing or abandoning *pardā* still requires nerve: each new encroachment on the male/public domain invites scrutiny, if not censure, by family and community members. Yet Mīrā is not enlisted as an exemplar: I have never heard her represented as an inspiration for social change. Rather, her departure has retained its transcendent rationale.[19] The fact that Mīrā did leave *pardā* and retain character could make her into an exemplar at some point: one never knows when a figure from the past will be picked up as an emblem of altered self-consciousness or group identity. But at the moment Rajput women who admire her are still troubled by what was then a clear-cut renunciation of marital duty.

Thus, Mīrā's spatial transgression, her entry into public space, has signified rejection of the *pativratā* role, which requires renunciation of personal desires for service of a husband. Today Rajput women consistently identify selfless obedience to their husbands and to their husbands' families (*sasurāls*) as the most important rule of female behavior. In fact, they frequently express the conviction that their caste affiliation makes them uniquely able to fulfill the trying role of *pativratā*. The reason is that the traditional duty of a Rajput was to sacrifice the self on behalf of others (in battle). This inherited and much-championed duty to sacrifice, a number of women remarked, makes Rajput women especially able to perform self-sacrificing *pativratā* duties.[20] Not infrequently Rajput women point to the tradition of *satī* immolation in their community as confirmation of this point. Many Rajputs believe that *satī* ritual is originally and appropriately a Rajput custom that demonstrates the self-sacrificing nature of the Rajput woman who follows her husband in death and shares his fate.[21]

Given this ideal of self-sacrifice on behalf of a husband, Mīrā's *bhakti* is particularly jarring. One woman who admired Mīrā because she attained enlightenment continued on to remark that "she wasn't a *pativratā:* she didn't sacrifice for her husband." Another woman was even more explicit: "Mīrā is too religious for me. . . . Why did she get married if she didn't want to live with her husband? Why make the man's life miserable?" Leaving *pardā* and the role it encompasses confirms that Mīrā has not sacrificed for her husband and that she strives to sacrifice all social ties to pursue her devotion to God and achieve liberation.[22]

It is instructive to compare the way in which Mīrā's violation of *pardā* compares with violations of *pardā* by Padminī and Hāḍī Rānī, the two other women Rajput women frequently mentioned as admirable. Both of these women are considered *pativratā*s, and both sacrificed their lives as *satī*s. Padminī, a queen of Mewar, through a Trojan-horse sort of ploy, led an army into battle and liberated her husband from captivity in the camp of his archenemy, Ala-ud-din. Then, knowing that the battle between her husband's forces and those of Ala-ud-din would end badly, she committed *jauhar:* she joined the other ladies of Chitor in offering herself as a *satī* to a mass sacrificial fire in the underground vaults of the palace. This story is told by Rajput women in the Udaipur area as the quintessential story of wifely devotion and sacrifice.[23]

Hāḍī Rānī was a princess recently married into a Mewar estate (*ṭhikāṇā*) when her husband was called to serve the king in battle. His affection for her kept him from leaving to fulfill his duty. He reluctantly agreed to go to war but asked his wife's servant to request from his wife some memento of her to take with him to battle. To make the point that he should put his affections aside and attend to his sacrificial duty, the wife grabbed a sword and sliced off her head, after giving instructions to her maidservant that it be offered as the requested memento. The husband then tied the queen's head to his saddle and, thus inspired, fought brilliantly, thereby gaining glory.

These stories illustrate normative behavior: all women should sacrifice their own welfare for the good of their husbands. But their sacrifices also surpass normative behavior: they are heroic.[24] Padminī commits *jauhar*, which keeps her husband from worrying about her welfare while fighting; Hāḍī Rānī amputates her head for precisely the same reason. Performing these sacrifices requires transgression of *pardā*. Both women leave home to go to war, Padminī still living but as a prelude to dying and Hāḍī Rānī having died so her husband could fight. Both women enter the battlefield, but they do so by way of expressing their sacrifice: their transgression of male space is but part of a sacrificial ritual that publicly displays their purity as *pativratās*.[25]

Thus their violation of *pardā* confirms their role as sacrificing wives, whereas Mīrā's confirms rejection of such a role. Mīrā's transgression represents closure to a chapter in Mīrā's life that began with noncompliance of the most fundamental sort: refusing to pay respect (*dhok*) to a her conjugal family's *kuldevī*. Honoring a *kuldevī* is typically the initial and initiatory gesture expected of a bride after she is welcomed into her new home. In sum, we see that Mīrā's abandonment of her place at home is the culmination of a set of behaviors that defy marital standards.

While Mīrā's transgression represents a devaluation of her identity as the wife of a human husband, it also indirectly reveals the nature and importance of *pativratā* duty.[26] For all who know her story, her nonconformity demarcates the limits of acceptable behavior and pinpoints the centrality of the norms she violates. As Hans Peter Duerr has shown in his eclectic study, those who transgress social boundaries (literally or figuratively) reveal to society what it holds sacred and fortifies its norms.[27]

Moreover, Mīrā also validates marriage and matrimonial duty on a transcendent plane. Many women who pointed out that Mīrā was no *pativratā* also said that she was in some sense a *pativratā* to Kṛṣṇa.[28] As one woman put it, Mīrā "was a *pativratā* in the sense that she considered herself married to Kṛṣṇa and thought of God as her husband. God was everything. She was therefore an absolutely devoted wife, although her husband wasn't flesh and blood. She didn't consider her husband her husband: she never looked at another man." Used in this context, the word *pativratā* inverts meaning; rejecting *pativratā* duty toward a human, she becomes a *pativratā* of God. This comports with the usage of *pativratā* to denote a female ascetic in Sri Lanka, as Obeyesekere's work has shown.[29] Such a usage lends titular legitimacy to women by encompassing their transgressive actions within the very category they transgress.[30] It also demonstrates the equally well-known observation that in the world of the gods, opposites can coexist. Hence, as Śiva can be an ascetic who engages in erotic behavior, Mīrā, as the wife of Kṛṣṇa, can be a good woman who transgresses the boundaries of marriage.[31] The miracle that ends the story shows how such behavioral transgression becomes sanctioned as transcendence.

Here I should also point out that of those women who referred to Mīrā as Kṛṣṇa's *pativratā*, some did so not to explain who Mīrā's "real" husband was but to set straight the nature of Mīrā's relationship with Kṛṣṇa. Whereas Rādhā is Kṛṣṇa's consort, Mīrā is Kṛṣṇa's wife.[32] The notion of a Rajput woman as consort does not play well in this community: Rajput women are expected to be wives.

Thus far I have focused on Mīrā's transgression of a woman's place, which is literally delimited by *pardā*. But what of the space she enters? As the narrative and comments make clear, in her life beyond *pardā* she frequents the woods and the roads. These loci reveal ongoing violations of marital duty and decorum.

First the woods. When Mīrā leaves home, she takes up unsupervised companionship with forest-dwelling ascetics. In mythology and in the popular imagination, ascetics, having enriched their sexual potency through their penances, are particularly tempting targets for women who dwell in the forest. Moreover, being exposed to such available women, they are particularly tempted to express their repressed sexuality. The forest is the traditional place of both sexual abstinence and sexual adventure.[33]

Concern over Mīrā's association with *sādhus* is conveyed in one vignette mentioned by several women I know. Even while Mīrā was still at Chitor, a *sādhu* asked her to prove her devotion to God by having sex with him. He claimed that, as a renouncer, he was God's living representative. Mīrā actually agreed to do so, for she could deny God no favor, but she stipulated that the union be performed in front of Kṛṣṇa's image. The *sādhu* became terrified and left. While Mīrā remained virtuous, the point is clear: as a female devotee, she is without a human protector, which is shown to be troublesome even while she is still at home. When she enters the forest, how much more problematic this becomes. One of the women who commented on the gossip Mīrā's wandering occasioned explained, "The Rajputs didn't like it when she went out with *sādhus*. Royalty didn't like this; they thought it was disgraceful."[34]

Mīrā is understood not only as consorting with renouncers but as being a renouncer. Her chaste devotion to Kṛṣṇa translates into celibacy among men. Yet because she is often described and depicted as wearing *suhāg* or *pativratā* clothing, that is, clothing worn by a woman who is sexually active, she does not appear as some asexual being. The fact that she is also described and depicted as extremely beautiful emphasizes her attractiveness in this regard.[35] Thus even more than is the case with male ascetics, Mīrā is not one-dimensional.[36] Sexuality may be repressed but not erased. The forest habitat emphasizes the sensuous nature of Mīrā's *bhakti*. This is particularly evident in that it is the place where Mīrā sings and dances, activities that occasioned more than a little concern in the commentary of Rajput women.[37]

The singing and dancing are not troublesome in themselves: women sing and dance at weddings and many holiday festivities. What is troublesome about them in this story is the public location in which they occur. Public performance of this nature is widely considered the height of shamelessness. A remark by one woman, who was defending Mīrā's action, shows how much Mīrā's public performance needs defending: "Maybe she sang in the streets, but at least she sang only songs of devotion!" Thus compounding Mīrā's sin of communing with renouncers in the forest is her immodest display "in the streets," the quintessential public place.

Thus, having crossed out of *pardā* and become a mendicant pilgrim enroute to Brindavan and Dvaraka, Mīrā makes rather a spectacle of herself: her behavior contrasts sharply with the shyness and decorum that Rajput women typically point to as characteristics of good Rajput women.[38] Once again we see how in crossing out of *pardā*, Mīrā crosses the line that demarcates the *pativratā* code. The connection is stated barely in the statement made by one woman that Mīrā "came out in the open singing and dancing—no *pardā* for her!" This remark, like so many others, counterposes her song and dance to her household life.

Until recently women who sang and danced publicly for God were not wives of men but wives of God (*devadāsī*s).[39] These women were honored temple servants, but they were also public women in that they were allowed and expected to take human lovers–patrons. Thus, while Mīrā's performances are understood to entice God, they are also seen as enticing men. Morris Carstairs, who worked in a village in Mewar, commented on the effect a Mīrā movie had on male moviegoers in the fifties:

> The film was "Mirabai" . . . and it was noticeable here, as in Udaipur, that it was the singing and dancing which most powerfully gripped the audience's attention: and both of these were at once religious and sensual. . . . [M]any of the villagers went each night to see the three-hour film over again.[40]

More recently Madhu Kishwar and Ruth Vanita have remarked on the "coy seductiveness" of Mīrā's singing in a more recent film on Mīrā.[41]

While Rajput women demonstrate concern about the scandalous nature of Mīrā's musical performance, they do not question its sacrality. As the remark that "at least she sang only songs of devotion" indicates, on the face of it her activity needs defending, but it is also defensible.

Mīrā is not a strumpet; she is a servant of God. Her song and dance are consistent with the *bhāvas* (attitudes and feelings) expressed in her *bhakti*.[42] Nonetheless, examined by themselves or in the context of other women performing religious songs and dances, her displays are starkly symptomatic of Mīrā's unfaithfulness to the *pativratā* ideal. In fact, it is what typically identifies Mīrā as Mīrā, whether on the cover of *bhajan* pamphlets or images in Kṛṣṇa temples. Her lute and dancing feet convey her identity.

In sum, Mīrā is a saint because and in spite of the fact that she transgresses the locus of *pardā* and the code that articulates a woman's place. Her existence at the margin is represented not only by her literal rejection of *pardā* as space but by her association with ascetics and by her defiant and public dancing and singing, behaviors at odds with the code that *pardā* delineates.

But Mīrā's marginality is also conveyed in numerous other ways. The remainder of this essay explores other aspects of Mīrā's marginality that are revealed most distinctly against the backdrop of the research on marital marginality presented by the other contributors to this volume. This exploration takes the form of a summary and application of findings that shed light on the complexity of Mīrā's nonconformity. My summary is not a synopsis of the central insights offered by the other contributors but, rather, a selective utilization of those ideas that have helped me as I have worked to understand and interpret Mīrā's story. Reviewing the various statuses along the margins of marriage analyzed by the other contributors has led me to marvel at how thoroughly Mīrā's story brings together varied and diverse aspects of marital experience and to wonder whether this fact might help account for the enormity of her popularity.[43]

Mīrā's Other Marginal Statuses

I begin by exploring the statuses of virgin and wife, which are supposed to be successive stages joined by the marriage ritual. Gloria Raheja's essay (see chapter 2, this volume) articulates key assumptions that underlie the transformation of a girl from one stage to the other. One of the basic notions upon which she builds is the idea that the gift of a virgin is only a step, albeit the most important one, in uniting bride with groom and groom's family. In theory, the gift of a virgin transforms her so that henceforth she belongs to her in-laws' family as a wife. This status will be confirmed many times over as her natal family gives her conjugal family gifts (*dān*) on appropriate occasions over a period of years. Continuing to give gifts, which secures a woman's status within the conjugal family, reveals the implicit assumption that the marriage process is ongoing: while a wife may no longer be a virgin, she is still a daughter and she retains that status as an integral, if ultimately diminishing, part of her identity. Marriage, then, accomplishes no alchemical transformation whereby personal attributes transmute into new ones, pristine and uncontaminated by the past. The dominant perspective, which sees the marriage ritual as changing the bride's person and personality to fit into her new place, is challenged by the actual experience of women.

In Mīrā's case we have a woman understood as a wife—she completed the marriage *saṃskāra*—but also as a virgin, as we have seen, and not or not just a daughter. Her ongoing virginity is specified in the narrative and is integral to her identity after marriage. Some of the women I interviewed strongly stressed the point that Mīrā "had no relations" with her husband. Thus Mīrā is understood as something more than she should be (she syncretizes virgin and wife statuses) and therefore less than she should be (she isn't much of a wife). Mīrā's ties to the transcendent require that her personality and person not be compromised in any way. Refusing to alter her identity as required by her marital status, she does not merely instantiate the challenge to the dominant view that comes out of women's experience, she manifests an idiosyncratic "morality beyond morality" that is outside both dominant and challenging frames of reference.[44]

In a way the narrative euphemizes her rejection of marriage by having her live with her husband as a sister. This conveys the idea that she remains a virgin. Yet by implicitly opposing the categories of wife and sister, the story shows that she remains in the sister (natal kin) category. This identity is transferred metaphorically: she becomes a sister to her husband and therefore good to him, for she has a sister's love. That their relationship is not tragically inimical is implied by the fact that he builds her a temple so she can pursue her devotion to Kṛṣṇa.[45] Thus Mīrā not only retains her virgin status but also performs her natal duty as sibling in the marital domain. This reveals not simply a fidelity to her previous identity but an unsubtle shaping of her new environment to conform with her self-perception and personal ambitions.[46]

Retaining her identity through celibacy, Mīrā forsakes the possibility of motherhood, a fact that has important implications. As Raheja has shown, one of the most important occasions for gift giving by a woman's natal kin after her marriage is the birth of a child. The gift giving confirms the woman's status as mother and so substantiates her status as other, one who has been incorporated into her conjugal family and can receive *dān* for it, even as the transaction subtly demonstrates her continued connection with her natal family. Childlessness in Mīrā's case is not merely the logical consequence of her virginal status but an important status, or nonstatus, in itself. Several of the women I interviewed specifically mentioned Mīrā's childlessness as a reason they could admire Mīrā despite her behavior. They said it would have been wrong for her to leave if she had had such ties to the family.[47] In short, as Hawley has put it, "Motherhood and Mīrā don't mix."[48] Her failure to produce a child challenges the notion that she is or is really a wife.

It may seem strange to think of motherhood as a marital threshold. Usually considered central to marriage, motherhood is often said to be the purpose for marriage and the excuse for carnal indulgence within marriage. But motherhood is marginal to the extent that the marriage initiated by ceremony is not deemed successful until children are born. Like virginity, it reflexively affirms the inchoate nature of the gift giving (*kanyā dān*) that marked a bride's entrance into her husband's household.[49]

Hence, rejecting marriage and lacking carnal and maternal experience, Mīrā appears to synthesize two statuses normally construed as distinguished by the marriage *saṃskāra*. It seems likely that the combination of these statuses makes Mīrā a sympathetic figure to women who have adjusted to married life while retaining their former loyalties and identities.[50] Yet at the same time it makes her someone beyond empathy, someone with experience beyond common experience, because the combination in fact requires rejection of the *pativratā* role that most women aspire to fill. It shows a failed marriage.

Ralph Nicholas (see chapter 6, this volume) shows that a failed marriage is indicative of a failed marriage *saṃskāra*. Even marriage ceremonies flawlessly performed can fail to be effective in this terrible Kali age.[51] There is no divorce *saṃskāra*, and hence we should not be surprised to find that Mīrā is not understood to be a divorcée, but as Nicholas shows, tradition has always recognized estrangement and separation, which reflect a failure to come together and become truly familiar. In the Mīrā narrative, husband and wife do not literally leave each other, but neither do they join together. At some point it becomes clear that the marriage is a flower that will not unfold.[52] The disintegration of the marriage after the ceremony shows that as a separate and uncoupled woman, a woman separated by will if not by distance, Mīrā stands on the boundary of marriage as a divorcée would. Her distance from her husband—her failure to have sex and bear children—is both destructive of marriage and demonstrative of an incomplete or otherwise improper entrance into marriage. Her wedding just did not do what weddings are supposed to do.

Nicholas notes that a *saṃskāra* such as marriage is intended to refine the person so as to initiate it into a new status. The notion that a failed *saṃskāra* reflects a lack of refinement is especially interesting when we consider the myth of the jungli rani treated in Ann Gold's essay (see chapter 5, this volume).[53] When her husband, the king, accompanies her to her home, or rather the illusion of a home provided for her by the Sun God, and then discovers that the home is really jungle, he realizes that she has had no proper family to give her as a bride, despite her claim that she is a Brahman's daughter. Her marriage is called dharmic, but the circumstances of it are less than ideal (her family is absent) and the way in which the narrator makes a point of its dharmic nature seems to protest too much.[54]

As the story has already revealed, well before the king's realization that her natal mansion is an illusion, the queen has manifested her continued "jungli" nature: her relationship with the Sun God, her forest companion, has made her responsible for various miracles. When the king is upset that the bread she cooked turned into gold, she reminds him that she came from the jungle. She does this to explain not who she was but who she is and why she can do what she can do. Marriage has not refined her; it has not taken the jungle and its mystery out of her personality and prepared her for wifely status.

The association of the queen with the jungle is mirrored in the Mīrā legend. Retaining her status as virgin despite the *saṃskāra,* Mīrā sets out for the wilderness, the home of her divine childhood groom. Thus, while she doesn't live as a denizen of the jungle before marriage, she does associate with the "jungli" god Kṛṣṇa before marriage.

The similarity between the stories does not end here. Both Mīrā and the jungli rani enter the wilderness as adults, which shows that they have retained their ties to their youth despite the criticism they have incurred on this account. Moreover, having failed to be transformed or refined adequately by marriage, both end up actually threatening the community. The jungli rani is suspected of sorcery, and Mīrā is held accountable for Mewar's decline. Their connection with the wilderness not only makes them odd brides, it renders them inauspicious and menacing.

Both queens' stories end without reconciliation. The jungli rani faces her husband's displeasure, while Mīrā contends with her *devar*'s. Posing unresolved problems, the stories would seem to reveal the ambivalence women can feel about marriage and the exclusive loyalty it theoretically imposes as well as the ambivalence that conjugal relations can feel about them. Brides may have ominous and poisonous powers: they can ruin a family's reputation or even work black magic.[55]

A final similarity should be noted. While, as we have seen, women's experience of marriage challenges the dominant conception that has women abandoning identities formed before, these women are not so much attached to natal families as they are bonded to deities they worshiped before marriage. Mīrā is attached to her natal family's god, Kṛṣṇa. In a sense her family—her mother—betroths Mīrā to him, as one woman specifically noted when narrating Mīrā's story. The jungli rani is devoted to the Sun God, whose status in relation to her is relatively unclear. As in the Mīrā story, the jungli rani's mother figures as the third in a triangle that joins her with daughter and the god, but in the jungli rani's case the mother competes with the deity for her daughter's loyalty and loses. The Sun God seems something of a paternal figure, one that stands in for the mysteriously missing father, and this may be the source of competition for the daughter's love.[56] But his affection could be construed as not strictly paternal. After all, he gives the girl wonderful food that she in turn gives to her husband-to-be. If, as Gold remarks, the feeding of delicious food connotes sexuality in the latter case, might it not also in the former?[57] If so, the Sun God stands implicitly in the role of first husband or divine husband with whom the daughter lives, having left her mother and "eloped."

Whatever the nature of the vague (and perhaps intentionally vague) relationship between the jungli rani and the Sun God, it is clear that, in both stories, gods threaten their protégées' social status and security. Uncompromised *bhakti,* as is often the case, requires a loyalty disruptive of or damaging to family. In these narratives it demonstrates an after-the-fact recognition that the *bhakta*s' marriages have failed to develop properly and that their fates will defy or transcend marital convention. Even the jungli rani, who feeds her husband "food" and then bears a son in nine months, chooses fidelity to the god of her maiden days over an ordinary married life, which leaves her future uncertain.[58] Importing gods is a dangerous business.

Elsewhere I have explored the ways in which brides may import *kuldevī*s (clan goddesses) and *iṣṭadevtā*s (family or personal deities) into conjugal households and have reflected on the results of such importations.[59] It seems to me much more work needs to be done to document the importation of various deities by brides and the influence that the importation of these deities has on the nature of ongoing household worship. Here I merely wish to note that loyalty to a deity should be considered an aspect of women's identity as brides cross the marriage threshold, an aspect that complements, for example, loyalty to a brother, which is so poignantly discussed by both Raheja and Wadley (see chapters 2 and 4, this volume).

Although loyalty to a brother is recognized in the dominant discourse, loyalty to a deity of one's youth is not. The *dān* a brother gives his sister at various ritual occasions implies that she is other, even as it also subverts this perspective by demonstrating her dependence upon and loyalty to him.[60] This subversion may be marked, even advertised, in various ways. Raheja mentions that wives wear tattoos of their brothers' names on their arms. Wadley notes that wives wear fraternal toe rings as well as ones for their husbands. By contrast, the subversion associated with attachment to a deity is often invisible. A *pativratā* is supposed to worship her husband as a god and ask his permission to worship (other) deities. Although he can ban importation of an icon, however, he cannot bar a deity's unseen entrance if the wife's loyalty persists, as women's narratives so vividly illustrate.[61]

Wadley's essay is of further interest for an understanding of marriage because it explores the conceptualization of widows and the implications of widowhood as experienced. Mīrā is, of course, a widow, and this status is extremely important in shaping her identity as wife and *bhakta*. A wife is held accountable for her husband's fate; her chastity protects his welfare and contributes to longevity. If her husband predeceases her, she may be suspected of unfaithfulness, in thought if not in deed. (In Hindi and related languages, a word for widow [*rāṇḍ*] also means whore.) Thus even aside from the fact that Mīrā "walks the streets" and frequents the forests after her husband's death, her widowhood is troublesome; it indicates a failure to be a respectable wife. For upper-caste women like Mīrā, losing a husband means losing not only security but respect as well. How much more scandalous is the woman who not only is a widow but is a widow who refuses to act like a widow. As one woman remarked about Mīrā: "She wore *suhāgin* [*pativratā*] clothes after her husband died; everyone criticized her and said she didn't care for her husband." Mīrā's status is even more tenuous in that she did not even give her husband a son before she became a widow. Her widowhood, like her childlessness and virginity, reflects her marginality from the beginning.

Although the story hints at her troubles maintaining her virginity, as the vignette about the lusty *sādhu* demonstrates and remarks that Mīrā was an attractive widow imply, it is clear that concern about her sexuality is directed mostly at her relationship with God. Being married to the prince makes her relationship with Kṛṣṇa adulterous. But before I treat this topic, so ubiquitous in Krishnite *bhakti* poetry, let me pause momentarily to speculate rather freely on sexual tension in another context.

The narrative expresses unusually ferocious tension between Mīrā and her *devar*. The wife–*devar* relationship is traditionally one that allows for a certain amount of sexual teasing while the husband lives, but the widow is supposed to be utterly insulated from any type of sexual tension. When Mīrā becomes a widow, she does so under the exact condition under which a levirate union might take place: she has produced no heir. Furthermore, she is still a virgin, which makes her potentially more available, though she is set on remaining celibate among men because of her love for God. Mīrā's defiance of convention and authority accounts for her *devar*'s displeasure, but might not Mīrā's availability and disinterest combined with her own denial of her widowhood help explain the extent of his wrath? If being a widow and refusing to act as a widow both connote potential depravity, would not Mīrā, so marginally married and so lovely, be not only insubordinate but tempting, rejecting, and infuriating?[62] Perhaps the unspoken assumptions about young widowhood, the sexual joking or tension that can be aspects of the relationship between a woman and her *devar*, and how these two conditions could combine might account in part for the young man's tremendous hostility and cruelty, which Rajput women emphasized and often condemned in their narratives.

Whether or not such motives can or should be imputed to the *devar* in their accounts, adultery remains a dominant theme throughout. Like the *gopīs* who attend Kṛṣṇa in Brindavan, Mīrā is the wife of another. The adultery that the *gopīs* commit is often interpreted allegorically: humans should put God above all other loyalties. But such an interpretation does not excuse their adultery, for if it did, the story would no longer demonstrate loyalty to Kṛṣṇa; meeting him would be just too easy. It is crucial that the *gopīs* are culpable of disregarding *dharma* when they cross into the forest and dance to Kṛṣṇa's music. Neither is Mīrā an innocent. It is tempting for us to treat Mīrā as a historical figure and see her adultery as metaphorical or somehow "merely mystical," such that trysting with Kṛṣṇa means just putting God first. But in the story Mīrā does not just put God first, she sings and dances for his pleasure, which are reprehensible activities in and of themselves. And these and other behaviors trouble people who believe that a woman's husband is her god and that he should get no competition from above. Their perspective is shared by many Puranic and epic stories that hold humans who tryst with gods guilty of adultery, as Wendy Doniger's essay (see chapter 7, this volume) and her work elsewhere illustrate.

As already noted, there is an important difference between Mīrā and the *gopīs*, including Rādhā (Kṛṣṇa's favorite). The *gopīs*' relationship with God is *parakīyā* (with the wife of another); Mīrā's is not only *parakīyā* but also *svakīyā* (with one's wife) because society sees her as married to a man but she is ultimately shown to be (also) married to God.[63] The coexistence of these relationships is possible in the realm of myth and legend but not in the social realm. Living in both worlds, Mīrā can and cannot be married to two males at once. Her double duplicity, cheating on both husbands according to shifting perspectives, makes her simultaneously saintly and shameless.

It also makes her inimitable. Mary Hancock has demonstrated the difficulties facing women who tackle the conundrum of how to live in both worlds at once, of how to be a wife and *bhakta* (see chapter 3, this volume). She describes the considerable strain that female *bhaktas* endure as they try to earn credibility and respect, both inside and outside their families. Their love for God, or in this case the Goddess, is associated with relinquishing various household duties and to some extent decreasing sexual relations with their husbands. Because they worship the Goddess, their *bhakti* is not understood as adulterous, but it does disrupt their relationships with their husbands and call into question their loyalties as *pativratās*.

Unlike Mīrā, these women do not completely renounce sexuality in the social realm. They do not leave home to pursue celibacy but stay home as *pativratās* (*cumaṅkalis*). Being intermittently or indefinitely celibate, they bring the boundary between marital sexuality and individualistic celibacy into the household sphere. For women this ends up resembling in some respects the compromise made by forest dwellers in the third stage of life (*vanaprastha*). At the edge of renunciation, forest dwellers live on the border of civilization and are still tied to family life in that they can still have relations with their wives. Like these hermits, these women live at the edge of matrimony, in their own homes. Staying inside, they retain respectability because they are still under male supervision. They avoid the troublesome judgment rendered by society on women who travel alone by bringing the outside realm, the realm that forsakes marital duty, into the home. The public comes into the home, which makes the home public and allows women exposure to outsiders, but the home remains a home and is ultimately understood as private. Public exposure is encompassed by residence.

The compromises implicit in homogeneous time (intermittent celibacy or celibacy now and then) and homogeneous space (the outside is inside) represent reshaping of the domestic realm and domestic convention to allow these women *bhaktas* the latitude to pursue their callings as mediums. This reshaping represents resistance to and release from conventional roles and rules, but it also demonstrates validation of conventional marriage, which subjugates women and limits their autonomy.

Thus Hancock's case histories, like the Mīrā narrative, demonstrate contrasting if syncretistic modes of marital experience. They exemplify violation of the dimensions of marriage while positively revaluing matrimony. As we have seen, the revaluation is abstract in Mīrā's case. Her defiance of the ordinary *pativratā* role shows the limits of decorum—it shows exactly the opposite of proper behavior and therefore establishes proper behavior—and her performance of the *pativratā* role on a transcendent plane is directly exemplary. Because of the tension between these two modes of illustration, however, there is ambiguity that permeates the narrative and that invites admirers' ambivalence. As Hancock argues, such ambiguity is an integral aspect of the character of *bhakti* devotionalism.

Before concluding this discussion of Mīrā's many-faceted marginality, I should like to explore a final status that may be implicitly associated with Mīrā: *satī* status. Like the *satī*, Mīrā is a widow who denies and escapes widowhood. *Satī* immolation, however, removes and disproves widow status by reclassifying a wife as a *sahagaminī* (one who accompanies her husband to the pyre and the afterlife), whereas Mīrā's death shows she cannot have been a widow relative to her husband because she miraculously joins her divine husband in heaven. Despite this difference, their deaths are semiotically joined. The *satī* stone, which is frequently draped with a sari, depicts the union and shared destiny of *satī* and husband, and the Kṛṣṇa image, draped with Mīrā's sari, depicts the union and shared destiny of Mīrā and her divine husband.[64]

Moreover, there is an interesting if indirect association made by one of the women I interviewed. She noted that Mīrā was tested by swallowing poison and goes on to compare Mīrā's test with Sītā's fire ordeal. Sītā is often called a *satī* because her trial by fire reveals her inner purity (*sat, sattva*). If Mīrā's poison ordeal is construed as a trial of purity, she certainly passes and meets the criterion for bearing the *satī* epithet in this context. These trials parallel the trial of the more typical *satī,* who dies on her husband's pyre.[65] Her death shows that her husband's death must not have been her fault and that therefore, by implication, she must have been a good woman (the literal meaning of *satī,* i.e., a woman who has goodness, or *sat*).[66] Vindication is especially necessary in Mīrā's case because, prior to her death, she was the widow of a human husband for whom she was not an ideal wife. Her mergence demonstrates that despite her unseemly behavior both inside and outside the palace, she was a good woman because she was a devout Kṛṣṇa *bhakta.*[67]

Further association of Mīrā with the category of *satī* is found in Paul Courtright's conclusion that Bāḷāsatīmātā is represented as an incarnation of Mīrā (see chapter 8, this volume). Bāḷāsatīmātā did not die as a *satī,* but because of her devotion, devotees say, she was able to live without eating, drinking, or sleeping.[68] These miracles (*camatkārs*) of ascetic prowess accomplish the same vindication as Sītā's fire ordeal and Mīrā's absorption—they prove that she embodies *sat.*

To summarize, Mīrā's marginality is manifold. Viewing her from the various stances on the periphery allows us to appreciate how the narrative provided might speak to as well as reflect the experiences of women with different statuses and diverging life stories. She is a wife but also, from other perspectives, an ascetic, a singing–dancing *dāsī,* a virgin, a widow, an adulteress, a *bhakta,* and in some sense a *satī.* She can be seen as subversive but also as indirectly and ultimately supportive of marriage, which is one reason she is so malleable in the hands of her interpreters, including academics. She transgresses but also traces the margins of Hindu marriage, which makes her a *bhakta* both transcendent and familiar, revered and uniquely troublesome.

NOTES

1. See my book *Religion and Rajput Women: The Ethic of Protection in Contemporary Narratives* (Berkeley: University of California Press, 1992). Portions of the analysis offered in this essay appear in this book, which is based on inter-

views conducted in 1984–85 and updated in 1987, 1989, and 1990–91. I was not particularly interested in Mīrā's *bhajans* because my purpose was to discover ways in which women understood Mīrā's story. This is easier to get at when women tell her story in their own words and interject interpretive commentary at their discretion.

2. Variants of this story are found throughout northern India. The Rajasthani Rajput narratives from which I am constructing this summary are quite consistent. Almost all the women who spoke of Mīrā insisted on relating the story to me in its entirety, presuming I would not know it. This was extremely helpful in that it allowed me to get a sense of the degree of standardization in the region.

3. See John Stratton Hawley, "Morality Beyond Morality in the Lives of Three Hindu Saints," in *Saints and Virtues,* ed. John Stratton Hawley (Berkeley: University of California Press, 1987), pp. 55–63, 70; John Stratton Hawley and Mark Juergensmeyer, *Songs of the Saints of India* (New York: Oxford University Press, 1988), pp. 122–29; Madhu Kishwar and Ruth Vanita, "Modern Versions of Mira," in *Manushi* (tenth anniversary issue), nos. 50–52 (1989), 100; and Kumkum Sangari, "Mirabai and the Spiritual Economy of *Bhakti,*" *Economic and Political Weekly* 25 (1990): 1465.

4. The narratives are consistent in holding that Mīrā's husband never became king and that his younger brother succeeded to the throne. This version is at odds with the tradition that Mīrā's husband was king and he ordered the assassination attempts or that Mīrā's father-in-law was king and he ordered the attempts. The narratives, like the majority of the women's narratives I gathered, leave out historical references, such as the identities of Mīrā's *sasurāl* members. For discussions of the identities of the latter, see Hawley and Juergensmeyer, *Songs of the Saints of India,* p. 125; and A. J. Alston, *The Devotional Poems of Mīrābāī* (Delhi: Motilal Banarsidass, 1980), pp. 1–9. On the lack of historical detail in women's narratives, see Harlan, *Religion and Rajput Women,* pp. 52–54; and A. K. Ramanujan, "Two Realms of Kannada Folklore, in *Another Harmony: New Essays on the Folklore of India,* ed. Stuart Blackburn and A. K. Ramanujan (Berkeley: University of California Press, 1986), pp. 44–46.

5. Mīrā is often blamed for the conquest of Mewar by Bahadur Shah and Akbar. See Sangari, "Mirabai and the Spiritual Economy of *Bhakti,*" p. 1465.

6. For a good discussion of exemplary versus transgressing saints, see Hawley's introduction to his edited collection *Saints and Virtues,* pp. xiii–xviii.

7. One woman remarked: "The highest line is *bhakti,* but then Mīrā was married."

8. On the general unattractiveness of Mīrā as an exemplar for women, see Madhu Kishwar and Ruth Vanita, "Poison to Nectar: The Life and Work of Mirabai," *Manushi* (tenth anniversary issue), 71, 91–92.

9. See Parita Mukta, "Mirabai in Rajasthan," *Manushi* (tenth anniversary issue), 94–99.

10. As always, the type of information one receives depends on the questions asked, how they are asked, and who is asking them. Interestingly enough, my survey bears out Mukta's observations about villagers. She finds that villagers have not joined aristocrats in accepting Mīrā. In a Rajput village I surveyed, Rajput women did not mention Mīrā as someone they admired. They

did not say they didn't admire her, however. When I asked them what they thought of Mīrā (after the survey), many said they knew little about her, which could indicate a rejection of her by them or by their ancestors. The village women I interviewed were much more familiar with Rajput heroines such as Padminī, whose story is given later in this essay.

11. I point this out because it is certainly not uncommon for admirers to denounce or censure some of the actions of those whom they admire. In this country many admire Thomas Jefferson and John Kennedy as leaders but decry their womanizing. Having offered this comparison, I note that Mīrā's case is distinguishable in that while most admirers of Jefferson and Kennedy admire them in spite of their indiscretions, Rajput admirers of Mīrā admire her not just in spite of her actions but because of them: they distinguish her as a saint. Admiration and ambivalence are attitudes that are often conjoined in the veneration of saints. (A good example of this is to be found in the Catholic church's attitudes toward Saint Francis of Assisi, who is admired because of *and* in spite of his outrageous behaviors, such as processing naked through town as penance for eating meat while recovering from an illness.) See Hester Goodenough Gelber, "A Theater of Virtue: The Exemplary World of St. Francis of Assisi," in Hawley, *Saints and Virtues*, pp. 15–35.

12. For interesting explorations of transgressive sacrality and marginality, see Alf Hiltebeitel, ed., *Criminal Gods and Demon Devotees: Essays on the Guardians of Popular Hinduism* (Albany: State University of New York Press, 1989).

13. Unlike maharajas, aristocrats did not tend to receive financial compensation when they lost properties and their powers of taxation after independence. Many have been selling off what land and valuables they still own to support themselves and have been living lifestyles stripped of the luxury their ancestors knew.

14. The word *backward* cropped up in a number of the interviews I conducted in English. Often women (including women from Udaipur) contrasted Udaipur women with Jaipur women in this regard.

15. This is undoubtedly an ancient worry. Some Rajputs said their anxiety is particularly acute because genealogists tend to have other full-time jobs and perform their traditional tasks in their off hours; no longer depending on their patrons as their sole source of sustenance, they may find bribery particularly tempting.

16. This nostalgia is consistent with the general notion that in times when the social order is perceived as threatened or chaotic, men often increase their control over women in the household. See Susan Snow Wadley, *Struggling with Destiny in Karimpur, 1925–1984* (Berkeley: University of California Press, 1994).

17. Here the woman was clearly implying a contrast between Mīrā and herself.

18. As one woman noted, "When Chitor was in trouble, they said it was because of her, so the nobles said, 'Go get her!' " Another said that the only time a woman who was in *pardā* should leave it is "feet first," that is, on her way to the funeral pyre.

19. Madhu Kishwar and Ruth Vanita have noted that women *bhakta*s do not inspire women to emulate their rebellion in pursuit of feminist ends. They

speculate that whereas low-caste men have everything to gain and nothing to lose in emulating male *bhaktas* who challenge hierarchy, women do have something to lose—respect. Unlike *śūdras* who are obedient and self-sacrificing, women with these characteristics are revered ("Poison to Nectar," p. 91).

20. For analysis of the connection between warrior self-sacrifice and wifely duty in fifteenth- and sixteenth-century Rajasthan, see Sangari, "Mirabai and the Spiritual Economy of *Bhakti*," p. 1466.

21. For further exploration of the question of what *satī* sacrifice accomplishes for the husband, family, and community, see Harlan, *Religion and Rajput Women*, pp. 120–38.

22. This conclusion is at odds with the representation of Mīrā in the comic Amar Chitra Katha, which portrays her as an ideal wife; see John Stratton Hawley, "The Saints Subdued: Domestic Virtue and National Integration in *Amar Chitra Katha*," in *Media and the Transformation of Religion in South Asia*, ed. Susan S. Wadley and Lawrence A. Babb (Philadelphia: University of Pennsylvania Press, 1995; Hawley, "Morality Beyond Morality," p. 70; and Kishwar and Vanita, "Modern Versions of Mira," p. 100.

23. The only woman who was directly critical of Padminī disliked her because the heroine wasn't self-sacrificing enough. She said that if Padminī had committed suicide early on, there would have been no war in the first place.

24. Unlike Mīrā, these women are ordinarily referred to as *vīraṅganās* (heroines). For more on *vīrāṅganās*, see Kathryn Hansen, "The Virangana in North Indian History: Myth and Popular Culture," *Economic and Political Weekly* 23 (April 1988): 25–33. and idem, "Heroic Modes of Women in Indian Myth, Ritual and History: The *Tapasvinī* and the *Vīrāṅganā*," in *Annual Review of Women in World Religions, vol. 2, Heroic Women*, ed. Arvind Sharma and Katherine K. Young (Albany: State University of New York Press, 1992), pp. 1–62.

25. One recent retelling of the Hāḍī Rānī tale expresses discomfort over the idea of the heroine's unveiled face. In it, Hāḍī Rānī's severed head accompanies the hero into battle, but it remains covered because the blood flowing from her head causes her sari to stick to her face, which preserves her modesty after she has left *pardā* (Ann Grodzins Gold, personal communication).

26. For various implications of Mīrā's distancing of herself from the social order yet not "disarticulating its order of reality," see Sangari, "Mirabai and the Spiritual Economy of *Bhakti*," especially pp. 1468–71.

27. In suggesting this comparison with Duerr's creatures haunting the margins—sprites, witches, and werewolves—I stipulate that Mīrā is rather like the good witch of Oz, for while she cannot be fit into the ordinary female mold because of her scandalous independence, she is not seen as a threat, as most of Duerr's nonconforming "others" are. See Duerr's *Dreamtime: Concerning the Boundary Between Wilderness and Civilization*, trans. Felicitas Goodman (Oxford: Basil Blackwell, 1985), especially pp. 32–39. Also see David Dean Shulman, "Outcaste, Guardian, and Trickster: Notes on the Myth of Kāttavarāyan," in Alf Hiltebeited, *Criminal Gods and Demon Devotees*, p. 57.

28. As one woman commented, "Mīrā was a *pativratā* of Kṛṣṇa. . . . She didn't consider her husband her husband."

29. Gananath Obeyesekere, *Medusa's Hair: An Essay on Personal Symbols and Religious Experience* (Chicago: University of Chicago Press, 1981).

30. It strikes me that a similar conceptualization or reconceptualization occurs in the many instances in which demons are transformed into divine guardians: they acquire deity status while holding onto demonic characteristics, which are essential to them if they are to fulfill their duties on the margin. See the essays in Hiltebeitel, *Criminal Gods and Demon Devotees*, including the analyses of Bhairava in Kathleen M. Erndl's essay, "Rapist or Bodyguard, Demon or Devotee? Images of Bhairo in the Mythology and Cult of Vaiṣṇo Devī" (pp. 239–50), and Sunthar Visuvalingam's essay, "The Transgressive Sacrality of the Dīkṣita: Sacrifice, Criminality and *Bhakti* in the Hindu Tradition" (pp. 427–62).

31. Wendy Doniger O'Flaherty, *Síva: The Erotic Ascetic* (London: Oxford University Press, 1973).

32. On the tension between wife and courtesan imagery in poetry commonly ascribed to Mīrā, see Sangari, "Mirabai and the Spiritual Economy of *Bhakti*," pp. 1470–72.

33. O'Flaherty, *Síva: The Erotic Ascetic.*

34. For commentary on the negative associations of wandering, even when wandering is part of religious pilgrimage, see Ann Grodzins Gold, *Fruitful Journeys: The Ways of Rajasthani Pilgrims* (Berkeley: University of California Press, 1988), pp. 260–61.

35. See Hawley and Juergensmeyer, *Songs of the Saints of India*, p. 139.

36. This is why she is depicted as wearing red (being sexually active) and as wearing saffron or ochre (being a renouncer) in song. For examples, see Alston, *The Devotional Poems of Mīrābāī*, p. 96; and Mukta, "Mirabai in Rajasthan," p. 97.

37. On the affront to family honor that Mīrā's performances among *sādhus* constitute in Mīrā songs, see Sangari, "Mirabai and the Spiritual Economy of *Bhakti*," pp. 1468, 1472.

38. When I interviewed Rajput women, I always began with an open-ended question about the nature of Rajput women. These characteristics recurred again and again in their responses. For specifics of the interview format, see Harlan, *Religion and Rajput Women*, pp. 229–35.

39. For comparisons of the different codes of the *pativratā* and the *devadāsī*, see Amrit Srinivasin, "Reform and Revival: The Devadasi and Her Dance," *Economic and Political Weekly* 20, no. 44): 1869–76. For general information on the auspicious nature of both occupations, see Frédérique Marglin, *Wives of the God-King: The Rituals of the Devadasis of Puri* (Delhi Oxford University Press, 1985).

40. G. Morris Carstairs, *The Twice-Born: A Study of High-Caste Hindus* (Bloomington: University of Indiana Press, 1967), p. 95.

41. Kishwar and Vanita, "Modern Versions of Mira," p. 100.

42. On these *bhāvas*, including the *dāsya* (servant) *bhāva*, in Mīrā's *bhajans*, see Kishwar and Vanita "Poison to Nectar," p. 88.

43. Here, as elsewhere, I am primarily concerned with understanding her appeal among Rajput women in Rajasthan. Because the particulars of her story vary throughout north India, I do not claim to be offering insights on her popularity everywhere. In narratives gathered elsewhere, she lacks certain of the statuses treated here. Nevertheless, while other narratives may not include all of these, they will include some of them and so shed light on traditions elsewhere.

44. On "morality beyond morality," see Hawley's introduction to *Saints and Virtues*, p. xvi, and his own contribution to the same volume: "Morality Beyond Morality in the Lives of Three Hindu Saints," pp. 52–72. On women *bhaktas'* difficulties in being married and their defiance of social norms, see A. K. Ramanujan, "On Woman Saints," in *The Divine Consort: Rādhā and the Goddesses of India*, ed. John Stratton Hawley and Donna Marie Wulff (Berkeley: Berkeley Religious Studies Series, 1982), pp. 316–24, 320–21; see also Hancock (chapter 3, this volume).

45. A couple of the women who commented on Mīrā's story explicitly used this incident to prove that Mīrā was not unkind to her husband.

46. Living with a husband "as a sister" was also one of the pieces of evidence produced for the public to prove that a teenage girl living near Udaipur had become a goddess in 1990. Understood to be an incarnation of Āvrī Mātā, this Rajput drew thousands of pilgrims to her village over the course of several months before her in-laws decided that she was not really an incarnation. The wife-as-sister theme appears frequently in stories about women who become goddesses.

47. One woman said that Mīrā's childlessness made her better than *satīs* who burn themselves and leave their children behind. Another said, "It's a sin to leave the house if you have children, but Mīrā had no tie-downs. It's one's duty to tend the innocent children you bring into the world."

48. See Hawley and Juergensmeyer, *Songs of the Saints of India*, p. 128.

49. In common parlance the virgin is given but not taken. In syncretizing the virgin and wife statuses, in robbing the *kanyā dān* gift of its transformative and temporal aspects, she conforms to the paradigm of female divinity and power (*śakti*) offered in the myths of goddesses such as Kālī, who are both virginal and married (and even maternal), according to context.

50. John Hawley has commented that the transnormative activities of saints make the norms observed in society seem less burdensome: "The saints' lives reveal a supernal standard against the background of which the limitations of ordinary morality seem easier to bear, even if nothing visibly changes in the near at hand" (introduction to *Saints and Virtues*, p. xvii).

51. On failed marriages as a characteristic of the Kali yuga, see also Sangari, "Mirabai and the Spiritual Economy of *Bhakti*," p. 1471.

52. There are variants from elsewhere in India that have the husband play the part of persecutor. In these his estrangement and resentment are patent.

53. I have retained the spelling of jungli rani found in Gold's essay to convey the force of the title in English. I have also left out diacritical marks to be consistent with her practice here and in other essays.

54. If her family can be confirmed as Brahman, her marriage is hypogamous or *pratiloma* (against the grain).

55. For an extensive treatment of this well-known theme, see Lynn Bennett, *Dangerous Wives and Sacred Sisters: Social and Symbolic Roles of High-Caste Women in Nepal* (New York: Columbia University Press, 1983).

56. In my fieldwork I came across a story of the goddess Daśamātā that follows the same basic story line; it identifies Daśamātā, clearly a multiform of the jungli rani, as daughter.

57. This question might be asked at either the literal or the subconscious level.

58. Interestingly enough, the jungli rani performs her marital role too well. For example, she makes not ordinary bread but golden bread, which is unnerving to people. She undermines her marriage by being abnormally good at her job.

59. Harlan, *Religion and Rajput Women*, pp. 54–106.

60. This increases her status and her power within the conjugal family.

61. For illustrations of this theme, see Harlan, *Religion and Rajput Women*, pp. 54–106.

62. As mentioned previously, in some versions the persecutor is the husband, which suggests that the *devar* acts as a multiform. This, it seems to me, further supports the speculation.

63. On the great differences implied by these two kinds of relationships in Kṛṣṇa mythology, see Frédérique Marglin, "Types of Sexual Union and Their Implicit Meanings," in Hawley and Wulff, *The Divine Consort*, pp. 298–315. On the competing themes of Kṛṣṇa as husband and Kṛṣṇa as lover in Mīrā songs, see Sangari, "Mirabai and the Spiritual Economy of *Bhakti*," pp. 1469–74.

64. David Shulman has suggested correspondence between *satī* symbolism and icon–*bhakta* mergence in his seminal work *Tamil Temple Myths: Sacrifice and Divine Marriage in the South Indian Śaiva Tradition* (Princeton, N.J.: Princeton University Press, 1980), p. 64. For further discussion of this correspondence, see Harlan, *Religion and Rajput Women*, p. 212.

65. The presumed widow status of *satīs* who have not yet died results in abusive behavior toward them in many *satī* stories. The *satī* curses the skeptics just before dying, and the harm engendered by the curses is taken as additional proof of the *satī*'s goodness while her husband lived.

66. On the usage of the *satī* epithet to apply to good women in general, see Kishwar and Vanita, "Poison to Nectar," p. 91; and Sonal Shukla, "Traditions of Teaching: Women Saint Poets of Gujarat," in *Manushi* (tenth anniversary issue), 71.

67. It is interesting to note that vindication of character among *satīs* who died on the pyre is symbolized either by saffron attire, which signifies purity and renunciation, or by red attire, which signifies auspiciousness. There is a close correlation between a woman's self-denial within the context of marriage and her auspiciousness as a wife: they merge in the *satī* figure.

68. For further information on Bāḷāsatīmātā, see Harlan, *Religion and Rajput Women*, pp. 172–75; and Paul Courtright, *The Goddess and the Dreadful Practice* (New York: Oxford University Press, forthcoming).

Glossary

Included are terms in Bengali, Hindi, Tamil, or Sanskrit that appear frequently in the essays. Literal translations are given in quotation marks.

adharma	violation of morality, law, or duty
ammaṉ	goddess
anuloma	"with the hair" (with the grain), in marriage; hypergamy
apiśekam	lustration
ātman	ontological or inner self that is not subject to *saṃsāra*
bacpan	childhood
bahan	sister
bahū	daughter-in-law
bahū kā rāj	"daughter-in-law's kingdom"; widowhood
banī kā gīt	bridal song
beṭī	daughter
bhaiyā dūj	ritual in which sisters honor their brothers
bhajan	devotional song
bhakta	religious devotee, celibate
bhakti	religious devotion
bhāt	gifts given by a brother at the marriage of his sister's children
bidā	ceremony of bride's departure from her natal place just after her wedding
bījnā	embroidered fan

bindī	forehead mark signifying marriage
brahmācāri	bachelor, student
Brahman	highest of the four ranked categories of castes
byāī gīt	birth song
ciṭṭhī	letter offering marriage
cumaṅkali	married woman living with her husband
dahej	dowry
dān	ritual gift
darśan	auspicious sight, viewing a sacred image or person
devadāsī	"servants of god," temple dancers
devar	husband's younger brother
dharma	morality, law, duty
dharmaśāstra	treatise on morality, law, duty
dhiyānī	married daughter or sister
gau dān	gift of a cow
gaunā	the ceremony consummating a marriage
ghar kā kām	housework
ghūṅghaṭ	a woman's veiling of her face in front of senior male in-laws and outsiders
gopī	cowherd maidens, devotees of Kṛṣṇa
gṛhastha	householder stage of life
hiṃsā	killing, injury, violence
jaccā	new mother
jajmānī	arrangement for the exchange of ritual and agricultural services, ritual gifts, shares of the harvest, etc.
jīvit satimātā	"living *satīmātā*"; a woman who seeks immolation but is restrained and later becomes venerated as a saint
jñāti	"shared body"; natal kin
kaṇjol	piece of white cloth, tied to the bride's clothing during the wedding ritual
kanyā dān	"gift of a virgin"; marriage
karma	action or experience understood as consequence of previous actions; fate
Kāyastha	accountant
khetī kā kām	field labor
kuṭumba	in-laws
laḍḍū	sweets made from chickpea flour, spices, sugar, and clarified butter; frequently offered on ritual and social occasions
laṛkī	girl
mā kā rāj	"mother's kingdom"; childhood

mantra	unit of speech understood to have transformative power when recited correctly
milāī	gift given by brother to his sister when visiting her in her conjugal village
mokṣa	liberation from life in and rebirth into the world
mukam	mask
nanad	husband's sister
neg	payment for ritual services
nicoṛ	wringing out, sum and substance
niyoga	practice allowing a widow to have sexual relations with her deceased husband's brother in order to bear children
nōṉpu	ritual observance undertaken by women for the benefit of their husbands
nyāre	separation of households, especially the breakup of a joint family
pardā	"curtain"; seclusion of women
pati	husband, lord
pativratā	virtuous wife
pativratādharma	moral action appropriate to wives
pativratya	practice of being a virtuous wife
pātra	appropriate recipient of ritual gifts
pherā	circling the fire at the wedding ceremony
pīhar	a woman's natal home, village
piyā	beloved
prasādam	food offered to deities and then distributed to devotees
pratiloma	"against the hair" (against the grain), in marriage; hypogamy
pūjā (Tamil: *pūja*)	ceremony of worshiping a deity or deities
purohit	Brahman priest
ronā	the time of crying, the third segment of a girl's marriage in north India
roṭ	thick, unsalted bread offered to deities
ṛtugamana	"following her fertile season"; the moral obligation of a husband to have sex with his wife during her fertile time of month
sādhu	holy man, renouncer
śādī	wedding, the ritual ceremony
sādhvinī	holy woman, renouncer
sagāī	betrothal ceremony
śakti	female creative energy, female consort
saṁnyāsin	renouncer

saṃsāra	round of rebirth
saṃskāra	life-cycle ritual
saṅkalp	resolution, vow of intention to perform an action
sās	husband's mother
sās kā rāj	"mother-in-law's kingdom"; marriage
sasurāl	conjugal home
sat	capacity for exemplary moral action; substance of moral perfection in married women
satī	dutiful wife, good woman, woman who is immolated on the funeral pyre of her husband
satīmātā, satīmā	woman who was immolated on the pyre of her husband and subsequently venerated by devotees, a saintly woman
sītnā	insult song
smṛti	classical texts on ritual practice and social behavior
strīdhan	female wealth, woman's property
śūdra	lowest of the four ranked categories of castes
suhāg	good fortune
sūsar	husband's father
sumaṅgalī	married woman living with her husband
ṭakkarpūrat	design drawn to create an auspicious place for a ritual
tapas	penance, ascetic practice
uttaravu	prediction, admonishment from the goddess
vādā	gift given to women as they travel between their natal and conjugal homes
vanaprastha	forest-dweller stage of life
varṇa	ranked category of castes
varṇāśramadharma	moral action appropriate to ranked categories of caste and stages in the life cycle
vigraham	deity, image
vrat	vow, a ritual performed by women, in which stories of a god's power are told, and ritual services offered, in the expectation that the worshiper will be granted a boon
vrat kathā	story illustrating the powers of a vow
yuga	one of the four cycles of history, thought to devolve from moral perfection to the present moral chaos

Bibliography

Abu Lughod, Lila. *Veiled Sentiments: Honor and Poetry in Bedouin Society.* Berkeley: University of California Press, 1986.

"The Romance of Resistance: Tracing Transformations of Power Through Bedouin Women." *American Ethnologist* 17, no. 1 (1990): 41–55.

Agrawal, Bina. "Women, Poverty and Agricultural Growth in India." *Journal of Peasant Studies* 13 (1986): 165–220.

Alston, A. J. *The Devotional Poems of Mīrābāī.* Delhi: Motilal Banarsidass, 1980.

Āpastamba Śrauta Sūtra. 3 vols. Calcutta: Asiatic Society of Bengal, 1882–1902.

Appadurai, Arjun, and Carol Breckenridge. "The South Indian Temple: Honor, Authority and Redistribution." *Contributions to Indian Sociology,* n.s., 10 (1976): 187–211.

Archer, W. G. *Songs for the Bride: Wedding Rites of Rural India.* New York: Columbia University Press, 1985.

Atharva Veda, with the commentary of Sāyaṇa. 5 vols. Hoshiarpur: Vishveshavaranand Vedic Research Institute, 1960.

Babb, Lawrence A. *The Divine Hierarchy.* New York: Columbia University Press, 1975. *Redemptive Encounters: Three Modern Styles in the Hindu Tradition.* Berkeley: University of California Press, 1987.

Bahri, Hardev. *Learner's Hindi-English Dictionary.* Delhi: Rajpal and Sons, 1989.

Banerji, Syama Charan, trans. *The Bṛhad-dharma Purāṇa.* Lucknow: The Indian Commercial Press, 1915.

Bennett, Lynn. *Dangerous Wives and Sacred Sisters: Social and Symbolic Roles of High-Caste Women in Nepal.* New York: Columbia University Press, 1983.

Beteille, Andre. *Caste, Class and Power: Changing Patterns of Stratification in a Tanjore Village.* Berkeley: University of California Press, 1965.

Bhāgavata Purāṇa, with the commentary of Śrīdhara. Calcutta: Pandita Pustakalaya, 1972.

Boddy, Janice. *Wombs and Alien Spirits: Women, Men and the Zar Cult in Northern Sudan.* Madison: University of Wisconsin Press, 1989.

Bourguignon, Erika. *Possession.* San Francisco: Chandler and Sharp, 1976.

Brahmavaivartta Purāṇa. Ed. Pancanana Tarkaratna. Calcutta: Navabharata Publishers, 1984.

Bṛhadarāṇyaka Upaniṣad. In *One Hundred and Eight Upanishads*. Bombay: Nirnaya Sagara Press, 1913.

Bṛhaddevatā of Śaunaka. Harvard Oriental Series, 5, Cambridge, Mass.: Harvard University Press, 1904.

Brubaker, Richard. "The Ambivalent Mistress: A Study of South Indian Village Goddesses and Their Religious Meaning." Ph.D. diss. University of Chicago, 1978.

Bühler, Georg, trans. *The Laws of Manu*. Sacred Books of the East, vol. 25. Delhi: Motilal Banarsidass, 1964.

Bussburger, Robert F., and Betty Dashew Robins. *The Everyday Art of India*. New York: Dover, 1968.

Butler, Judith, and Joan Scott, eds. *Feminists Theorize the Political*. New York: Routledge, 1992.

Caplan, Patricia. *Class and Gender in India*. London: Tavistock, 1985.

Carroll, Lucy. "Law, Custom and Statutory Social Reform: The Hindu Widows' Remarriage Act of 1856." In *Women in Colonial India: Essays on Survival, Work and the State*, ed. J. Krishnamurty, 1–26. Delhi: Oxford University Press, 1989.

Carstairs, G. Morris. *The Twice-Born: A Study of High-Caste Hindus*. Bloomington: University of Indiana Press, 1967.

Cenkner, William. *A Tradition of Teachers: Śankara and the Jagadgurus Today*. Delhi: Motilal Banarsidass, 1983.

Chakravarti, Uma. "Pati-vratā." *Seminar* 318 (1986): 17–21.

Chowdry, Prem. "Customs in a Peasant Economy: Women in Colonial Haryana." In *Recasting Women: Essays in Colonial History*, ed. Kumkum Sangari and Sudesh Vaid, 302–36. New Delhi: Kali for Women, 1989.

Claus, Peter. "The Siri Myth and Ritual: A Mass Possession Cult in South India." *Ethnology* 14, no. 1 (1975): 47–58.

Courtright, Paul B. "The Iconographies of Satī." In *Satī: The Blessing and the Curse*, ed. John Stratton Hawley, 27–53. New York: Oxford University Press, 1994.

———. *The Goddess and the Dreadful Practice*. New York: Oxford University Press, forthcoming.

Crapanzano, Vincent, and Jane Garrison, eds. *Case Studies in Spirit Possession*. New York: John Wiley, 1977.

Das, Veena. "Masks and Faces: An Essay on Punjabi Kinship." *Contributions to Indian Sociology* n.s., 10 (1976): 1–30.

Datta, V. N. *Satī: A Historical, Social and Philosophical Enquiry into the Hindu Rite of Widow Burning*. Riverdale, Md.: The Riverdale Company, 1988.

Dave, J. H., ed. *The Laws of Manu*. 6 vols. Bombay: Bharatiya Vidya Bhavan, 1972–84.

David, Kenneth, ed. *The New Wind: Changing Identities in South Asia*. The Hague: Mouton, 1977.

Denton, Lynn Teskey. "Varieties of Female Asceticism." In *Roles and Rituals for Women*, ed. I. Julia Leslie, 211–32. London: Pinter Press, 1991.

Desai, Vishakha N., and Darielle Mason. *Gods, Guardians, and Lovers: Temple Sculptures from North India, A.D. 700–1200*. New York: Asia Society Galleries, 1993.

Dirks, Nicholas. *The Hollow Crown: Ethnohistory of an Indian Kingdom*. Cambridge: Cambridge University Press, 1987.

Doniger, Wendy. "When God Has Lipstick on His Collar." Mackay Lecture, St. Lawrence University, 1991.

Doniger, Wendy, with Brian K. Smith. *The Laws of Manu*. Harmondsworth, Eng.: Penguin, 1991.

Dreze, Jean. "Social Insecurity in India." Paper presented at the Workshop on Social Insecurity in Developing Countries. London School of Economics, 1988.

Dube, Leela. "On the Construction of Gender: Hindu Girls in Patrilineal India." *Economic and Political Weekly* (April 30 1988): 11–19.

Duerr, Hans Peter. *Dreamtime: Concerning the Boundary Between Wilderness and Civilization*. Trans. Felicitas Goodman. Oxford: Basil Blackwell, 1985.

Dumont, Louis. *Hierarchy and Marriage Alliance in South India*. Royal Anthropological Institute Occasional Paper, no. 12. London: Royal Anthropological Institute, 1957.

———. "World Renunciation in Indian Religion." *Contributions to Indian Sociology*, n.s., 4 (1960): 33–62.

———. "Marriage in India: The Present State of the Question. III: North India in Relation to South India." *Contributions to Indian Sociology*, n.s., 9 (1966): 90–114.

———. *Homo Hierarchicus: The Caste System and Its Implications*. Chicago: University of Chicago Press, 1970.

———. *Affinity as a Value: Marriage Alliance in South India, with Comparative Essays on Australia*. Chicago: University of Chicago Press, 1986.

———. *A South Indian Subcaste: Social Organization and Religion of the Pramalai Kallar*. Delhi: Oxford University Press, 1986.

Dyson, Tim, and Mick Moore. "On Kinship Structure, Female Autonomy, and Demographic Behavior in India." *Population and Development Review* 9 (1983): 35–60.

Eastman, Alvan Clark. *The Nala-Damayanti Drawings*. Boston: Museum of Fine Arts, 1959.

Eck, Diana L. *Darśan: Seeing the Divine Image in India*. 2nd rev. ed. Chambersburg, Pa.: Anima Press, 1985.

Eglar, Zekiye. *A Punjabi Village in Pakistan*. New York: Columbia University Press, 1960.

Egnor, Margaret Trawick. "The Changed Mother, or What the Smallpox Goddess Did When There Was No More Smallpox." *Contributions to Asian Studies*, n.s., 18 (1982): 24–45.

———. "On the Meaning of Śakti to Women in Tamil Nadu." In *The Powers of Tamil Women*, South Asia Series, no. 6, ed. Susan Wadley, 1–34. Syracuse: Maxwell School of Citizenship and Public Affairs, 1982.

———. "Internal Iconicity in Paraiyar Crying Songs." In *Another Harmony: Essays on the Folklore of India*, ed. Stuart Blackburn and A. K. Ramanujan, 294–344. Berkeley: University of California Press, 1986.

———. "Spirits and Voices in Tamil Songs." *American Ethnologist* 15(1988): 193–213.

Erndl, Kathleen. "Rapist or Bodyguard? Demon or Devotee? Images of Bhairo in the Mythology and Cult of Vaiṣṇo Devī." In *Criminal Gods and Demon Devotees: Essays on the Guardians of Popular Hinduism*, ed. Alf Hiltebeitel, 239–50. Albany: State University of New York Press, 1989.

———. *Victory to the Mother: The Hindu Goddess of Northwest India in Myth, Ritual, and Symbol*. New York: Oxford University Press, 1993.

Foucault, Michel. *The History of Sexuality*. Vol. 1: *An Introduction*. New York: Random House, 1978.

Freitag, Sandria. *Collective Action and Community: Public Arenas and the Emergence of Communalism in North India*. Berkeley: University of California Press, 1989.

———, ed. *Culture and Power in Banaras: Community, Performance and Environment, 1800–1980*. Berkeley: University of California Press, 1989.

Fruzzetti, Lina, M. *The Gift of a Virgin: Women, Marriage, and Ritual in a Bengali Society*. New Brunswick, N.J.: Rutgers University Press, 1982.

Fuller, Christopher, J. "Sacrifice in the South Indian Temple." In *Religion and Society in South India*, ed. V. Sudarsen, G. Prakash Reddy, and N. M. Suryanarayana, 21–36. Delhi: B. R. Publishing Company, 1987.

———. *The Camphor Flame: Popular Hinduism and Society in India*. Princeton, N.J.: Princeton University Press, 1992.

Geertz, Clifford. *The Interpretation of Cultures*. New York: Basic Books, 1973.

Gelber, Hester Goodenough. "A Theater of Virtue: The Exemplary World of St. Francis of Assisi." In *Saints and Virtues*, ed. John Stratton Hawley, 15–35. Berkeley: University of California Press, 1987.

Gold, Ann Grodzins. *Village Families in Story and Song: An Approach Through Women's Oral Tradition in Rajasthan*. Indiakit Series, Outreach Educational Project, South Asia Language and Area Center. Chicago: University of Chicago, 1982.

———. *Fruitful Journeys: The Ways of Rajasthani Pilgrims*. Berkeley: University of California Press, 1988.

———. "Gender and Illusion in a Rajasthani Yogic Tradition." In *Gender, Genre and Power in South Asian Expressive Traditions*, ed. Arjun Appadurai, Frank Korom, and Margaret Mills, 102–35. Philadelphia: University of Pennsylvania Press, 1991.

———. *A Carnival of Parting: The Tales of King Gopi Chand and King Bharthari as Sung and Told by Madhu Natisar Nath of Ghatiyali, Rajasthan*. Berkeley: University of California Press, 1992.

———. "Mother Ten's Stories." In *Religions India in Practice*, ed. Donald S. Lopez, Jr. Princeton, N.J.: Princeton University Press, in press.

———. "Sexuality, Fertility, and Erotic Imagination in Rajasthani Women's Songs." In Gloria Goodwin Raheja and Ann Grodzins Gold, *Listen to the Heron's Words: Relmagining Gender and Kinship in North India*. Berkeley: University of California Press, 1994, pp 30–72.

Good, Anthony. "The Actor and the Act: Categories of Prestation in South India." *Man*, n.s., 17 (1982): 23–41.

Goody, Jack. "Bridewealth and Dowry in Africa and Eurasia." In *Bridewealth and dowry*, by Jack Goody and S. J. Tambiah, Cambridge Papers in Social Anthropology 7, 59–169. Cambridge: Cambridge University Press, 1973, pp. 1–58.

———. *The Oriental, the Ancient and the Primitive.* Cambridge: Cambridge University Press, 1990.

Gough, Kathleen. "Brahmin Kinship in a Tamil Village." *American Anthropologist* 58 (1956): 826–53.

Granoff, Phyllis. "When Miracles Become Too Many: Stories of the Destruction of Holy Sites in the *Tāpi Khaṇḍa* of the *Skanda Purāṇa.*" *Annals of the Bhandarkar Oriental Research Institute* 77 (1992): 47–71.

———. "Halāyudha's Prism: The Experience of Religion in Medieval Hymns and Stories." In *Gods, Guardians and Lovers: Temple Sculptures from North India,* A.D. 700–1200, ed. Vishakha N. Desai and Darielle Mason, 66–93. New York: Asia Society Galleries, 1993.

Guha, Ranajit, and Gayatri Chakravorty Spivak, eds. *Selected Subaltern Studies.* New York: Oxford University Press, 1988.

Hancock, Mary. Saintly Careers Among South India's Urban Middle Classes." *Man,* n.s., 25, (1990): 505–20.

———. "Crafting Culture for the Nation." In *Culture as a Contested Site,* ed. Sandria Freitag. Forthcoming.

Hansen, Kathryn. "The Virangana in North Indian History: Myth and Popular Culture." *Economic and Political Weekly* 23 (1988): 25–33.

———. "Heroic Modes of Women in Indian Myth, Ritual and History: The *Tapasvinī* and the *Vīrāṅganā.*" In *Annual Review of Women in World Religions.* vol. 2: *Heroic Women,* ed. Arvind Sharma and Katherine K. Young, 1–62. Albany: State University of New York Press, 1992.

Harlan, Lindsey. *Religion and Rajput Women: The Ethic of Protection in Contemporary Narratives.* Berkeley: University of California Press, 1992.

Hawley, John Stratton. "Introduction: Saints and Virtues." In *Saints and Virtues,* ed. John Stratton Hawley, xi–xxiv. Berkeley: University of California Press, 1987.

———. "Morality Beyond Morality in the Lives of Three Hindu Saints." In *Saints and Virtues,* ed. John Stratton Hawley, 52–72. Berkeley: University of California Press, 1987.

———. "The Saints Subdued: Domestic Virtue and National Integration in *Amar Chitra Katha.*" In *Media and the Transformation of Religion in South Asia,* ed. Susan S. Wadley and Lawrence A. Babb. Philadelphia: University of Pennsylvania Press, 1995.

Hawley, John Stratton, and Mark Juergensmeyer. *Songs of the Saints of India.* New York: Oxford University Press, 1988.

Hawley, John Stratton, and Donna Marie Wulff, eds. *The Divine Consort.* Berkeley: Berkeley Religious Studes Series, 1982.

Haynes, Doug, and Gyan Prakash, eds. *Contesting Power: Resistance and Everyday Social Relations in South Asia.* Berkeley: University of California Press, 1992.

Hazra, Rajendra Chandra. *Studies in the Puranic Records on Hindu Rites and Customs.* Bulletin no. 20. Dacca: University of Dacca, 1940.

———. *Studies in the Upapurāṇas.* Vol. 2: *Śākta and Non-Sectarian Upapurāṇas.* Research Series, no. 22. Calcutta: Sanskrit College, 1963.

Hershman, Paul. "Virgin and Mother." In *Symbols and Sentiments: Cross-cultural*

Studies in Symbolism, ed. I. M. Lewis, 269–92. London: Academic Press, 1977.

———. *Punjabi Kinship and Marriage*. Delhi: Hindustan Publishing, 1981.

Hiltebeitel, Alf. "Draupadī's Hair." *Puruṣārtha* 5 (1981): 179–214.

———, ed. *Criminal Gods and Demon Devotees: Essays on the Guardians of Popular Hinduism* Albany: State University of New York Press, 1989.

Inden, Ronald. *Marriage and Rank in Bengali Culture: A History of Caste and Clan in Middle Period Bengal*. Berkeley: University of California Press, 1976.

Inden, Ronald, and Ralph Nicholas. *Kinship in Bengali Culture*. Chicago: University of Chicago Press, 1977.

Jacobson, Doranne. "Women and Jewelry in Rural India." In *Family and Social Change in Modern India*, ed. Giri Raj Gupta, 135–83. Delhi: Vikas, 1976.

———. "Flexibility in North Indian Kinship and Residence." In *The New Wind: Changing Identities in South Asia*, ed. Kenneth David, 263–83. The Hague: Mouton, 1977.

———. "The Chaste Wife: Cultural Norm and Individual Experience." In *American Studies in the Anthropology of India*, ed. Sylvia Vatuk, 94–138. New Delhi: Manohar Books, 1978.

Jeffery, Patricia, Roger Jeffery, and Andrew Lyon. *Labour Pains and Labour Power: Women and Childbearing in India*. London: Zed Books, 1989.

Kakar, Sudhir. *The Inner World: A Psycho-analytic Study of Childhood and Society in India*. Delhi: Oxford University Press, 1978.

———. *Intimate Relations: Exploring Indian Sexuality*. Chicago: University of Chicago Press, 1990.

Kāmasūtra of Vātsyāyana, with the commentary of Śrī Yaśodhara. Bombay: Laksmivenkatesvara Press, 1856.

Kessler, Clive. "Conflict and Sovereignty in Kelatenese Malay Spirit Seances." In *Case Studies in Spirit Possession*, ed. Vincent Crapanzano and Jane Garrison, 295–331. New York: John Wiley, 1977.

Kinsley, David. *Hindu Goddesses: Visions of the Divine Feminine in the Hindu Religious Tradition*. Berkeley: University of California Press, 1986.

Kishwar, Madhu, and Ruth Vanita. "Modern Versions of Mira." *Manushi* (tenth anniversary issue) 50–52 (1989): 100–101.

———. "Poison to Nectar: The Life and Work of Mirabai." *Manushi* (tenth anniversary issue) 50–52 (1989): 75–93.

Koenig, Michael, and Gillian H. C. Foo. "Patriarchy and High Fertility in Rural North India." Paper presented at the Rockefeller Foundation Workshop on Women's Status and Fertility, Mt. Kisco, N.Y., June 1985.

Kolenda, Pauline. "Region, Caste and Family Structure: A Comparative Study of the Indian 'Joint' Family.' " In *Structure and Change in Indian Society*, ed. Milton Singer and Barnard Cohn, 339–96. Chicago: Aldine, 1968.

———. "Widowhood Among 'Untouchable' Chuhras." In *Concepts of Person: Kinship, Caste and Marriage in India*, ed. A. Östör, Lina Fruzetti, and Steve Barnett, 172–220. Cambridge, Mass.: Harvard University Press, 1982.

———. "Untouchable Chuhras Through Their Humor: 'Equalizing' Marital Kin Through Teasing, Pretence, and Farce." In *Divine Passions: The Social Construction of Emotion in India*, ed. Owen Lynch, 116–53. Berkeley: University of California Press, 1990.

Kurtz, Stanley. *All Mothers Are One: Hindu India and the Reshaping of Psychoanalysis.* New York: Columbia University Press, 1992.

Lakshman, N. "Interview with Jayendra Saraswati, Sankaracharya of Kanchipuram." *Illustrated Weekly of India,* September 13, 1987.

Leslie, I. Julia. Suttee or *Satī:* Victim or Victor?" In *Roles and Rituals for Hindu Women,* ed. I. Julia Leslie, 173–92. London: Pinter Publishers, 1991.

Lewandowski, Susan. *Migration and Ethnicity in Urban India: Kerala Migrants in the City of Madras.* New Delhi: Manohar Books, 1980.

Lewis, I. M. *Ecstatic Religion: An Anthropological Study of Spirit Possession and Shamanism.* Harmondsworth, Eng.: Penguin, 1971.

———. *Religion in Context: Cults and Charisma.* Cambridge: Cambridge University Press, 1986.

Lorenzen, David. "The Kabir-Panth and Social Protest." in *The Sants: Studies in a Devotional Tradition of India,* ed. Karine Schomer and W. H. McLeod, 281–303. Delhi: Motilal Banarsidass, 1987.

Macdonell, Arthur Anthony Macdonnell and Arthur Barriedale Keith. *Vedic Index,* 2 vols. London: John Murray, 1958.

McGee, Mary. "Feasting and Fasting: The Vrata Tradition and Its Significance for Hindu Women." Ph.D. diss. Harvard University, 1987.

Madan, T. N. "Is the Brahmanic *gotra* a Grouping of Kin?" *Southwestern Journal of Anthropology* 18 (1962): 59–77.

———. *Family and Kinship: A Study of the Pandits of Rural Kashmir.* Bombay: Asia Publishing House, 1965.

———. *Non-Renunciation: Themes and Interpretations of Hindu Culture.* Delhi: Oxford University Press, 1987.

Mahābhārata. Critical edition. Ed. V. S. Sukthankar et al. Poona: Bhandarkar Oriental Research Institute, 1933–69.

Maitrāyaṇī Saṃhitā. Wiesbaden: Hassarowitz, 1970.

Majumdar, R. C., ed. *The History of Bengal.* Vol. 1: *The Hindu Period.* Dacca: The University of Dacca, 1943.

Mandelbaum, David. *Society in India: Continuity and Change.* Berkeley: University of California Press, 1970.

Mani, Lata. "Production of an Official Discourse on *Sati* in Early Nineteenth Century Bengal." *Economic and Political Weekly* 21 (1986): 32–40.

———. "Contentious Traditions: The Debate on SATĪ in Colonial India." *Cultural Critique* (Fall 1987): 119–56.

———. "Cultural Theory, Colonial Texts: Reading Eyewitness Accounts of Widow Burning." In *Cultural Studies,* ed. Lawrence Grossberg, Gary Nelson, and Paula Breichler, 392–408. New York: Routledge, 1991.

———. *Contentious Traditions: The Debate on Sati in Colonial India, 1780–1833.* Berkeley: University of California Press, forthcoming.

Marglin, Frédérique A. "Three Types of Sexual Union and Their Implicit Meanings." In *The Divine Consort: Rādhā and the Goddesses of India,* ed. John Stratton Hawley and Donna Marie Wulff, 298–315. Berkeley: Berkeley Religious Studies Series, 1982.

———. *Wives of the God-King: The Rituals of the Devadasis of Puri.* Delhi: Oxford University Press, 1985.

Marriott, Mckim, and Ronald Inden. "Towards an Ethnosociology of North

Indian Caste Systems," in *The New Wind: Changing Identities in South Asia* ed. Kenneth David, The Hague: Mouton, 1977. 227–38.
Mehta, Rup Kunwar. *Śrī satī mātā caritāmṛt.* Jodhpur: Sushma Prakashan, 1986.
Meyer, Eveline. *Aṅkāḷaparmēcuvari: A Goddess of Tamilnadu, Her Myths and Cult.* Stuttgart: Steiner Verlag, 1986.
Mies, Maria. *Indian Women and Patriarchy.* Delhi: Concept Publishing Company, 1979.
Misra, B. B. *The Indian Middle Classes.* Delhi: Oxford University Press, 1961.
Mukta, Parita. "Mirabai in Rajasthan." *Manushi* (tenth anniversary issue) 50–52 (1989): 94–99.
Muthiah, S. *Madras Discovered.* New Delhi: Affiliated East-West Press, 1987.
———, ed. *A Social and Economic Atlas of India.* Delhi: Oxford University Press, 1987.
Nandy, Ashis. *The Intimate Enemy: Loss and Recovery of Self Under Colonialism.* Delhi: Oxford University Press, 1983.
Narayana Rao, Velcheru, David Shulman, and Sanjay Subrahmanyam. *Symbols of Substance: Court and State in Nāyaka Period Tamilnadu.* Delhi: Oxford University Press, 1992.
Needham, Rodney. "Polythetic Classification: Convergence and Consequences." *Man,* n.s., 10 (1975): 349–69.
Nicholson, Linda, ed. *Feminism/Postmodernism.* New York: Routledge, 1991.
Niranjana, T., P. Sudhir, and Vivek Dhareshwar, eds. *Interrogating Modernity: Culture and Colonialism in India.* Calcutta: Seagull Books, 1993.
Obeyesekere, Gananath. *Medusa's Hair: An Essay on Personal Symbols and Religious Experience.* Chicago: University of Chicago Press, 1981.
O'Flaherty, Wendy Doniger. *Śiva: The Erotic Ascetic.* London: Oxford University Press, 1973.
———. *The Origins of Evil in Hindu Mythology.* Berkeley: University of California Press, 1976.
———. *Women, Androgynes, and Other Mythical Beasts.* Chicago: University of Chicago Press, 1980.
———, ed. *The Rig Veda: An Anthology of One Hundred and Eight Hymns.* Harmondsworth, Eng.: Penguin, 1980.
Ojha, Catherine. "Feminine Asceticism in Hinduism: Its Tradition and Present Condition." *Man in India* 61 (1981): 254–85.
Omvedt, Gail. "Patriarchy: The Analysis of Women's Oppression," *Insurgent Sociologist* 13 (1986): 30–50.
Östör, Akos, Lina Fruzzetti, and Steve Barnett, eds. *Concepts of Person: Kinship, Caste and Marriage in India.* Cambridge, Mass.: Harvard University Press, 1982.
Pandian, M. S. S. "From Exclusion to Inclusion: Brahminism's New Face in Tamilnadu." *Economic and Political Weekly* 25 (1990): 1938–39.
Pandey, Raj Bali. *Hindu Saṃskāras.* Delhi: Motilal Banarsidass, 1976.
Papanek, Hanna. "Family Status Production: The 'Work' and 'Non-Work' of Women." *Signs* 4, no. 4 (1979): 775–81.
———. "Purdah: Separate Worlds and Symbolic Shelter." In *Separate Worlds: Studies in Purdah in South Asia,* ed. Hanna Papanek and Gail Minault, 3–53. Delhi: Chanakya Publications, 1982.

Parry, Jonathan. *Caste and Kinship in Kangra.* London: Routledge and Kegan Paul, 1979.

———. "Ghosts, Greed and Sin: The Occupational Identity of the Benares Funeral Priests." *Man,* n.s., 15 (1980): 88–111.

———. "*The Gift,* The Indian Gift and the 'Indian Gift'." *Man,* n.s., 21 (1986): 453–73.

Pathak, R. C. *Bhargava's Standard Illustrated Dictionary of the Hindi Language.* Varanasi: Barghava Book Depot, 1986.

Peterson, Indira. "The Tie That Binds: Brothers and Sisters in North and South India." *South Asian Social Scientist* 41 (1988): 25–52.

Raheja, Gloria Goodwin. "Kinship, Caste, and Auspiciousness in Pahansu." Ph.D. diss. University of Chicago, 1985.

———. *The Poison in the Gift: Ritual, Prestation, and the Dominant Caste in a North Indian Village.* Chicago: University of Chicago Press, 1988.

———. "Negotiating Kinship and Gender: Essentializing and contextualizing Strategies in North Indian Song and Narrative Traditions" Paper presented at the conference "Language, Gender, and the Subaltern Voice: Framing Identities in South Asia" University of Minnesota, April, 1991.

Raheja, Gloria Goodwin, and Ann Grodzins Gold. *Listen to the Heron's Words: Reimagining Gender and Kinship in North India.* Berkeley: University of California Press, 1994.

Rajgarhiya, Campadevi. *Bārah mahīno kā tyauhār.* Calcutta: Hari Art Press, n.d.

Ramanujan, A. K. *Speaking of Śiva.* Harmondsworth, Eng.: Penguin, 1973.

———. "The Indian Oedipus." In *Oedipus: A Folklore Casebook,* ed. Lowell Edmunds and Alan Dundes, 234–61 New York: Garland, 1984.

———. *Poems of Love and War: From the Eight Anthologies and the Ten Long Poems of Classical Tamil.* Delhi: Oxford University Press, 1985.

———. "On Woman Saints." In *The Divine Consort: Rādhā and the Goddesses of India,* ed. John Stratton Hawley and Donna Marie Wulff, 316–24. Berkeley: Berkeley Religious Studies Series, 1982.

———. "Two Realms of Kannada Folklore." in *Another Harmony: New Essays on the Folklore of India,* ed. Stuart Blackburn and A. K. Ramanujan, 41–75 Berkeley: University of California Press, 1986.

———. *Folktales from India: A Selection of Oral Tales from Twenty-two Languages.* New York: Pantheon Books, 1991.

Rāmāyaṇa of Valmīki, ed. G. H. Bhatt et al. Baroda: Oriental Institute, 1960–75.

Randhawa, M.S. *Kangra Paintings on Love.* New Delhi: The National Museum, 1962.

Rapp, Rayna. "Family and Class in Contemporary America: Notes Toward an Understanding of Ideology." In *Rethinking the Family: Some Feminist Questions,* ed. Barrie Thorne, with Marilyn Yalom, 168–87. New York: Longman, 1982.

Rawson, Philip. *Erotic Art of the East.* New York: Putnam, 1968.

Raya, Nihararanjana. *Bāṃālī hindur varṇa-bheda.* Calcutta: Visvabharati University, 1945.

Reynolds, Holly Baker. "The Auspicious Married Woman." In *The Powers of Tamil Women,* South Asia Series, no. 6, ed. Susan S. Wadley, 35–60.

Syracuse, N.Y.: Maxwell School of Citizenship and Public Affairs, 1982.

———. "Sisters Protect Brothers: Two Tamil Women's Rituals." Paper presented at the conference "Women's Rites, Women's Desires," Harvard University, 1988.

Ṛg Veda, with the commentary of Sāyaṇa. 6 vols. London: H. Frowde, 1890–92.

Roland, Alan. *In Search of Self in India and Japan: Toward a Cross-Cultural Psychology*. Princeton, N.J.: Princeton University Press, 1988.

Rudolph, Lloyd, and Susanne Rudolph. *The Modernity of Tradition: Political Development in India*. Chicago: University of Chicago Press, 1967.

Sangari, Kumkum. "Mirabai and the Spiritual Economy of *Bhakti*." *Economic and Political Weekly* 25 (1990): 1464–75, 1537–52.

Sangari, Kumkum, and Sudesh Vaid. "*Satī* in Modern India: A Report." *Economic and Political Weekly* 16 (1981): 1284–88.

———, eds. *Recasting Women: Essays in Indian Colonial History*. New Brunswick, N.J.: Rutgers University Press, 1990.

Śaṅkhāyana Gṛhya Sūtra. Delhi: Munshi Ram Manoharlal, 1960.

Śatapatha Brāhmaṇa. Benares: Chowkhamba Sanskrit Series, 96, 1964.

Sax, William. *Mountain Goddess: Gender and Politics in a Himalayan Village*. New York: Oxford University Press, 1991.

Schomer, Karine, and W. H. McLeod, eds. *The Sants: Studies in a Devotional Tradition of India*. Delhi: Motilal Banarsidass, 1987.

Sharma, Krishna. *Bhakti and the Bhakti Movement: A New Perspective*. New Delhi: Munshiram Manoharlal, 1987.

Sharma, Ursula. "Women and Their Affines: The Veil as a Symbol of Separation." *Man*, n.s., 13 (1978): 218–33.

———. "Purdah and Public Space." In *Women in Contemporary India and South Asia: Traditional Images and Changing Roles*, ed. Alfred de Souza, 213–39. New Delhi: Manohar Books, 1980.

———. *Women, Work and Property in North West India*. London: Tavistock, 1980.

———. "Dowry in North India: Its Consequences for Women." In *Women and Property—Women as Property*, ed. Renee Hirshon, 62–74. New York: St. Martin's Press, 1984.

———. *Women's Work, Class and the Urban Household: A Study of Shimla, North India*. London: Tavistock, 1986.

Shukla, Sonal. "Traditions of Teaching: Women Saint Poets of Gujarat." *Manushi* (tenth anniversary issue) 50–52 (1989): 62–73.

Shulman, David. *Tamil Temple Myths: Sacrifice and Divine Marriage in the South Indian Śaiva Tradition*. Princeton, N.J.: Princeton University Press, 1980.

———. "Outcaste, Guardian, and Trickster: Notes on the Myth of Kāttavarāyan." In *Criminal Gods and Demon Devotees: Essays on the Guardians of Popular Hinduism*, ed. Alf Hiltebeitel, 35–67. Albany: State University of New York Press, 1989.

Singer, Milton. *When a Great Tradition Modernizes: An Anthropological Approach to Indian Civilization*. Chicago: University of Chicago Press, 1972.

———. ed. *Traditional India: Structure and Change*. Austin: University of Texas Press, 1959.

Śiva Purāṇa. Benares: Pandita Pustakalaya, 1964.

Spellman, Elizabeth V. *The Inessential Woman: Problems of Exclusion in Feminist Thought*. Boston: Beacon Press, 1988.

Srinivasan, Amrit. "Reform and Revival: The Devadasi and Her Dance." *Economic and Political Weekly* 20, no. 44 (1985): 1869–76.

Sullivan, Bruce M. *Kṛṣṇa Dvaipāyana Vyāsa and the Mahābhārata: A New Interpretation*. Leiden: E. J. Brill, 1990.

Tagare, Ganesh Vasudeo, trans. *The Bhāgavata Purāṇa*. 4 vols. Delhi: Motilal Banarsidass, 1976.

Taittirīya Brāhmaṇa. Calcutta: Bibliotheca Indica, 1859.

Taittirīya Saṃhitā. Calcutta: Bibliotheca Indica, 1860.

Tambiah, Stanley. "Dowry and Bridewealth and the Property Rights of Women in South Asia." In *Bridewealth and Dowry*, by Jack Goody and Stanley J. Tambiah, Cambridge: Cambridge Papers in Social Anthropology 7, 59–169. Cambridge: Cambridge University Press, 1973.

———. "From *Varṇa* to Caste Through Mixed Unions." In *The Character of Kinship*, ed. Jack Goody, 191–229. Cambridge, Mass.: Harvard University Press, 1982.

———. "*Bridewealth and Dowry* Revisited: The Position of Women in Sub-Saharan Africa and North India." *Current Anthropology* 30, no. 4 (1989): 413–435.

Tarabout, Giles. *Sacrifier et donner à voir en pays Malabar: Les Fêtes de temple au Kerala (Inde du Sud)*. Paris: Ecole Française d'Extrême-Orient, 1986.

Thapar, Romila. "Death and the Hero." In *Mortality and Immortality: The Anthropology and Archaeology of Death*, ed. S. C. Humphreys and Helen King. 293–315. London, Academic Press, 1981.

Trautmann, Thomas. *Dravidian Kinship*. Cambridge: Cambridge University Press, 1981.

Turner, Victor. *The Ritual Process: Structure and Anti-Structure*. Chicago: Aldine, 1969.

van der Veen, Klaas. *I Give Thee My Daughter: A Study of Marriage and Hierarchy Among the Anaval Brahmans of South Gujarat*. Assen: Van Gorcum, 1972.

———. "Reply." *Current Anthropology* 30 (1989): 431–32.

van der Veer, Peter. "The Power of Detachment: Disciples of Body and Mind in the Ramanandi Order." *American Ethnologist* 16, no. 3 (1989): 458–70.

Vanaik, Achin. "The Rajiv Congress in Search of Stability." *The New Left Review* 154 (1985): 55–63.

Vatuk, Sylvia J. *Kinship and Urbanization: White-Collar Migrants in North India*. Berkeley: University of California Press, 1972.

———. "Gifts and Affines." *Contributions to Indian Sociology*, n.s., 5 (1975): 155–96.

———. "The Aging Woman in India: Self-Perceptions and Changing Roles." In *Women in Contemporary India and South Asia: Traditional Images and Changing Roles*, ed. Alfred de Souza, 287–309. New Delhi: Manohar Books, 1980.

Vatuk, Sylvia, and Ved Prakash Vatuk. "On a System of Private Savings Among North Indian Village Women." *Journal of Asian and African Studies* 6 (1971): 179–90.

———. "The Social Context of Gift Exchange in North India." In *Family and*

Social Change in Modern India, ed. Giri Raj Gupta, 207–32. Delhi: Vikas, 1976.

Vatuk, Ved, and Sylvia Vatuk. "The Lustful Stepmother in the Folklore of Northwestern India." In *Studies in Indian Folk Traditions*, ed. Ved Vatuk, 190–221. New Delhi: Manohar Books, 1979.

Véquaud, Yves. *Women Painters of Mithila*. London: Thames and Hudson, 1977.

Visaria, Pravin, and Leela Visaria. "Indian Households with Female Heads: Their Incidence, Characteristics and Level of Living." In *Tyranny of the Household: Investigative Essays on Women's Work*, ed. D. Jain and N. Banerjee, 50–83. New Delhi: Shakti Books, 1985.

Viṣṇu Purāṇa, with the commentary of Srīdhara. Calcutta: Sanatana Sastra, 1972.

Visuvalingam, Sunthar. "The Transgressive Sacrality of the Dīkṣita: Sacrifice, Criminality and *Bhakti* in the Hindu Tradition." In *Criminal Gods and Demon Devotees: Essays on the Guardians of Popular Hinduism*, ed. Alf Hiltebeitel, 427–62. Albany: State University of New York Press, 1989.

Wadley, Susan Snow. *Shakti: Power in the Conceptual Structure of Karimpur Religion*. Chicago: University of Chicago Department of Anthropology, 1975.

———. "Brothers, Husbands and Sometimes Sons: Kinsmen in North Indian Ritual." *Eastern Anthropologist* 29 (1976): 149–70.

———. "Texts in Contexts: Oral Traditions and the Study of Religion in Karimpur." In *American Studies in the Anthropology of India*, ed. Sylvia Vatuk, 309–41. New Delhi: Manohar Books, 1978.

———. "The 'Village Indira': A Brahman Widow and Political Action in Rural North India." In *Balancing Acts: Women and the Process of Social Change*, ed. Patricia Lyons Johnson, 65–87. Boulder, Colo.: Westview Press, 1992.

———. *Struggling with Destiny in Karimpur, 1925–1984*. Berkeley: University of California Press, 1994.

———. "Women and the Hindu Tradition." In *Women in India: Two Perspectives*, Susan S. Wadley and Doranne Jacobson, 111–36. New Delhi: Manohar Books, 1977.

———, ed. *The Powers of Tamil Women*. South Asia Series 6. Syracuse, NY: Maxwell School of Citizenship and Public Affairs, 1982.

Wadley, Susan Snow, and Bruce Derr. "Karimpur Families over 60 Years." *South Asian Anthropologist* 9 (1988): 119–32.

Washbrook, David. "Caste, Class and Dominance in Modern Tamil Nadu." In *Dominance and State Power in Modern India*, ed. Francine Frankel and M.S.A. Rao, 204–64. Delhi: Oxford University Press, 1989.

Weissman, Lee. "Who Is Pankaru?" Paper presented at the Conference on Religion in South India, Research Triangle Park, N.C., June 1988.

White, Charles, S.J. "Mother Guru: Jnanananda of Madras, India." In *Unspoken Worlds: Women's Religious Lives in Non-Western Cultures*, ed. Nancy Aver Falk and Rita M. Gross, 22–37. San Francisco: Harper and Row, 1980.

Wiser, William. "Social Institutions of a Hindu Village in North India," Ph.D. diss., Cornell University, 1933.

Wiser, William, and Charlotte Viall Wiser. *Behind Mud Walls, 1930–1960,* with a sequel, "The Village in 1970," and a new chapter by Susan S. Wadley, "The Village in 1984"; foreword by David G. Mandelbaum. Berkeley: University of California Press, 1989.

Yalman, Nur. "On the Purity of Women in the Castes of Ceylon and Malabar." *Journal of the Royal Anthropological Institute* 93 (1963): 25–58.

Index

Adultery, 160–80; passim in Vedic texts, 161–62; in *Manu*, 163; violating guru's bed, 163–65; Bṛhaspati, 165–69; sanctioned, 170–72; the *niyoga*, 172–74, 177–79; Vyāsa and Dīrghatamas, 174–77; Vyāsa and Ṛṣyaśṛṅga, 177–79; later history of levirate, 179–80; and Mīrā Bāī, 219
Advaitavedānta, 64
Age of widows, 100, 103, 106
Agriculture: as male activity, 96; women in, 98
Ambaṣṭhās, the, 148–49, 151–52
Annapūrṇā, 69
Apiśekam (ritual bathing of deity's image), 66, 68, 73; and the household, 73
Atharva Veda, 161–62
Auspiciousness: of women, 7; and *cumaṅkalis*, 82

Bāḷāsatīmātā, 190–203, 221; story of, 194–201; significance of, 202
Bane kā gīt (bridegroom's song), 43–44
Banī kā gīt (young bride's song), 27
Behri Yogin, 130–31
Bengal: lady magicians of, 130, 132; marriage and divorce in, 137–57; *saṃskāra* rites in, 139; myth of Veṇa and Pṛthu, 144–49; *Bṛhaddharma Purāṇa*, 149–53; *satī* in, 185
Bhāgavata Purāṇa, 166–67
Bhakta (devotee of god), 219; among Smārta Brahmans, 61; and divinity, 84–85; ambivalence toward caste and household, 85; Mīrā Bāī as, 206, 209
Bhakti (religious devotion), 15; in social context, 60–63; ambiguities of, 62; reasons for turning to, 62–63, 79; in three lives, 63–73; and gender, 70, 72–73; and currents of domestic life, 73–81; and femininity and domesticity, 81–87; disruptive to marriage, 217, 219–20
Bharata (king), 168–69
Bharati, Agehananda, 184, 186, 187
Bhāt (gifts at marriage of sister's children), 38; songs of, 38–40, 51
Biography, *caritāmṛta* as, 193–94
Birth: as act of kinship, 154–55; and *saṃskāra* rites, 155; duality of, 169
Brahmā, 170–72
Brāhmaṇas, 161, 162
Brahmans, 5; Smārta, 60–87 passim; stages in life of, 82; in Karimpur, 95; and castes of Pṛthu, 148–49; relation to kings, 149–50
Bṛhaddevatā, 168, 174
Bṛhaddharma Purāṇa, 144–49; analysis, 149–53
Bṛhaspati, 165–72
Bride: as bearer of inauspiciousness, 29–30; burning of, 20, 57–58n63; bride-price, 143–44; importation of deities by, 217
British: use of *dharmáśāstras* by, 22; *satī* during colonial period of, 185
Brother: tie with sister, 25, 32–34, 36, 97–98; later relation of sister to, 32, 33: *milāī* from, 34–35; *vādā* from, 35; songs on relationship with, 37; of widows, 114 and *niyoga*, 163, 165, 172–74, 177–80; vs. loyalty to deity, 217
Budha, 167
Byāī gīt ("birth song"), 40–43

Candra, 172
Caritāmṛta, 193–94
Carstairs, G. Morris, 212
Caste, 17n7; and *bhakta*s, 61, 63, 72–73; and control of women, 95; and widows, 100, 114; and divorce, 138, 142, 143; and dowry, 144; created by Veṇa, 145–47; and Pṛthu, 147–49; of Bengal, 144–49; and *saṃskāra* rites, 153–57